Urban Hope and Spiritual Health

The Adolescent Voice

Leslie J. Francis
and
Mandy Robbins

✚ EPWORTH

British Library Cataloguing in Publication data

A catalogue record for this book is available from the British Library

07162 0609 9
978 07162 0609 5

First published in 2005
by Epworth
4 John Wesley Road
Werrington
Peterborough PE4 6ZP

Typeset by Regent Typesetting, London
Printed and bound in Great Britain by
William Clowes Ltd, Beccles, Suffolk

Contents

Preface

This study is an example of empirical theology and of the collab-
orative approach to research in practical theology modelled within the Welsh National Centre for Religious Education, University
of Wales, Bangor. We wish to express our gratitude to the many
schools and to the thousands of pupils who provided the data; to
the colleagues who prepared the data for analysis; to Karen Lord,
Douglas Turton and Emyr Williams who helped with the presen-
tation; to Susan Thomas who took responsibility for shaping the
manuscript; to Carol Roberts who checked the materials and provided the indices; to Helen Patterson and Ann Morisy who provided the challenge and the inspiration to undertake the analyses;
to Gwyther Rees who worked with us on the preliminary report;
to Steven Pearce and Doug Swanney who have linked the research
to pastoral practice; to Natalie Watson who commissioned and
guided the book; and to John Fisher whose friendship and scholarship have shaped our understanding of spiritual health.

Leslie J. Francis and Mandy Robbins

Feast of St Michael and All Angels 2005

Foreword

As Leslie Francis and Mandy Robbins put it in their concluding chapter to this book, 'Hope stands at the very heart of the Christian gospel.' As a contribution to exploring the basis for such hope, they analyse here in some detail the spiritual health of young people, understood in terms of the establishment and maintenance of their right relationships with their selves, with others, with the environment, and with God. They then seek to assess the influence on this psychological and spiritual state of a range of different factors that impact on the lives of adolescents. The ultimate purpose of this study is revealed in Francis' and Robbins' well-grounded assumption that 'good spiritual health properly generates hope and confidence in the future of urban living' (from the Introduction).

Hope is a matter of expectation and desire, and a state that is marked by the stance of confidence. Most would agree that it is 'a good thing'. It is good for people, especially young people, to be hopeful. We want them to be both confident and assured in themselves, and confident and assured towards others; we desire that they be expectant about the future, and that they come to believe that many things (if not, with Mother Julian, all things) 'will be well'.

Fundamentally, hope is an expression of a person's belief *in* something – for many, we might say, it expresses a belief in everything. Like faith and love, which are the other central Christian virtues (the so-called 'theological virtues'), hope is 'a dynamic quality of living' (R. E. C. Browne). Understood as a dimension of spirituality, it is 'a personal experience, an attitude of mind, a way of approaching life' (Rex Chapman). In both characterisations, hope is in its essence a *positive* aspect of our human orientation. 'Hope does not empty out one's life but rather fills it', writes Jürgen Moltmann. He adds, 'whoever loses hope, loses God', and 'we love only so far as we can hope'.

It is not surprising, therefore, that hope is frequently regarded as a crucial marker of the good health both of individuals and of society. We know that we need it. And we also know that if the next generation are to grow up, in our towns and cities, with hope in themselves and their society – and their futures under God, this can only be as an organic expression of a wholeness of spirit that *we* must help to nurture and allow to flourish. Certainly, we all dread the 'hopeless' alternative of the stunted and withered spirit, knowing that gives rise only to despair. And despair breeds disaster. If the city of tomorrow is to flourish, then, we must pay more heed than we often do to the shaping of its soul, particularly in the persons of its young people.

I believe that this study is an important contribution to our better understanding of this critical task.

Jeff Astley
North of England Institute for Christian Education
Durham
October 2005

Introduction

Setting the context

This study has its origins in the Commission on Urban Life and Faith and builds on the report *Spiritual Health and the Well-Being of Urban Young People* (Rees, Francis and Robbins, 2005) launched by the Commission in association with The Children's Society in July 2005.

The Commission on Urban Life and Faith was established to mark the twentieth anniversary of the Church of England's report *Faith in the City* produced by the Archbishop of Canterbury's Commission on Urban Priority Areas (1985). The Commission was tasked to re-visit some of the issues that were at the heart of *Faith in the City* and to explore the changing nature of urban life. Its purpose is to 'promote a vision of urban life which analyses and addresses the realities of its glories, injustices and needs'. As part of its response, the Commission on Urban Life and Faith identified the voices of young people living in urban areas as crucial insight into the ways in which urban living is perceived.

The report *Spiritual Health and the Well-Being of Urban Young People* drew on the unique database assembled by our research group in University of Wales, Bangor in order to publish new analyses from our survey of over 34,000 13- to 15-year-old pupils living throughout England and Wales. That report highlighted a number of key issues. This new book builds on the earlier report in two ways. It narrows and intensifies the focus on the issue of spiritual health and broadens and expands the ways in which individual differences in spiritual health are analysed and interpreted. The key argument of the present book is as follows. The data demonstrate that there are good indicators of spiritual health among young people living and growing up in urban areas throughout England and Wales. In turn good spiritual health properly generates hope and confidence in the future of urban living. At the same time, however, the data point to a range of indicators signalling areas in which spiritual health is low. Such indicators need to be taken seriously and listened to with care. This study allows the adolescent voice to be clearly heard. The challenge is for politicians, teachers, religious leaders and parents to listen, to interpret and, where appropriate, to act.

Shaping the study

The present study has been constructed on the basis of three key theoretical perspectives, concerning research methodology, concerning research content, and concerning the interrogation of research data. Each of these three theoretical perspectives will be examined in turn.

Regarding research methodology, there are two main traditions concerned with listening to the voices of young people in educational and social research: one employs qualitative techniques and the other employs quantitative techniques. There are strengths and weaknesses with both approaches. The qualitative technique is perhaps best displayed through one-to-one interviews or through focus groups enabling several voices to clarify and to amplify what is being said and heard. The real strength of this method is that issues can be explored in depth and approached with flexibility from a variety of angles. The weakness is that it may be difficult to know how secure it is to generalise from the findings. Susie Fisher and Susan Holder's (1981) classic study of young people at the beginning of the 1980s provides a good example of this approach under the title *Too Much Too Young: today's generation speaks out on being young in the eighties*. A more recent example is provided by Monica Barry's (2001) study, *Challenging Transitions: young people's views and experiences of growing up.*

The quantitative technique is perhaps best displayed through the self-completion surveys based largely on selecting pre-coded responses or rating intensity of responses. The real strength of this method is that the responses young people give to well-honed questions can be analysed with precision and confidence levels can be established regarding the reliability and generalisability of the information generated. The weakness is that it may be difficult to penetrate behind the well-framed questions to establish the deeper underlying meaning. Adrian Furnham and Barrie Gunter's (1989) classic study of young people in the mid-1980s provides a good example of this approach under the title *The Anatomy of Adolescence: young people's social attitudes in Britain.* More recent examples are provided by Sarah Beinart, Barry Anderson, Stephanie Lee and David Utting (2002) in their study, *Youth at Risk? a national survey*, and by Alison Park, Miranda Phillips and Mark Johnson (2004) in their study, *Young People in Britain: the attitudes and experiences of 12 to 19 year olds.*

The theoretical perspective adopted by the present study prefers the quantitative approach. Chapter one provides a full introduction to this approach and describes when and how the data on which the present study is based were gathered.

Regarding research content, the Commission on Urban Life and Faith was concerned to illuminate the life perspectives of young people living and growing up in urban environments. But the Commission was concerned to do more than that. Other studies had already let young people have their say on their social attitudes (Roberts and Sachdev, 1996), on how they feel (Gordon and Grant, 1997) or on their views and experiences of growing up (Barry, 2001). Broader political interest was already focused on shaping educational and technical skill or on promoting citizenship and pro-social values and behaviour. What, however, seemed much more lacking in contemporary research, debate and policy concerned an in-depth analysis of the spiritual dimensions of adolescent life.

Indeed, closer review of the literature revealed concern with social and moral development, with emotional intelligence and interpersonal skills, and with psychological wellbeing and quality of life indicators. By way of comparison, research in the areas of spiritual and religious development of young people seemed to be much less adequately documented within England and Wales, although beginning to flourish in the USA (Roehlkepartain, King, Wagener and Benson, 2005; Dowling and Scarlett, 2006). At the same time, it might seem somewhat odd if a Commission on Urban Life and Faith established by the Church of England were not to take an interest in spiritual and religious matters.

The theoretical perspective adopted by the present study prefers to focus on the more broadly defined area of spiritual development rather than on the more narrowly defined area of religious development. Chapter two provides a full discussion of what the present study understands by *spiritual health* and why it prefers this formulation to cognate constructs like spirituality and spiritual development. In essence preference is shown for the way in which recent research has offered a tight and illuminating definition of spiritual health as concerning the right relationships with the following four domains: self (the personal domain), other people (the communal domain), the physical and human world on local and global planes (the environmental domain), and those aspects of life which transcend the ordinary and everyday account of the physical environment (the transcendental domain whether or not conceived in theistic terms).

Regarding the interrogation of the research data, the theoretical perspective adopted by the present study builds on the individual differences approach of social psychology. After chapter three has examined an overview of the spiritual health of urban adolescents as a whole, the remaining chapters of this book focus on how both internal and external factors can function as predictors of individual differences in the levels of spiritual health experienced by different groups of young people.

There is a range of different ways in which the individual differences approach could be employed to analyse the present rich source of information on the spiritual health of urban adolescents. The approach preferred employs statistical significance testing to examine the difference between two or more groups and does so by examining each designated predictor variable in turn rather than within a multivariate model. The strength of this approach is that it allows each predictor variable to be seen with clarity and to be discussed separately. The weakness of this approach is that it fails to take into account the potentially contaminating effect of intervening variables. The theoretical perspective adopted by the present study maintains that for the purposes of the enquiry the strengths outweigh the weaknesses. It is, however, important to be clear about the kind of question which such analysis is able to answer with clarity.

By examining the predictor variables one by one it is the following question which is being posed. Suppose we knew only one thing about the young people, say whether they were male or female, or whether they were living in the north or in the south, or whether they were growing up in an intact or broken home, how much would that single piece of information help to predict individual differences in spiritual health? The statistical test used to check whether the difference between groups is likely or unlikely to have occurred by chance is chi square.

Selecting the factors

The range of individual differences which could have been explored in the present study is vast. Constraints imposed by the length of the book, by the attention span of the authors, and by the tolerance of the reader meant that some clear (and difficult) decisions had to be made at the outset regarding the issues to which attention would be given. Five main groups of factors were isolated for analysis.

The first group of factors concentrates on the two key personal individual differences of sex and age. Both psychological and sociological theories try to account for individual differences between men and women, between boys and girls. Psychological theories may prefer to concentrate on fundamental differences, say in the personality profile or in the cognitive functioning processes of the two sexes, while sociological theories may prefer to concentrate on the different social experiences of the two sexes in order to account for the observed difference. Chapter four examines the extent to which levels of spiritual health differ between males and females.

Chapter five turns attention to the second key personal difference included in the study, namely age. Although the age range covered by the study is narrowly focused on year-nine and year-ten pupils (between the ages of 13 and 15 years), previous research has indicated just how much change takes place over these two years of compulsory schooling. This chapter examines whether significant differences can be detected in levels of spiritual health between year nine and year ten.

The second group of factors concentrates on three aspects which help to shape the home background of the young people in the survey. The first of these issues concerns the well-worn debate regarding the north–south divide. Chapter six divides the young people living in England into two groups depending on which side they live of a line dividing the country into north and south, and then examines the extent to which levels of spiritual health vary between these two groups.

The second of the home-background issues concerns the differences between households in which the male parent-figure is unemployed and households in which the male parent-figure is employed. Chapter seven examines the extent to which levels of spiritual health vary between these two groups.

The third of the home-background issues concerns the differences between young people who have grown up in intact families and those who have experienced parental divorce, separation or break-up and who are not living with their original set of parents. Chapter eight examines the extent to which levels of spiritual health may vary according to this factor.

The third group of factors concentrates on the influence of the type of school attended. The potential for analysis here is quite large, given the variety of types of schools both within the state-maintained and the independent sectors of education. Given the concern of the study with religion and spirituality, the focus of the analyses was restricted to three types of school with a religious foundation. The three types of school singled out for scrutiny were Anglican schools within the state-maintained sector, Roman Catholic schools within the state-maintained sector, and the much more recently established Christian schools within the independent sector. Chapters nine, ten and eleven compare pupils educated in one of these three types of school having a religious foundation with pupils educated in non-denominational state-maintained schools.

The fourth group of factors concentrates on two theoretical perspectives which may help to account for individual differences in the general wellbeing of young people. The first theoretical perspective concerns the place of social engagement in enhancing wellbeing. Chapter twelve examines the relationships between social engagement and levels of spiritual health. The second theoretical perspective concerns the place of religious faith in enhancing wellbeing by focusing on prayer. Prayer is conceptualised as a specific example of religious behaviour which presupposes (consciously or unconsciously) a religious view of the universe. Chapter thirteen compares the levels of spiritual health enjoyed by young people who pray daily with the levels of spiritual health enjoyed by young people who never pray.

The fifth group of factors concentrates on the place of self-assigned religious affiliation in shaping individual differences in spiritual health. Taking in turn five of the six categories of religious affiliation incorporated in the pre-coded check list for the 2001 census in England and Wales, chapters fifteen, sixteen, seventeen, eighteen and nineteen compare with unaffiliated young people those who identified themselves as Christians, Muslims, Jews, Hindus and Sikhs. Unfortunately, the number of young people who identified themselves as Buddhist proved to be too small to sustain statistical analysis. These chapters allow differences in levels of spiritual health to be discussed according to faith groups.

These chapters concerned with individual differences can be pursued in whatever order captures the interest and attention of the reader. The chapters all follow the same structural pattern. The first section situates the new research within the wider context of theory and evidence. The second section discusses the method used to examine the database to generate new insights. The next four sections examine each of the domains of spiritual health in turn. The final section draws together the broad findings from the new research. Some readers may be more interested in the statistical detail and others in the broad findings.

1

Listening to young people

Setting the context

The present study is part of a well-established research programme pioneered by Leslie J. Francis in the late 1970s and developed consistently by his research team for nearly thirty years. Working within the individual differences traditions of quantitative social psychology and of empirical theology, the research programme set out to provide a thorough conceptual and empirical map of values relevant to the secular and religious worldviews of young people. Different theoretical perspectives have been able to draw on this values map in a variety of ways. The present study does so in order to illuminate and to interrogate the spiritual health of a sample of 34,000 young people between the ages of 13 and 15 years. Some history of the wider research programme is, however, necessary in order to situate the present analysis.

Mapping values

The research programme had its roots during the late 1970s in a Leverhulme-sponsored project coordinated by the London Central YMCA (Centymca) and the Department of Community Medicine at the Westminster Medical School. The aim was to generate insight into the worldviews of young people living, working or studying in the city centre. The values map was designed as the primary tool through which to gain access to those worldviews. The quantitative approach facilitated by means of self-completion questionnaires was adopted in order to enable the individual differences approach to examine the key predictors of how values and worldviews were being shaped differently among different groups of young people. The values map was developed as a consequence of four interrelated processes (see Francis, 1982a).

The first process involved a careful and exhaustive review of previous empirical research concerned with values and related constructs among school pupils, adolescents, students and young adults. The review embraced such classic studies as Reed (1950), McLeish (1970), Yankelovich (1974), Glock, Wuthnow, Piliavin and Spencer (1975), Austin (1977), McCann-Erickson (1977), Market and Opinion Research International (1979) and Kitwood (1980). What became quite clear from this review was that at that time no inventory of values assessed an appropriate range of issues and areas.

The second process involved consultation with a wide variety of people and organisations who were concerned with the development of values among young people during the final years of schooling and into work or higher education. Particular attention was given to schools and teachers, to work and employers, and to the voluntary sector. London Central YMCA and the National Council of YMCAs were central to facilitating this network. These contributions helped to define the precise areas within which research would be useful.

The third process involved settling down alongside young people in schools, in the YMCA and elsewhere, to listen to the issues that they were discussing and to the matters that were important to them. In this way a conceptual map began to develop of values and attitudes which properly helped to define the young person's worldview. At the same time this map was able to reflect the language and ideas of young people themselves.

The fourth stage involved drawing up a series of pilot inventories and field testing the items. After considerable modification the first edition of the Centymca Attitude Inventory was ready to set to work. This first edition was employed in three studies: *Youth in Transit* (Francis, 1982a), *Experience of Adulthood* (Francis, 1982b) and *Young and Unemployed* (Francis, 1984a). Learning from the experience of these three studies slight revision was undertaken for a fourth study reported by Francis (1984b) under the title *Teenagers and the Church*. This version was translated into Dutch and used by van Driel and Kole (1987). A second revision was undertaken to reflect the changing culture of the 1990s and used by Francis and Kay (1995) in their study *Teenage Religion and Values*. This version was translated into Czech and used by Quesnell (2000, 2002). The five studies conducted in England and Wales will be reviewed in turn.

Youth in Transit

Youth in Transit, the first study to employ the Centymca Attitude Inventory, reported by Francis (1982a), provides a profile of 16- to 25-year-old young people. Data were provided by 1,085 members of London Central YMCA who fell within the age category and who completed a copy of the inventory sent to them by post. These 1,085 respondents constituted a response rate of 57%.

Research among the 16- to 25-year-old age range is notoriously difficult to conduct given the diverse and mobile nature of the population. There were many strengths associated with basing the study on membership of London Central YMCA. The sample included a good mix of young men and young women from a wide variety of educational, social and geographical backgrounds. Students and young workers met side by side. Individuals from the north of England, from the south of England, from Wales and from the rest of the world congregate in central London. At the same time, however, there are serious weaknesses in basing a study on such a population since there is no evidence that young people who move to central London are really representative of

11

young people throughout England and Wales. For this reason Francis (1982a) expressed greater confidence in employing the data to report on the relationship between values and other factors than in using the data to generalise to the level of support given for specific value areas by young people in general.

In *Youth in Transit* nine main comparisons were made between different groups of young people. For example, the comparison between men and women identified a lower level of wellbeing and a greater anxiety over health-related issues among women. The women showed a greater interest in religion and a greater level of concern over social issues. The women showed less ambition in their work and a lower level of interest in sport.

The comparison between 16- to 21-year-old participants and 22- to 25-year-old participants identified a significant growth in self-esteem and confidence between the two age groups. The older group took more interest in politics and less interest in having a good time. The older group shared less interest in religion and less concern with their horoscope. The older group became more liberal in their moral values but stricter in their attitude to the law over issues like drinking and driving. The older group showed a greater level of social concern and greater satisfaction with their leisure activities.

The comparison between different social classes demonstrated that those in higher social class employment enjoyed a higher level of psychological wellbeing and a more positive attitude toward work and toward politics.

The comparison between different educational levels showed a very clear correlation between higher educational attainment and psychological wellbeing, positive work-related attitudes and interest in politics. Higher levels of education were also associated with lower levels of religious belief and greater moral liberalism. Higher levels of education were associated with greater concern about world development and environmental politics.

Experience of Adulthood

Experience of Adulthood, the second study to employ the Centymca Attitude Inventory, reported by Francis (1982b), provided a profile of 26- to 39-year-old young adults. This time data were provided by 2,074 members of London Central YMCA who fell into the older age category. The strengths and weaknesses of basing a study of young adulthood on the membership of a voluntary association are similar to those discussed in respect of the 16- to 25-year-old cohort. Once again the main emphasis in the analysis published in this volume is on the comparison between different groups. The ten comparisons made in this volume are between men and women, between those in their twenties and those in their thirties, between the married and the single, between different employment categories, between different social classes, between those born overseas and those born in Britain, between those living in different types of accommodation, between those living in different types of social groups, between different educational levels, and between different denominational groups.

The comparison between different denominational groups showed that Anglicans enjoyed a higher level of wellbeing than either Roman Catholics or those who had no religious affiliation.

Anglicans were less likely to be worried over personal matters than Roman Catholics. In comparison with Roman Catholics, Anglicans placed less value on religion and less importance on moral issues. Anglicans were more tolerant of abortion, euthanasia and pornography. Anglicans were more right wing in their politics.

The comparison between the married and the single demonstrated a higher level of wellbeing among the married, and overall a lower level of worry. The married were generally more conservative in their moral outlook. The married were also more politically alert and more concerned about some of the social trends in society. The married were more content and stable in their work.

The comparison between different age groups begun in *Youth in Transit* now enabled comparisons to be made between four age groups: those aged 16 to 21, 22 to 25, 26 to 29 and 30 to 39. Comparing the youngest and oldest of these two groups revealed a significant improvement in wellbeing, although some increase in age-related concerns. The older group demonstrated a much greater concern with politics and with moral issues. Religious belief and belief in horoscopes continued to decline across the age span. The older group showed more tolerance for soft drugs and less tolerance for hard drugs. The older group continued to display more law abiding attitudes. The older group continued to grow in concern for world development issues. The older group was beginning to show less contentment and less ambition at work.

Young and Unemployed

In *Young and Unemployed*, Francis (1984a) returned to the database of 1,085 16- to 25-year-old young people used in *Youth in Transit* in order to shape an analysis specifically concerned with learning about the socio-psychological features associated with unemployment among this age group. Two main types of analysis were undertaken in the study.

The first type of analysis concentrated on identifying the characteristics of the young people most vulnerable to experiencing unemployment. Discriminant analysis profiled those most vulnerable to unemployment as the 16- to 19-year-old women who were born overseas and were relative newcomers to England, who left school at sixteen without any academic qualifications, whose parents were divorced, who were living with their partners in a bedsit, and who were currently working in low status and poorly paid employment.

The second type of analysis concentrated on identifying the value correlates of having experienced unemployment. Factor analysis identified two main factors which transcended the value areas. These factors can be described as social conservatism and personal wellbeing. Young people who had experienced unemployment were characterised by more radical social values and by less positive personal values and a lower sense of wellbeing.

Teenagers and the Church

In *Teenagers and the Church*, Francis (1984b) employed a revised form of the Centymca Attitude Inventory with a view to profiling the values of young churchgoers between the ages of 13 and 20 years. The sample was defined as the young people between these ages who attend churches within carefully specified geographical areas on a given Sunday. A lot of care was taken in preparing the ground for churches to help identify these young churchgoers. By this method a total of 1,902 names and addresses were assembled. Questionnaires were distributed by post. The response rate of 70% produced 1,328 questionnaires completely and thoroughly answered.

The key interest in the analysis of the data produced by this project concerned the similarities and differences between the young people shaped by three different denominational traditions: the Anglican Church, the Roman Catholic Church, and the Free Churches. For example, in the area of sexual ethics, 15% of the young Roman Catholics followed their church's teaching and agreed that contraception is wrong, compared with 7% of the Free Church teenagers and 4% of the Anglicans. Over half (55%) of the Free Church members agreed that sex outside marriage is wrong, compared with 32% of Roman Catholics and 28% of Anglicans. On the subject of homosexuality, 55% of the Free Church members said that it is wrong, compared with 40% of the Anglicans and 40% of the Roman Catholics. Similar striking differences occurred between the denominations over a wide range of value areas.

Teenage Religion and Values

In *Teenage Religion and Values*, Francis and Kay (1995) employed a further revision of the Centymca Attitude Inventory with the view to profiling the values of young people between the ages of 13 and 15 years. The sample was derived from year-nine and year-ten pupils across a wide range of schools. Drawing on a database of just over 13,000 teenagers this book examined the relationship between values and three different conceptualisations of religion within a Christian context. Adherents of other world faiths were intentionally excluded from this analysis. The first conceptualisation of religion was based on reported frequency of church attendance, distinguishing between those who attended weekly, those who attended less often than weekly, and those who never attended. The second conceptualisation of religion was based on levels of belief in God among those young people who never attended church, distinguishing between theists, agnostics and atheists. The third conceptualisation of religion was based on denominational affiliation among those young people who attended church weekly, distinguishing between Roman Catholics, Anglicans and members of the Free Church. The relationship between religion and values can be illustrated by reference to three value areas, namely environmental concern, the use of substances, and abortion.

Regarding environmental concern, all three indicators of religion proved significant. Thus, 74% of weekly churchgoers reported concern about pollution, compared with 59% of those who never attended church. Among the nonchurchgoers, 66% of the theists reported concern about pollution, compared with 55% of the atheists. Among the weekly churchgoers, 77% of the Free Church members reported concern about pollution, compared with 73% of the Roman Catholics.

Regarding substances, 53% of the weekly churchgoers considered that it is wrong to smoke cigarettes, compared with 42%

of those who never attended church. Among the nonchurch-goers, 45% of the theists considered that it is wrong to smoke cigarettes, compared with 40% of the atheists. Among the weekly churchgoers, 56% of the Free Church members considered that it is wrong to smoke cigarettes, compared with 48% of the Roman Catholics.

Regarding abortion, 50% of the weekly churchgoers judged abortion to be wrong, compared with 35% of those who never attended church. Among the nonchurchgoers, 43% of the theists judged abortion to be wrong, compared with 32% of the atheists. Among the weekly churchgoers, 66% of the Roman Catholics judged abortion to be wrong, compared with 38% of the Anglicans.

The new survey

Against this background a new survey was conceived which would be able to provide secure information about the values of year-nine and year-ten pupils during the final decade of the twentieth century and as schools prepared to shape values education for the third millennium. The aim was the ambitious one of assembling a database of over 30,000 respondents. There were two reasons behind this ambition. First, a database of this size would allow analysis as presented in *The Values Debate: a voice from the pupils* (Francis, 2001a) to claim authority. Second, a database of this size would allow secondary analyses to focus on properly defined minority subsets of young people, like young Jehovah's Witnesses or young people who had suffered the death of a parent.

The instrument

The revision of the Centymca Attitude Inventory employed in this survey was designed to profile values over fifteen areas defined as personal wellbeing, worries, counselling, school, work, religious beliefs, church and society, supernatural, politics, social concerns, sexual morality, substance use, right and wrong, leisure and the local area. Each area comprised a set of short well focused statements designed for Likert scaling (see Likert, 1932). Pupils were required to grade their agreement with each statement on a five point scale anchored by agree strongly, agree, not certain, disagree and disagree strongly. A five point scale was chosen for two reasons. First, the odd number of response categories allows a middle position of uncertain to be available. This is an important and legitimate option since the survey contains areas and issues on which some young people may not have reached a clear decision. Second, a five point scale permits a finer range of responses than is available through a more basic three point scale.

Alongside the battery of Likert-type items the instrument included a number of forced choice questions designed to profile the respondents' background, beginning with forced choice questions on sex and age.

Before turning attention to the method of data collection, each of the fifteen areas covered by the instrument will be introduced briefly in turn.

Personal wellbeing Personal wellbeing is concerned with how young people feel about themselves. How much do they value themselves as individuals? To what extent do they feel that their life has a sense of purpose? Do they feel life is really worth living? On the other hand, how much are they aware of feelings of depression in their lives? How many of them have been driven to consider taking their own life?

Worries The questions on worries bring together the issues which are known to trouble some young people. How many young people growing up in today's world are worried about getting AIDS? How many of them are worried about their relationships, how they get on with other people, or how attractive they are to

18

the opposite sex? Are they worried about their sex lives? To what extent are young people worried about going out at night in their area, or about being attacked by pupils from other schools?

Counselling This section is concerned with the value that young people associate with their need to talk things through with others. How many young people long for someone to turn to for advice? How many of them find it helpful to talk about their problems with their father, with their mother, or with close friends? How do young people perceive the caring professionals and how willing are they to discuss their problems with a school teacher, a youth leader, a doctor, a priest or minister, or a social worker?

School This section is concerned with school-related values. What do the pupils think of their school and how happy are they there? What do they think of the people with whom they go to school and how positive are they about teachers? How much do they worry about their school work and about exams at school? What proportion of young people are worried about being bullied at school these days?

Work This section is concerned with work-related values. Would young people today rather be unemployed than be working in a job they do not like? Or are young people fearful of being unemployed? Do they think that a job brings with it a sense of purpose? Are they committed to working hard and ambitious to get to the top in their work when they get a job? Do they think that most unemployed people could really get a job if they tried?

Religious belief This section is concerned with the value that young people place on religion. What proportion of young people believe in God? How many believe that Jesus really rose from the dead? Who believes in life after death? In what kind of God do young people believe? Do they believe that God punishes people who do wrong? Do they believe in a God who made the world in six days and rested on the seventh? Who thinks that Christianity is the only true religion?

Church and society This section is concerned with the value young people place on the role of the Church in society. How do they perceive the relevance of the Church for life today, or the relevance of the Bible for life today? What proportion of young people still see a role for the Church in major rites of passage like marriage or christenings? Indeed, how do young people perceive the Church and the clergy? While still at school what view have they formed about the value of statutory religious education and the daily religious assembly?

Supernatural This section is concerned with the value young people place on the supernatural as a whole. Do young people, in any numbers, believe in black magic or in the possibility of contacting the spirits of the dead? Do they believe in their horoscopes or in fortune-tellers? Would they be frightened of going into a church alone? Do they believe in the devil?

Politics This section is concerned with the political values of young people. Do young people have confidence in the main political parties? Are they sceptical about the whole political process and think that it does not really matter which party is in power? What do young people think about private schools and about private medical practice outside the National Health Service? How racist are young people today and what are their views on immigration policies?

Social concerns This section is concerned with the social values of young people. To what extent do young people feel that they are empowered to help solve the world's problems and what do they consider those problems to be? How concerned are they about environmental pollution, about the poverty of the third world or about the risks of nuclear war? What do young people feel about violence on television or about the availability of pornography?

Sexual morality This section is concerned with the sexual values of young people. What view do young people take on issues like sexual intercourse outside marriage or sexual intercourse under the legal age? What view do young people take on homosexuality? How do young people feel about issues like contraception, abortion and divorce?

Substance use This section examines young people's values on the use of substances. What view do young people take on the use of substances like glue, marijuana, alcohol, butane gas, cigarettes and heroin? Which of these substances do pupils feel that it is most wrong to take? Is alcohol thought to be more socially acceptable than tobacco, or vice versa?

Right and wrong This section examines young people's values on law and order. It is concerned with down-to-earth practical matters. How many pupils think there is nothing wrong with shoplifting, or travelling on public transport without buying a ticket, or buying alcohol or cigarettes under the legal age? Is writing graffiti generally thought to be all right? Is playing truant actually wrong? What do they think about riding a bicycle at night without lights? What do young people feel about the police?

Leisure This section is concerned with the value that young people place on their leisure. How satisfied are they with their leisure time? How many wish for more things to do with their leisure time or feel that they just hang about with friends doing nothing in particular? How do they perceive their parents' attitude to what they do in their leisure time? Does this meet with parental approval or disapproval?

21

My area The final section is concerned with the neighbourhood where the young people live. How content are young people in their neighbourhood? Do they feel that their area actually cares about them as young people? Looking around how many of them perceive that there is in their area a growth in crime, vandalism or violence? Do they feel that drug taking or alcohol abuse is on the increase? How do they perceive the employment prospects in their area?

Data collection

The intention to build up a database of over 30,000 young people sets the present study apart from many comparable studies in two ways. First, the majority of studies have based their findings on a much smaller sample of young people. For example, in their study on health issues Shucksmith and Hendry (1998) interviewed 44 young people individually. The study on social attitudes among 12- to 19-year-old adolescents reported by Roberts and Sachdev (1996) employed a database of 580 interviews. The study of young people in the 1980s published by the Department of Education and Science (1983) was based on 635 14- to 19-year-old adolescents. Simmons and Wade (1984) in their study of attitudes, values and beliefs of 15-year-old adolescents drew information from 820 pupils. The study of young people's social attitudes reported by Furnham and Gunter (1989) employed data from over 2,000 young people. The study of young people's involvement in sport edited by Kremer, Trew and Ogle (1997) drew data from 2,400 children between the ages of 7 and 16 years. The study of young people's leisure and lifestyle undertaken by Hendry, Shucksmith, Love and Glendinning (1993) assembled 9,916 responses in their 1987 survey. The national survey of risk factors, protective factors and problem behaviours among young people in England, Scotland and Wales reported by Beinart, Anderson, Lee and Utting (2002) assembled 14,666 responses.

Second, because a larger database has been generated, a longer period of time has been required to assemble, code, check and analyse these data. What is offered, therefore, is a thorough profile of young people in the late 1990s rather than a snapshot of a particular year.

Data were provided from 163 schools throughout England and Wales, from Pembrokeshire to Norfolk, and from Cornwall to Northumberland. A proper mix of rural and urban areas was included, as was a proper mix of independent and state-maintained schools. Within the state-maintained sector proper attention was given to the balance between Roman Catholic voluntary schools, Anglican voluntary schools and non-denominational schools.

Participating schools were asked to follow a standard procedure. The questionnaires were to be administered in normal class groups to all year-nine and year-ten pupils throughout the school. Pupils were asked not to write their name on the booklet and to complete the inventory under examination-like conditions. Although pupils were given the choice not to participate very few declined to do so. They were assured of confidentiality and anonymity. They were told that their responses would not be read by anyone in the school, and that the questionnaires would be despatched to the University of Wales for analysis.

Participating schools were also given assurance that their data would not be published independently. However, before data from each school was merged with the growing database, a confidential profile was made available to the school.

As a consequence of this process thoroughly completed questionnaires were processed for 33,982 pupils. Of these respondents, 51% were male and 49% were female; 53% were in year nine and 47% were in year ten. Of those educated within the state-maintained sector, 86% were in non-denominational schools, 9% in Roman Catholic schools and 5% in Anglican schools. Of the total sample of pupils, 10% were being educated outside the state-maintained sector.

Posing questions

A database of 33,982 adolescents provides a valuable and almost inexhaustible resource. The first taste of the rich source of information available from this survey was published in *The Values Debate: a voice from the pupils* (Francis, 2001a). A set of more tightly focused chapters were published in *Religion, Education and Adolescence* (Francis, Robbins and Astley, 2005). Other aspects of the survey have been, and will continue to be, published through a variety of journals. A view of young people growing up in rural England and Wales was published in *Rural Youth* (Francis and Martineau, 2001).

The findings in the present volume draw on the information provided by the 23,418 young people living in urban areas. The selection of issues explored among this group of young people has been shaped by an understanding of the markers most helpful to provide insights into spiritual health. The understanding of spiritual health which shaped the selection is discussed and debated in the following chapter.

It is fully recognised that the dataset on which the analysis is based is already aging. The Commission on Urban Life and Faith, however, took the view that more secure generalisations could be based on a survey of this size, scope and professionalism than could be derived from a much smaller and specifically commissioned new study. While opinions and fashions are ephemeral and volatile, values and worldviews are much more deep-seated and more stable. At this level fundamental changes and shifts are measured in decades rather than in days. Planning based on these kinds of data is not dissimilar from planning based on the statistical data provided by the decadal census.

The research team is now committed to compiling a comparable database to provide a profile of young people at the end of the first decade of the twenty-first century.

2

What is spiritual health?

Setting the context

The purpose of chapter two is to examine why the present study decided to focus on the notion of *spiritual health* and to discuss what the study understands by that construct. The argument develops in three main stages. First, it is argued that the place of religion in the twenty-first century in England and Wales remains ambiguous and contested and that this situation has allowed the notion of spirituality to occupy a more central and less contested place in public discourse. Second, attention is drawn to the way in which the notion of spiritual development has come to play a particularly important role in educational debate in light of the 1988 Education Reform Act (Department of Education and Science, 1989). It is argued, however, that lack of agreement regarding how this construct is interpreted in educational debate renders the notions of spirituality and spiritual development as too imprecise for the present study. Third, it is argued that the notion of spiritual health provides a more robust and precise term to guide empirical research. In particular, attention is drawn to John Fisher's conceptualisation of spiritual health in terms of four domains and to the ways in which this conceptualisation has proved helpful in earlier studies reported, for example, by Fisher, Francis and Johnson (2000, 2002). It is this definition which provides the theoretical framework for the subsequent chapters.

Religion and spirituality

The place of religion in the twenty-first century in England and Wales remains ambiguous and contested. The so-called secularisation debate, well-stimulated in the 1960s by the opposing perspectives of Bryan Wilson (1966) and David Martin (1967), has left a lasting impression on popular understanding. This lasting impression is reflected in two fundamental controversies, concerning whether or not religion remains a matter of social significance and whether or not religion is a proper matter for public scrutiny.

The first controversy focuses first and foremost on the changing profile of the Christian churches. At the very beginning of the 1980s the title of Alan Gilbert's (1980) book proclaimed with confidence, *The Making of Post-Christian Britain*. More recently Callum Brown (2001) pronounced the obituary with his title, *The Death of Christian Britain*. For Steve Bruce (2002) the message is even more inclusive with his title *God is Dead*. At one level the case seems cut and dried. If the social significance of Christianity in today's society were to rest largely on the visibility of Sunday church attendance, the message given by closed churches and closed chapels, and by the dwindling and aging congregations within those that remain open, is quite clear. However, if the social significance of Christianity in today's society were to rest elsewhere, then the case may be far less than cut and dried. Two key pieces of evidence challenge the view that Christianity has lost social significance.

The first piece of evidence comes from the 2001 census. For the first time ever in England and Wales the 2001 census asked a question about religious affiliation. The nearest precedent in the past was in 1851 when a head count was taken of church attendance to coincide with the national census. In 2001 72% of the population of England and Wales were described as Christian within the census returns. The census returns also draw public attention to the growing numbers and growing strengths of the other major faith communities in England and Wales.

The second piece of evidence comes from the careful research that shows both churchgoing Christians and nonchurchgoing Christians develop a distinctively different profile of social attitudes and values in comparison with those who are associated with no religious group. Robin Gill's (1999) seminal work, *Churchgoing and Christian Ethics*, made good use of the British Social Attitudes Survey datasets to demonstrate the social significance of church attendance in shaping a range of personal and social values. Building on Gill's method of analysis, Francis (2003) demonstrated from the same dataset the power of religious affiliation to predict individual differences of social and practical significance. In other words, religious affiliation is not an empty category but an important aspect of personal identity which helps to shape the kind of people we become. Such findings are consistent with Reginald Bibby's (1985) earlier work in Canada which speaks in terms of 'religious encasement'. To know about an individual's religious affiliation is to know a great deal that is of social and public significance.

At present the balance of evidence regarding the first controversy suggests that the obituary for religion in England and Wales has been published prematurely. Churchgoing is irrefutably in decline, but the public significance of religion remains quite strong.

The second controversy focuses on whether or not religion is a proper matter for public scrutiny. This controversy came to the fore in the public debate preceding the decision to include the religious question in the 2001 census. One view suggests that religion should be treated as an intensely personal matter. On this account, it is inappropriate to pry into the souls of others. What they believe about God and what they do about such beliefs should, it is argued, be protected as a personal matter between them and their God. The opposite view suggests that religion is so much part of an individual's self-identity that it provides an essential component descriptor of society. On this account, it is thoroughly appropriate to ask about religion in a public census. A question about religion, it is argued, is not fundamentally different from a question about sex, age, or ethnicity, and such issues have long been accepted as legitimate components of public enquiry in general and the public census in particular.

In an important essay preparing the ground for the religious question in the 2001 census, Fane (1999) attempted to clarify the problem by refining distinctions well-established in the social scientific study of religion between the constructs of religious belief, religious practice and religious affiliation. Belief and practice, she argues, are properly to be regarded as private and personal matters, while affiliation on the other hand, like ethnicity, belongs to a very different domain of discourse. If this distinction can be maintained, public discussion about religion becomes much easier to handle.

At present, the balance of evidence regarding the second controversy suggests that the case has been largely won for questions about religious affiliation to find a proper place in the public domain. The Office for National Statistics is supporting the case for the religious question to go forward to the 2011 census.

While the latter part of the twentieth century witnessed considerable nervousness in England and Wales regarding the public debate of religion, the notion of spirituality provided good opportunity for a parallel debate to prosper. Those in favour of religion and those against religion seemed able to reach greater agreement discussing spirituality.

Spiritual development

One clear example of the way in which the notion of spirituality has enabled secular and religious discourse to appear to have reached some consensus is provided by the 1988 Education Reform Act (Department of Education and Science, 1989). A spiritual basis for education in state-maintained schools through-out England and Wales is enshrined in the well-known legal requirement that the curriculum of each school should be one which:

a promotes the spiritual, moral, cultural, mental and physical development of pupils at the school and of society; and

b prepares such pupils for the opportunities, responsibilities and experiences of adult life.

These clauses from the 1988 Education Reform Act (Department of Education and Science, 1989) have been involved in a number of subsequent Government circulars to encourage or to admonish teachers and educational administrators. The circular on *Religious Education and Collective Worship*, issued in draft form in 1993, claimed as follows.

The Government is concerned that insufficient attention has been paid explicitly to the spiritual, moral and cultural aspects of pupils' development, and would encourage schools to address how the curriculum and other activities might best contribute to this crucial dimension of education.

The same foundation clauses are pressed into service to provide the basis for a renewed policy for sex education in the Government circular *Sex Education in Schools*, also issued in 1993. 'The Government believes that all pupils should be offered the opportunity of receiving a comprehensive, well-planned programme of sex education during their school careers.' Any such programme is 'in fulfilment of the requirement' that the curriculum must 'promote the spiritual [and] moral development ... of pupils' and prepare them 'for their responsibilities and experiences of adult life'.

Nowhere, however, in initial Government documentation was there any attempt to offer a definition of 'spiritual development'. In the absence of any agreed definition considerable literature has developed from a range of different perspectives. In a penetrating analysis of the situation which arose in educational debate following the 1988 Education Reform Act, Adrian Thatcher (1996: 118) argued that 'accounts of "spiritual development" appear to have proliferated out of control'. Using Wittgenstein's model of language-games, Thatcher argues that there is a wide diversity of meanings attributed to the notion of spiritual development since a number of different language-games are being played by different players.

There are many players, theologians, philosophers, psychologists and anthropologists; representatives of all major religious traditions who speak of their own tradition's spirituality; religious people, humanists and atheists; teachers of religion, of personal, social and moral education, indeed of all subjects . . .; politicians, civil servants and headteachers. It is hard to think of an equivalent homonym which has spawned such diversity of use, spreading cognitive chaos in its wake (Thatcher, 1996: 118–19).

When in April 1993 the National Curriculum Council (1993) published its discussion paper, *Spiritual and Moral Development*, the attempt was to make the term as wide as possible. According to this discussion document 'The potential for spiritual development is open to everyone.' It is 'not confined to the development of religious beliefs', since this would 'exclude from its scope the majority of pupils in our schools'. The discussion document proceeded to argue as follows.

The term needs to be seen as applying to something fundamental in the human condition which is not necessarily experienced through the physical senses and/or expressed through everyday language. It has to do with relationships with other people and, for believers, with God. It has to do with the universal search for individual identity – with our responses to challenging experiences, such as death, suffering, beauty and encounters of

30

good and evil. It has to do with the search for meaning and purpose in life and for values by which to live (National Curriculum Council, 1993: 3).

Spiritual health

Partly in reaction to the sometimes vague and imprecise ways in
which the term 'spiritual development' has been used in recent
years, another research tradition has set out to establish a more
rigorous usage of the cognate term 'spiritual health'. At the fore-
front of this pioneering work, and operating specifically within
the educational arena, is the Australian researcher John Fisher.
Fisher set out both to establish a coherent conceptual model of
spiritual health and to develop a set of reliable and solid psychometric instruments capable of operationalising that model (see
for example, Fisher, 1998, 2000, 2001, 2004; Fisher, Francis and
Johnson, 2000, 2002; Gomez and Fisher, 2003, 2005).

Fisher has begun his conceptual analysis by fully recognising
that the concept of 'spiritual health' is doubly problematic in view
of the way in which the two terms 'spiritual' and 'health' have
themselves undergone considerable development in recent years.
To begin with Fisher argues that classical definitions of spirituality tended to concentrate on the religious and the ecclesiastical,
or on matters concerned with the soul. Current studies in spirituality, however, have tended to adopt much wider definitions,
integrating all aspects of human life and experiences, as represented, for example, by the work of Muldoon and King (1995) in
their essay on 'spirituality, health care and bioethics'. For Fisher,
a definition of spiritual health has to make sense within both sides
of this divide.

Fisher then proceeds to argue that there has been a similar
widening in understanding of what counts as health. There has
been a shift in emphasis in medicine introducing greater concern
for the whole person, rather than just the treatment of disease.

For Fisher, a definition of spiritual health needs to recognise the way in which the words 'health', 'healing' and 'wholeness' are all derived from the same root. He cites with approval the definition offered by Coward and Reed (1996: 278) that 'healing is defined as a sense of wellbeing that is derived from an intensified awareness of wholeness and integration among all dimensions of one's being'.

Prior to Fisher's work several attempts had been made to link the two concepts of spiritual and health, most generally within the idea of 'spiritual wellbeing'. For example, in setting out to define and measure spiritual wellbeing, Ellison (1983: 332) suggested that spiritual wellbeing 'arises from an underlying state of spiritual health and is an expression of it, much like the colour of one's complexion and pulse rate are expressions of good (physical) health'. In a similar vein, Fehring, Miller and Shaw (1997: 664) argued that 'spiritual wellbeing is an indication of individuals' quality of life in the spiritual dimension, or simply an indication of their spiritual health'.

Ellison's (1983) Spiritual Well-Being Scale (The SWBS) stimulated a great deal of research during the 1980s. The measure proved to be useful both in population studies concerned with mapping individual differences in wellbeing and in clinical settings. The review of ten years' work with this instrument, published by Bufford, Paloutzian and Ellison (1991), provided general support for the reliability and validity of the measure and for the usefulness of the construct over a wide range of studies. The main constraint on this instrument, and on the conceptualisation on which it builds, concerns the explicitly religious context in which it was shaped. In effect, the Spiritual Well-Being Scale is a 20-item self-report instrument with two subscales. One subscale, defined as the Religious Well-Being subscale, contains 10 items which refer to God and assess what it describes as the vertical dimension of spirituality. The other subscale, defined as the Existential Well-Being subscale, contains 10 items designed to assess what is described as the horizontal dimensions of wellbeing in relation to the world around us, and embraces notions like a sense of life purpose and satisfaction with life. As a consequence of this design good spiritual wellbeing as assessed by the Spiritual Well-Being Scale is tightly aligned with a particular theological view of spirituality.

Fisher's aim was both to build on Ellison's helpful notion of thinking in terms of conceptually discrete dimensions of spiritual wellbeing and to develop a dimensional model of spiritual wellbeing which would value both religious and non-religious perspectives. His solution to this problem was to discuss spiritual health in four domains, to develop a series of tools capable of assessing these four domains (including the SH4DI: the Spiritual Health in Four Domains Index), and to distinguish among four different spiritual health perspectives, represented by what he describes in terms of ideal types as personalists, communalists, environmentalists, and religionists.

Four domains of spiritual health

In developing his conceptual framework for spiritual health, Fisher drew on the discussion advanced by the National Interfaith Coalition on Aging (1975) which argued that 'spiritual health is the affirmation of life in a relationship with God, self, community and environment that nurtures and celebrates wholeness'. The four sets of relationships identified by the National Interfaith Coalition on Aging, of a person with self, others, the environment, and with God (or Transcendent Other), are also variously mentioned in contemporary discussions of spiritual health. For example, Hateley (1983) wrote about relation to self, integration and self-esteem; moral development, empathy in the community and religion; mystery of creation; relationship with God. Young (1984) mentioned the inter-relatedness of body, mind and spirit within the context of inner peace; relations with and love of others; relation with nature; God as the focus of belief. Goodloe and Arreola (1992) spoke of meaning and purpose, with self-transcendence; social and spiritual action with others; oneness with nature; disembodied spirits, abstract and personal relations with God. According to Hood-Morris (1996: 440), 'the spiritual component includes transcendent and existential features pertaining to an individual's relationship with the self, others, and a higher being ... coupled with interaction with one's environment'.

Working with these four sets of relationships, Fisher (1998) analysed the responses from interviews with 98 teachers in a range of state, Catholic and other non-government schools near Melbourne, Australia. On the basis of these analyses, Fisher proposed that spiritual health is a fundamental dimension of people's overall health and wellbeing, permeating and integrating all the other dimensions of health (including the physical, mental, emotional, social and vocational). In addition, Fisher (1998: 191) argues that spiritual health is a dynamic state of being, shown by the extent to which people live in harmony within relationships in the following domains of spiritual wellbeing.

First, the *personal domain* is concerned with internal relationships with the self. At this level the human spirit creates self-awareness, and is concerned with matters of self-esteem and self-identity. Good spiritual health in the personal domain is reflected in a sense of self-worth, and in a sense of meaning, purpose and value in life.

Second, the *communal domain* is concerned with external relationships with other people. At this level the human spirit creates constructive and satisfying relationships with other people, and is concerned with matters of accepting others and being accepted by them. Good spiritual health in the communal domain is reflected in qualities like love, justice and hope in interpersonal dealings and in faith in humanity.

Third, the *environmental domain* is concerned with relationships with the physical and human world on both local and global planes. At this level the human spirit recognises the unity and connectedness between the self and the rest of the universe. Good spiritual health in the environmental domain is reflected in accepting responsibility for matters of environmental concern and for matters of global and sustainable development.

Fourth, the *transcendental domain* is concerned with relationships with those aspects of life which transcend the ordinary everyday account of the physical environment. The transcendental domain embraces matters of ultimate concern, cosmic forces, transpersonal phenomena, and (in traditional theistic categories) God. Good spiritual health in the transcendental domain is reflected in a life-enhancing rather than a life-diminishing view of relationships with whatever it is that is conceived as existing beyond the human level, whether this is expressed in terms of a personal God, in terms of an impersonal life force, or in terms of the unpredictable power of luck or fate.

The model of spiritual health presented by Fisher proposes two inter-related aspects of *knowledge* and *inspiration*, for each of the four domains of spiritual wellbeing. Knowledge provides the framework, whereas inspiration involves 'essence' and 'motivation' (Carr, 1995: 89) for the development of spiritual wellbeing in each domain. The quality of relationship in each domain constitutes a person's *spiritual wellbeing* in that domain. An individual's *spiritual health*, the state of being, is seen to be indicated by the combined effect of spiritual wellbeing in each of the domains embraced by the individual. The four domains are not isolated, but are inter-related. Therefore, it is assumed that spiritual health is enhanced by developing positive relationships in each domain and increased by embracing more domains.

The notion of progressive synergism was proposed to help explain the relationship between the domains. For example, the communal domain is seen to build on the personal domain as well as building it up. In other words, the meaning, purpose and values developed through self-awareness are precursors to, yet enhanced by, the development of morality and culture through in-depth inter-personal relationships. Similarly, connectedness with nature should build on, and build up, self-awareness and in-depth inter-personal relationships, with faith embracing the other three relationships and being fostered by them (Fisher, 1998: 192).

Ideal types

While Fisher (1998) argues that spiritual health is enhanced by developing all four domains, he also recognises that many individuals give priority to one domain over the others. It is such individuals who enable us to see more clearly the unique qualities associated with each domain. The list of ideal types given below, therefore, is an attempt at describing the unique characteristics of the people embracing each of the domains *as* spiritual wellbeing.

Personalists are people embracing the personal domain *as* spiritual wellbeing. Personalists are individuals who believe their spiritual wellbeing is brought about entirely from within their own resources (or being), that is, that their human spirit provides the motivation to seek meaning, purpose, and values in life. They feel wholly self-sufficient, thus self-centred, regarding the development of their personal spiritual wellbeing, even though they might acknowledge a need for inter-personal relationships for other dimensions of their wellbeing, such as social, emotional or vocational.

Communalists are people embracing the communal domain *as* spiritual wellbeing. Communalists recognise the need to have harmony in the personal domain, to have stated meaning, purpose and values clarified, and lived out. As well as this basic facet of spiritual wellbeing, communalists acknowledge a need for quality and depth in inter-personal relationships, which transcend morality, and culture. They recognise that the whole is much greater than the sum of the parts. They believe that when people interrelate at depth, it has a significant impact on their spiritual wellbeing. Burke (1993: 35) reported that research is showing the importance of connectedness of people to others for spiritual and emotional wellbeing.

Environmentalists are people embracing the environmental domain *as* spiritual wellbeing. Environmentalists have an appreciation of the knowledge and inspirational aspects of the personal and communal domains, together with, at least, a sense of awe and wonder about the environment. They go beyond responsible management of the physical, eco-political and social aspects of the environment to a sense of connectedness of the individual or group with it. They are so in tune with nature that their relationship with it adds meaning to the other domains. Worldviews of many indigenous people would fit in this category (Hammond, 1991; Regnier, 1994).

Religionists are people embracing the religious domain *as* spiritual wellbeing. They have a primary focus on their relationship with God, even though they recognise the importance of relationships with self, others and the environment in the development of spiritual health. Growth in this domain requires the experience, exercise, or both of a faith dimension expressed through communication with some-thing, or some-one, beyond the human level. Marfleet (1992: 25) proposed that 'our spiritual nature is actualised [when] our psycho-spiritual being [comes] into harmony with God'. When a person has connected with the ultimate source of being in the universe, it should have a profound effect on his or her sense of identity and destiny, and on relations with others and the environment (Robinson, 1994: 3).

Measuring spiritual health

Fisher has offered a broad theory of spiritual health and advanced broad definitions of the four domains which he conceptualises as core to his model of spiritual health. Much of Fisher's subsequent research has concentrated on testing different operationalisations of this theory. For example, an early study reported by Fisher, Francis and Johnson (2000) described the Spiritual Health in Four Domains Index developed for use among teachers. Fisher (2004) described the Feeling Good Living Life Instrument developed for use among children as young as five years. It is recognised that, although such instruments provide only approximate indicators of the underlying constructs, the information generated offers useful insights into the spiritual health of groups and of individuals and provides reliable and valid predictors of a wide range of human individual differences.

It is against this background that chapter three now proceeds to propose indicators of spiritual health across the four domains capable of generating insight into the lives of urban adolescents and helpful in identifying tensions between hope and despair, between strengths and weaknesses, and between success and failure in urban life today.

3

Overall health check

Setting the context

John Fisher's model of spiritual health has advanced the view that a good level of spiritual health can be defined in terms of establishing good relationships across four areas of life which he characterises as the personal domain, the communal domain, the environmental domain, and the transcendental domain.

For different individuals these four domains are likely to assume different levels of significance. Those whom Fisher describes as personalists give priority to the personal domain as being key to their understanding of spiritual health. They may strive hard to promote their personal self-understanding and self-acceptance, but they would not be living spiritually healthy lives if they felt out of relationship with others, with the environment or with whatever they conceive as the transcendent. Those whom Fisher describes as communalists give priority to the communal domain as being key to their understanding of spiritual health. They may strive hard to promote a positive view of their relationship with other people, but they would not be living spiritually healthy lives if they felt out of relationship with themselves, with the environment or with whatever they conceive as the transcendent. Those whom Fisher describes as environmentalists give priority to the environmental domain as being key to their understanding of spiritual health. They may strive hard to promote a positive view of the global physical and human environment, but they would not be living spiritually healthy lives if they felt out of relationship with others, with themselves or with whatever they conceive as the transcendent. Those whom Fisher describes as religionists give priority to the transcendental domain as being key to their understanding of spiritual health. They may strive hard to celebrate their right relationship with their God, but they would not be living spiritually healthy lives if they felt out of relationship with their own inner self, with others around them, or with the global physical and human environment.

The values map included in the survey provides multiple indicators of each of these four domains. Our aim has been to select just seven indicators for each of the four domains, a total of 28 key questions. At one level this is clearly a totally inadequate sample of indicators to represent such broad conceptual categories. At another level, however, concentrating on a small number of well-chosen indicators permits proper care and due weight to be given to the discussion of each one, and allows the full set of indicators to be run against quite a wide range of factors, like those which form the structure for the following chapters of this book.

The aim of the present chapter now is to discuss the seven items selected to represent the four domains and to assess what these indicators have to say about the overall level of spiritual health among young people living and growing up in urban England and Wales today.

Personal domain

The personal domain is concerned with what young people believe about themselves and with what young people feel about themselves. There are certain recurrent things that young people are likely to say about themselves when they are enjoying a good level of spiritual health within the personal domain. First and foremost, they are likely to affirm their self-worth and to put forward a confident and secure self-image. Their self-esteem will be high and they are unlikely to endorse the first indicator in this section: 'I feel I am not worth much as a person.'

Young people who have developed a positive self-image and a high level of self-esteem are in the habit of trusting their own judgements and of placing confidence in their own abilities. While not shaping self-sufficient lives in an insular and threatened sense, they have grown to stand on their own feet rather than to be over-reliant on the support of others. Such young people are unlikely to endorse the second indicator in this section: 'I often long for someone to turn to for advice.'

Young people who enjoy a good level of spiritual health within the personal domain are likely to be content with their lives and with their day-to-day experiences. Their perceived quality of life will be good and they are likely to endorse the third indicator in this section: 'I find life really worth living.'

School occupies a high proportion of the young person's life and defines a considerable part of their activities, experiences and relationships. Young people who enjoy a good level of spiritual health within the personal domain are likely to have made good sense of their time at school and to feel affirmed by the experience of school. They are likely to endorse the fourth indicator in this section: 'I am happy in my school.'

Spiritual health in the personal domain is inadequately conceptualised if the definition remains content with indicators of general personal happiness and quality of life. Spiritual health in the personal domain goes deeper than that as the individual life seeks meaning and purpose. Young people who enjoy a good level of spiritual health within the personal domain are likely also to endorse the fifth indicator in this section: 'I feel my life has a sense of purpose.'

Classic discussions of psychological wellbeing and psychological health speak in terms of balanced affect (Bradburn, 1969). On this account positive affect is not understood as the bipolar opposite of negative affect. Empirically positive affect and negative affect are orthogonal phenomena. Accordingly, good psychological wellbeing is defined in terms of the presence of positive affect and the absence of negative affect. In a similar way good spiritual health in the personal domain should be reflected in the absence of negative affect as well as in the presence of positive affect. Young people who enjoy a good level of spiritual health within the personal domain are unlikely to endorse the sixth indicator in this section: 'I often feel depressed.'

The ultimate indicator of negative affect in the personal domain is provided by the life-denying and life-threatening image of suicidal ideation. The extreme precariousness of spiritual health in the personal domain is signalled by the young people who endorse the seventh indicator in this section: 'I have sometimes considered taking my own life.'

The statistics presented in table 3.1 provide mixed messages regarding the spiritual health of young people living and growing up in urban areas of England and Wales as far as the personal domain of spiritual health is concerned. On the surface things seem to be going well for the majority of young people. Levels of self-esteem and self-worth are high, with only 13% of the young people feeling that they are not worth much as a person. Levels of perceived satisfaction with life are high, with 70% finding life really worth living and 71% being happy in their school. Below the surface, however, there is a somewhat less positive view. If a sense of meaning and purpose in life is taken as a key indicator of spiritual health, then not much over half the young people (56%) passed that test. Living life without a sense of purpose can be discouraging and debilitating. Confidence in self and in self-direction is not as high as it may seem. Only 39% of the young people denied that they are often longing for someone to turn to for advice. The darker side of the spiritual health of the young people living and growing up in urban areas of England and Wales is illustrated by the facts that over half (52%) often felt depressed, and over a quarter (27%) sometimes considered taking their own life.

As far as the personal domain of spiritual health is concerned, the key areas to be addressed concern the need to help more young people identify and name a sense of purpose for their lives and to help young people deal with suicidal ideation in a non-life-threatening way. As suicide, attempted suicide and self-harm become increasingly visible problems in teenage culture, so the issues of enhancing the sense of purpose in life and of dealing with suicidal ideation become more pressing matters of concern.

Communal domain

The communal domain is concerned with what young people believe about those with whom, in one sense or another, they share their lives and with what young people feel about those relationships. There are certain recurrent things that young people are likely to say about others when they are enjoying a good level of spiritual health within the communal domain. First and foremost they are likely to affirm their relationships and to feel positively about other people.

In some ways the dynamics underpinning the communal domain are quite different from those underpinning the personal domain. In the personal domain the spiritually healthy adolescent is busily engaged in constructing his or her own identity. In the communal domain the focus of power is much more outside the individual's own control. At this level spiritual health may often be in the hands of others. The three key areas of experience which access this dimension of spiritual health among adolescents concern relationships with parents, relationships with friends, and relationships at school.

Young people who enjoy a good level of spiritual health within the communal domain are likely to feel at ease with their parents, feel that they can approach their parents and feel that they can trust their parents. Their perceived quality of relationships with their parents will be good and they are likely to endorse the first two indicators in this section: 'I find it helpful to talk about my problems with my mother' and 'I find it helpful to talk about my problems with my father.'

Young people who enjoy a good level of spiritual health within the communal domain are likely to be supported and surrounded by sufficient friends whom they trust. The need for friends will vary from one young person to another depending on their basic personality profile. Extraverts will prefer a group of friends with whom they can interact at different levels. Introverts will prefer one or two really close friends with whom they can form in-depth relationships. Neither spiritually healthy introverts nor spiritually healthy extraverts thrive in isolation. Thus, young people who enjoy a good level of spiritual health within the communal domain are likely to endorse the third indicator in this section: 'I find it helpful to talk about my problems with close friends.'

Young people who enjoy a good level of spiritual health within the communal domain are likely to have confidence in their inter-personal relationships, both in a general sense and in respect of members of the opposite sex in particular. They are likely to approach other people with confidence and expect to find themselves accepted by others. Their confidence will be high and they are unlikely to endorse the fourth indicator in this section: 'I am worried about how I get on with other people.'

Forming relationships with members of the opposite sex generates one of the major areas of trauma during adolescence. Young people who enjoy a good level of spiritual health within the communal domain are unlikely to suffer excessive angst in this area. Confident about the nature of relationships they are unlikely to endorse the fifth indicator in this section: 'I am worried about my attractiveness to the opposite sex.'

Since school is such a central part of life for young people the experiences of school are really formative in shaping spiritual health in the communal domain. Young people who get on well with their fellow pupils are well on the road to enjoying higher levels of spiritual health in the communal domain. Young people who are ill at ease with their peers in the classroom and in the playground may be doomed to experience lower levels of spiritual health in the communal domain. It is for this reason that the sixth indicator in this section points in the direction of good spiritual health: 'I like the people I go to school with.' The seventh indicator in this section points in the direction of poor spiritual health: 'I am worried about being bullied at school.'

The statistics presented in table 3.2 suggest that overall the spiritual health of young people living and growing up in urban areas of England and Wales may not be that strong as far as the communal domain of spiritual health is concerned. To begin with, the bonds with parents are not particularly good. Just half of the young people felt sufficiently close to their mother to be able to say that they find it helpful to talk about their problems with their mother (50%). Just a third of the young people felt sufficiently close to their father to be able to say that they find it helpful to talk about their problems with their father (32%).

Overall the young people suffered considerable anxiety about relationships. Half of them were worried about how they get on with other people (51%) and a third were worried about their attractiveness to the opposite sex (34%). Such statistics reveal a significant lack of confidence in forming and sustaining relationships.

At a superficial level the experience of school life seems good, creative and empowering, with 90% of the young people reporting that they like the people with whom they go to school. A little deeper below the surface, however, lurks something much darker. The fear of being bullied at school casts a shadow over the lives of one young person in every four (28%). Clearly there is little hope of a good level of spiritual health in the communal domain among those young people whose daily life at school is threatened by bullies.

The really good news from these statistics is that two out of every three of the young people living and growing up in urban areas of England and Wales (64%) reported that they have close friends with whom they find it helpful to talk about their problems. The less good news is that one in three of the young people (36%) could not affirm that this is the case within their own experience. It is difficult to posit a good level of spiritual health in the communal domain for young people who cannot draw on the insights, friendships and support which comes from someone who is close to them.

As far as the communal domain of spiritual health is concerned, the key areas to be addressed concern the need to help more young people establish the relationship skills necessary to navigate the precarious transition from childhood to adulthood. This involves seeing parents in a new light, negotiating relationships which enrich both the self and the other, and the development of perspective-taking and empathic capabilities on which mutual respect and trust can be built. A key message for schools which emerges from these data is that the on-going campaign to remove bullying from the classroom, the playground and the school bus has not yet reached its goal. Bullying continues to damage the spiritual health of young people across urban areas of England and Wales.

Environmental domain

The environmental domain is concerned with what young people believe about their connectedness with and interdependence with the natural, physical and human global environment and with what young people feel about that domain. The environmental domain raises fundamental questions about global citizenship and about sustainable development. There are certain recurrent things that young people are likely to say about the world in which they live when they are enjoying a good level of spiritual health within the environmental domain. First and foremost, they are likely to recognise the importance and significance of global issues and register appropriate levels of concern for the issues which threaten global sustainability.

Young people who enjoy a good level of spiritual health in the environmental domain will be aware of the impact on the eco system of factors like industrial waste, intensive farming methods, and consumption of fossil fuels. They are likely to endorse the first indicator in this section: 'I am concerned about the risk of pollution to the environment.'

Young people who enjoy a good level of spiritual health in the environmental domain will have a view on matters concerned with international development, on fair trade and economic justice across the economies of the world. They are likely to endorse the second indicator in this section: 'I am concerned about the poverty of the third world.'

A realistic view of life in the twenty-first century recognises the potential fragility of world stability. Conflicts continue to arise between nations as political power shifts across the globe. At the same time, elusive and amorphous global terrorism undermines hopes for world peace and stability, threatening high levels of spiritual health in the environmental domain. The third indicator in this section provides a measure of such global uncertainty: 'I am concerned about the risk of nuclear war.'

In twenty-first century urban life in England and Wales, globalisation does not remain an abstract theoretical construct about what happens overseas and in other places. Overall England and Wales have become and are recognised as fully multicultural societies. Many towns and cities are now rich centres for ethnic, cultural and religious diversity. Young people who enjoy a good level of spiritual health in the environmental domain are unlikely to endorse the fourth indicator in this section: 'There are too many black people living in this country.'

One political strategy of controlling and containing the

progressive movement toward multiculturalism in England and Wales focused on immigration into Britain. The ethical, political and economic arguments are well-developed on both sides of this contentious and divisive debate. An important insight into the young person's spiritual health in the environmental domain is provided by the fifth indicator in this section: 'I think that immigration into Britain should be restricted.'

Life in twenty-first century England and Wales has been and remains subject to all kinds of social pressures and changes. Standards of behaviour and values do not remain static over time. Some may argue that England and Wales are becoming more violent societies and that changes in standards promoted by the media are at least partly responsible for normalising the acceptability of violence. Young people who enjoy a good level of spiritual health in the environmental domain are unlikely to welcome growth in violence and may well endorse the sixth indicator in this section: 'There is too much violence on television.'

Young people who enjoy a good level of spiritual health in the environmental domain are likely to feel that their actions and their voices count toward making the world a better place in which to live. They are unlikely, therefore, to endorse the seventh indicator in this section: 'There is nothing I can do to help solve the world's problems.'

The statistics presented in table 3.3 suggest that overall in the environmental domain the spiritual health of young people living and growing up in urban areas of England and Wales remains far from secure. On the one hand, nearly two-thirds of the young people registered concern for the risks of pollution to the environment (64%) or for the poverty of the third world (59%). On the other hand, this means that over a third of the young people were not really concerned about environmental pollution (36%) or about the poverty of the developing nations (41%).

The world inhabited by more than half the young people is one in which global peace remains illusory: 55% were concerned about the risk of nuclear war. It is very hard to enjoy a high level of spiritual health in the environmental domain if you perceive the international political scene as volatile and unstable. Perhaps fear of terror attacks has taken over from fear of internecine conflict between world super-powers.

Closer to home racist attitudes undermine peaceful co-existence within the fabric of a multicultural and multiethnic society. Nearly one in five of the young people said that there are too many black people living in this country (17%). A third of the young people thought that immigration into Britain should be restricted (32%).

Discontent with contemporary society is signalled by the 20% of young people who believed that there is too much violence on television. These are young people who feel out of step with the society of which they are part.

One in four of the young people felt that there is nothing they can do to help solve the world's problems (26%). These are the young people who feel completely disempowered in today's world and who are fully alienated by life in the urban location. Those who feel so disempowered are signalling a low level of spiritual health in the environmental domain.

As far as the environmental domain of spiritual health is concerned, one key area to be addressed is the need to help more young people grasp the challenges and opportunities of living within a multicultural nation as part of a global economy. Education for global citizenship and for sustainable development has begun to play a more important part in the school curriculum but needs to be brought into an even more central place if schools are to make a proper contribution to the spiritual development of pupils within the environmental domain. The second key area to be addressed concerns the critique of racist attitudes and racist behaviours. The third key area to be addressed concerns ways of empowering young people to recognise their responsibilities for the environment and for the global future and to seize opportunities to impact the future. Here is an agenda for political parties, for development agencies, and for environmental pressure groups as well as for schools.

Transcendental domain

The transcendental domain is concerned with what young people believe about those aspects of life which transcend the ordinary everyday account of the physical environment, and with what young people feel about that domain. The transcendental domain embraces matters of ultimate concern, cosmic forces, transpersonal phenomena, and (in traditional theistic categories) God. In some senses the transcendental domain is more complex to operationalise than the other three domains. The added complexity is a function of the way in which conceptualisation in this area is not independent of fundamental theological assumptions. Given the concern of the Commission on Urban Life and Faith with the role of the faith communities and explicit religiosity in shaping spiritual health, regeneration and hope in the urban regions of England and Wales, the conceptualisation of the transcendental domain adopts a theistic view of spiritual health and posits a social context in which belief in God is viewed as normative rather than as marginal or abnormal.

There are certain recurrent things that young people are likely to say about the transcendental domain when they are enjoying a good level of spiritual health within a social context that values a theistic interpretation of life. First and foremost they are likely to affirm the existence of God and to endorse the first indicator in this section: 'I believe in God.'

A religious view of the world is differentiated from a non-religious view in a number of ways. From a psychological perspective one of the most important differences concerns the nature of human life in general and the significance of human mortality in particular. A number of religious worldviews offer the possibility or the promise of some form of immortality, some form of life beyond the grave, some form of transcendent existence. Such a worldview offers a transformative view of the significance and purpose of life before death, however the possibilities of the afterlife are conceived. Young people who enjoy a good level of spiritual health in the transcendental domain conceived within a theistic context are likely to endorse the second indicator in this section: 'I believe in life after death.'

One of the important consequences of the experience of living in a pluralist, multicultural and multifaith society has been reflected in ways in which religious leaders and theologians have reflected on the positive synergies between denominational perspectives and between faith traditions. Different denominations and different faith traditions increasingly affirm what they share in common rather than what separates them. In such a social context the big division comes between individuals of faith and individuals of no faith rather than between denominational groups or faith groups. In a social and theological context of this nature, young people who enjoy a good level of spiritual health in the transcendental domain are unlikely to endorse the third and fourth indicators in this section: 'The Church seems irrelevant for life today' and 'The Bible seems irrelevant for life today.'

The range of spiritual ideas available to young people living and growing up in urban areas in England and Wales is now very wide. Alongside the belief systems of the major world faiths, there exist the popular beliefs of a post-Christian culture and the assorted beliefs of the New Age perspective. From a traditional Christian theological perspective some of these beliefs would be regarded as less spiritually healthy than others. For example, young people who adopt belief in apparently innocuous horoscopes may in fact be developing into a worldview which surrenders their locus of control to extraneous irrational forces. On this account, young people who enjoy a good level of spiritual health in the transcendental domain are unlikely to endorse the fifth indicator in this section: 'I believe in my horoscope.'

Other beliefs which may detract from responsible and mature acceptance of responsibility for the future and the development of a mature internal locus of control centre around forms of determinism. Such beliefs may include the power of fortune-tellers and the influence of the spirits of the deceased. On this account, young people who enjoy a good level of spiritual health in the transcendental domain are unlikely to endorse the sixth and seventh indicators in this section: 'I believe fortune-tellers can tell the future' and 'I believe it is possible to contact the spirits of the dead.'

The statistics presented in table 3.4 indicate that when spiritual health in the transcendental domain is conceived in traditional theistic terms, the spiritual health of young people living and growing up in the urban areas of England and Wales is far from being consistently good. Just a little over two-fifths of the young people said that they believe in God (43%) or that they believe in life after death (45%). In one sense these statistics may seem to confront the churches and the faith communities with bad news as they are forced to recognise that fewer young people live with a religious worldview than live without a religious worldview. In another sense, however, these statistics may offer considerable hope and promise to the churches and to the faith communities. These statistics concerning religious belief are so much more encouraging in comparison with routine observations concerning the number of young people who practise faith by attending public occasions of worship. Moreover, the proportion of the young people who consciously rejected religious beliefs is relatively low. Just one in four rejected belief in God (26%) and fewer than one in five rejected belief in life after death (17%).

Hostility to organised religion is reflected in the proportion of young people who rejected religious institutions as irrelevant for life today. Between a quarter and a third of the young people felt that the Church seems irrelevant for life today (27%) and that the Bible seems irrelevant for life today (30%). If good spiritual health in the transcendental domain involves positive affirmation of the spirituality of others, these dismissive attitudes may be indicative of less than satisfactory levels of spiritual health.

The statistics suggest that almost as many young people living and growing up in urban environments in England and Wales believed in their horoscope as believed in God (35% compared with 43%). One in five of the young people believed fortune-tellers tell the future (20%) and one in three believed it is possible to contact the spirits of the dead (31%). Such statistics may present the churches with mixed messages. On the positive side, they show young people who are open to the transcendental domain. On the less positive side, they show young people who are creating a theological worldview of their own operating outside the framework of rational theological discourse. If positive spiritual health in the transcendental domain involves a rational scrutiny of religious beliefs and the acceptance of personal autonomy, these particular beliefs in the supernatural may be indicative of less than satisfactory levels of spiritual health.

As far as the transcendental domain of spiritual health is concerned, the key areas to be addressed concern the educational task of enabling young people to make informed and rational judgements about religious matters. Preparing young people for their life in a multicultural and multifaith society, the role of religious education in school may be more important than ever before. The task for religious education is three-fold: to help young people to see the consequences of the choices they make about transcendental beliefs; to help young people to make rational choices about the belief systems which they adopt and about the belief systems which they reject; and to examine their prejudices about religion and religious groups.

Conclusion

The present analysis gives some good grounds for hope in the spiritual health of the young people living and growing up in urban areas of England and Wales at the beginning of the twenty-first century. Perhaps more importantly, however, it has identified flaws in the spiritual health of these young people which could significantly threaten the quality of life in urban England and Wales. For example, the data drew attention to the following issues: in the personal domain an unacceptably high level of suicidal ideation; in the communal domain an unacceptably high level of racist attitudes; in the environmental domain an unacceptably high level of political powerlessness; and in the transcendental domain a range of beliefs which may damage aspects of human growth and development. Within each of these domains strategies have been suggested which could help to enhance the spiritual health of young lives and bring greater hope to the urban landscape of England and Wales.

Urban planners may need to take seriously and to address the signs of poor spiritual health which characterise young people living and growing up in urban areas of England and Wales. Young people whose lives are threatened by suicidal ideation need to be enabled to find meaning, purpose and hope. Young people who threaten community integration by racist attitudes and behaviours need to be enabled to accept and to respect racial differences. Young people who feel powerless to impact the world in which they live need to be empowered and charged with vision for positive change and development. Young people who are fearful or uncertain about the transcendent forces that shape their universe need to be enabled to test and to make rational judgements about their beliefs.

4

Male and female

Setting the context

This chapter poses the deceptively simple question regarding the relationship between Fisher's four domains of spiritual health and being either male or female. Sex is a basic human difference taken seriously both by psychology and sociology. In his classic review of sex as a key variable in social investigation, Morgan (1986) described this variable as 'both ubiquitous and hidden'. It is ubiquitous in the sense that it is one of the most common variables to be included in social surveys, almost as a matter of routine. It is hidden in the sense that the full potential of this variable is often ignored in the analysis and interpretation of data. When, however, sex is identified as a key variable in the analysis of individual differences, this generally emerges as a highly fruitful and valuable exercise, not only in studies among adults but among young people as well.

In research of this nature the distinction between sex and gender is important. The distinction between sex and gender was defined by Oakley (1981: 41) in the following terms. 'Sex refers to biological division into female and male; gender to the parallel and socially unequal division into femininity and masculinity.'

A similar distinction was made by Matthews (1982: 31) as follows. 'Sex is defined as the biological dichotomy between female and male, chromosomally determined and, for the most part, unalterable, while gender is that which is recognised as masculine and feminine by a social world.'

Following this use of language the present chapter is concerned with sex differences rather than with gender differences.

A number of quantitative studies concerned with the world-views of young people have examined the part played by sex in shaping individual differences. A good example of what has been found by such analysis is provided by the report on young people's social attitudes compiled and edited by Roberts and Sachdev (1996). The seven contributors to this report focused on the following topics: rights, rites and responsibilities; gender matters; prejudice and racial discrimination; crime, justice and punishment; educational issues; politics and the media; and religion and morality. Some of these areas may offer clues regarding the relationship between sex and spiritual health.

In his analysis of rights, rites and responsibilities, Newman (1996) found some interesting sex differences in shaping the age at which young people thought it appropriate to accept adult responsibilities. A higher proportion of young men (27%) than young women (20%) wished to lower the age for driving cars to 16 years. Young men were rather more confident than young women at being left alone for the evening: 22% of young men felt that this was appropriate between the ages of 8 and 12, compared with 17% of young women.

In her analysis of gender matters, Oakley (1996) found young men revealing themselves as more conventional and pro-marriage than young women. For example, 66% of young women maintained that one parent can bring up a child as well as two parents, compared with 45% of young men. While 22% of young men took the view that, when there are children in the family, parents should stay together even if they do not get along, the proportion fell to 14% of young women. When asked to rate their main ambition in life, young women and young men revealed some key differences. Both placed being happy at the top of the list, but young women did this a little more emphatically than young men (47% compared with 40%). More young men than young women gave emphasis to being well off (14% compared with 3%).

In her analysis of crime, justice and punishment, McNeish (1996) found that young women displayed more fear of crime in comparison with young men. For example, 67% of young women were worried that they or others living with them might become the victim of crime, compared with 56% of young men. Only 5% of young women felt very safe walking alone after dark in their area, compared with 22% of young men. As a consequence of this greater fear, young women were more likely than young men to take precautions to avoid crime. For example, 30% of young women did not go out alone, compared with 12% of young men. Similarly, 16% of young women never answered the door, compared with 7% of young men.

In their analysis of views on education, Hughes and Lloyd (1996) found that a higher proportion of young men than young women rated having a good education as essential for doing well in life (29% compared with 22%). Young women were more likely than young men to feel that a lot of bullying occurred in their present or most recent school (30% compared with 25%).

In his analysis of views on politics and the media, Walker (1996) found less interest in politics among women: 64% of young women said that they either had no interest or not very much interest in politics, compared with 52% of young men. These data also demonstrated that young women were less likely than young men to read a newspaper at least three times a week (41% compared with 50%).

In her analysis of religion and morality, Roberts (1996) highlighted sex differences in both areas. Young women were more likely than young men to regard themselves as belonging to a particular religious group (52% compared with 39%) and to believe in God (61% compared with 56%). When asked if they would pocket money found in an empty street, young men were more likely to do so irrespective of the value specified. Thus, 81% of young men would keep £5, compared with 73% of young women; 61% of young men would keep £20, compared with 49% of young women; 27% of young men would keep £100, compared with 22% of young women.

A great deal of research among children, adolescents and adults conducted in Christian and post-Christian cultures demonstrates that females are more religious than males across a range of indicators including religious affiliation, public religious practice, personal religious practice, religious beliefs and religious attitudes. Indeed in their classic review of the social psychology of religion, Argyle and Beit-Hallahmi (1975) concluded that sex differences constitute one of the most widely supported empirical findings within the psychology of religion. Argyle and Beit-Hallahmi's conclusion was supported by the more recent review of the literature published by Francis (1997).

While there is general agreement that, within Christian and post-Christian contexts, women tend to be more religious than men, there remains considerable disagreement regarding why this might be the case. The arguments fall into two broad categories. On the one hand, strands of sociological theory argue in terms of women's role in society or society's expectations placed on women. On the other hand, strands of psychological theory argue in terms of fundamental differences in personality between men and women which lead women into greater religiosity. Francis (1997) argued that the sociological arguments designed to account for sex differences in religiosity have worn proportionately thinner as the roles of men and women have become more equal in society. At the same time a sequence of empirical studies, reported by Thompson (1991), Francis and Wilcox (1996, 1998) and Francis (2005b), has begun to organise an impressive body of evidence to support the strength of the psychological arguments designed to account for sex differences in religiosity in terms of the psychological constructs of masculinity and femininity rather than in terms of biological sex. In this sense religiosity emerges as consistent with well-developed personality characteristics of femininity in men as well as in women.

Clearly there is sufficient empirical evidence from previous studies to suggest that sex differences are worth taking seriously and that the examination of sex differences in spiritual health is worth exploring further.

Method

In order to examine the relationship between sex and spiritual health, the dataset was simply divided between the males and the females and the chi square test was employed to examine the statistical significance of differences between the two groups.

Personal domain

The statistics presented in table 4.1 reveal just how much spiritual health in the personal domain is a function of sex differences. Overall, males enjoy a significantly higher level of spiritual health in this domain compared with females. The difference between the sexes is particularly stark in respect of the indicators in this section concerned with negative affect. For example females were significantly more likely than males to report suffering from depression. Thus, three-fifths of the females said that they often feel depressed (60%), compared with 45% of the males. Differences in levels of depression were also reflected in levels of suicidal ideation. Nearly a third of the females have sometimes considered taking their own life (31%), compared with a quarter of the males (24%).

Self-confidence and self-reliance were significantly less strong among the females than among the males. While 12% of the males felt that they were not worth much as a person, the proportion rose to 15% among the females. While 29% of the males often longed for someone to whom to turn for advice, the proportion rose to 41% among the females.

These significant differences in depression and self-confidence are also seen in the young people's overall evaluation of their personal lives. The females were significantly less likely than the males to feel positively about their experience of life. While three-quarters of the males found life really worth living (74%), the proportion fell to 65% among the females.

Just two of the indicators in this section contradict the general trend. The females were not significantly less likely than the males to feel that their life has a sense of purpose (55% and 56% respectively). The females were marginally, but significantly, more likely than the males to be happy in their school (72% compared with 70%).

Communal domain

The statistics presented in table 4.2 reveal just how much spiritual health in the communal domain is also a function of sex differences. Three main differences emerge. The first main difference concerns the negative affect component of the communal domain. The females experienced a significantly higher level of relationship anxiety in comparison with the males. Thus, 55% of the females were worried about how they get on with other people, compared with 47% of the males. Similarly, 40% of the females were worried about their attractiveness to the opposite sex, compared with 29% of the males. Negative affect in the communal domain is also reflected in fear of bullying. While a quarter of the males were worried about being bullied at school (25%), the proportion rose to 31% among the females.

In some senses these higher levels of negative affect may be offset by higher levels of positive affect reflected by responses to other indicators. The second main difference between the sexes concerns the positive affect component of the communal domain. The females experienced a significantly higher level of support from their friends in comparison with the males. Thus,

79% of the females found it helpful to talk about their problems with close friends, compared with 48% of the males. The same kind of difference is reflected in the fact that 91% of the females liked the people with whom they go to school, compared with 88% of the males.

The third main difference between the sexes within the communal domain of spiritual health concerns relationships with parents. While the mother remained the preferred confidant among both males and females, the difference was not that great among the males, with 43% of the males finding it helpful to talk about their problems with their mother and 39% of the males finding it helpful to talk about their problems with their father. The gap widened considerably among the females, with 57% of the females finding it helpful to talk about their problems with their mother and 25% of the females finding it helpful to talk about their problems with their father.

Environmental domain

The statistics presented in table 4.3 suggest that overall in the environmental domain females may enjoy a better level of spiritual health than males. A primary indicator to this effect is that the females were significantly more likely than the males to feel engaged with world issues and to recognise their potential to influence the course of events. While a third of the males said that there is nothing they can do to help solve the world's problems (31%), the proportion fell to a fifth among the females (21%).

Second, females were much more tolerant than males of life in a multicultural and multiracial community. While 24% of the males argued that there are too many black people living in this country, the proportion fell to 10% of the females. While 41% of the males thought that immigration into Britain should be restricted, the proportion fell to 22% of the females.

Third, females showed more concern than males about the problems of violence on both a local and a global level. Although 54% of the males were concerned about the risk of nuclear war, the proportion rose slightly, but significantly, to 56% among the females. Similarly 24% of the females registered concern that there is too much violence on television, compared with 16% of the males.

Fourth, females showed more concern than males for the problems and poverty of the developing world. Two-thirds of the females were concerned about the poverty of the third world (65%), compared with 54% of the males. On the other hand, males and females displayed equal levels of concern for the environment. Nearly two-thirds of the males were concerned about the risk of pollution to the environment (64%), and so were 63% of the females.

Transcendental domain

The statistics presented in table 4.4 reveal that in the transcendental domain in some senses females enjoy a better level of spiritual health than males. Females were more likely than males to hold to traditional religious beliefs. While 40% of the males believed in God, the proportion rose to 46% among the females. While 44% of the males believed in life after death, the proportion rose to 46% among the females.

This greater tendency for females to believe in traditional religion is also reflected in a more positive attitude toward religious institutions. While a third of the males dismissed the Bible as irrelevant for life today (35%), the proportion fell to 25% among the females. While a third of the males dismissed the Church as irrelevant for life today (33%), the proportion fell to 22% among the females.

There are other ways, however, in which the females seem to experience a lower level of spiritual health in the transcendental domain compared with the males. Not only were the females more likely than the males to show greater acceptance of traditional religious beliefs, they also showed greater acceptance of non-traditional religious beliefs. The females were twice as likely as the males to believe in their horoscope (47% compared with 24%). The females were twice as likely as the males to believe that fortune-tellers can tell the future (26% compared with 14%). The females were also slightly more likely than the males to believe that it is possible to contact the spirits of the dead (33% compared with 29%).

Conclusion

This analysis has confirmed the importance of sex in shaping individual differences in spiritual health. In terms of Fisher's four ideal types, males are more likely than females to be personalists, having better spiritual health in the personal domain with a greater sense of self-worth. Males are also more likely than females to be communalists, having better spiritual health in the communal domain with fewer anxieties on relational matters. On the other hand, females are more likely to be environmentalists, having better spiritual health in the environmental domain with a greater sense of connectedness with local and global issues of citizenship and sustainable development. Females are also more likely than males to be religionists, having better spiritual health in the transcendental domain defined in traditional theistic terms. In these ways males and females may be offering different insights into hope for the urban future.

Urban planners may need to recognise and to value the distinctive perspectives, values and skills brought to urban living by young women and by young men, and to provide opportunities for the voices of both sexes to be heard in public debate and policy.

5

Growing older

Setting the context

This chapter poses a second deceptively simple question regarding the relationship between Fisher's four domains of spiritual health and age. Age is a second basic human difference taken seriously both by psychology and sociology. Because of the nature of the dataset employed in the present study, the question is tightly focused on the differences between two year groups of secondary school pupils: year nine (13- to 14-year-old pupils) and year ten (14- to 15-year-old pupils). The value of examining the way in which responses change between these two age groups has been well documented by a series of studies published by the Schools Health Education Unit based in the University of Exeter.

For example the 1992 report of the Schools Health Education Unit (Balding, 1993), based on the responses of 20,218 pupils between the ages of 11 and 15, enables close comparison to be made between the views of year-nine and year-ten pupils on eight themes defined as diet, doctor and dentist, health and safety, activities after school, drugs, money, sport, and social and personal issues.

Regarding attitudes toward diet and food, the data demonstrated two somewhat opposing trends between year-nine and year-ten pupils. On the one hand, there was a slight increase in the proportion of young people who said that they never considered their health when choosing what to eat, from 10% in year nine to 14% in year ten. On the other hand, there was a slight increase in the proportion of young people who had elected never to eat meat or to eat meat only occasionally, from 13% in year nine to 16% in year ten.

Regarding attitudes toward doctors and dentists, there was a slight increase in self-confidence between year nine and year ten. While 55% of year-nine pupils felt at ease with the doctor on their most recent visit, the proportion grew slightly to 58% among year-ten pupils.

Regarding attitudes and practices related to health and safety, the data showed a slight decrease in remedies and medication taken between year nine and year ten. Among year-nine pupils 53% had taken remedies within the past week for asthma, colds, diabetes, allergies and skin problems. The proportion fell slightly to 50% among year-ten pupils. Among year-nine pupils 73% had taken within the past week iron tablets, vitamins, antibiotics, painkillers or other remedies or medicines. The proportion fell slightly to 70% among year-ten pupils.

Regarding time spent on activities after school, there were some considerable differences between year-nine and year-ten pupils. Over this period time spent listening to music and being with friends increased, while time spent doing homework or reading decreased. Thus, the proportion of pupils who had listened to music the previous day increased from 60% to 69%, and the proportion who had met with friends increased from 42% to 51%. The proportion of pupils who had spent time on homework the previous day decreased from 76% to 70%, and the proportion who had read a book decreased from 37% to 28%.

Regarding drugs and substances, the proportion of pupils who could claim that they had never smoked fell from 48% in year nine to 38% in year ten. The proportion of pupils who had consumed alcohol within the past week grew from 43% in year nine to 56% in year ten. The proportion of pupils who had purchased alcohol for themselves within the past week grew from 12% in year nine to 24% in year ten.

Regarding money, the proportion of pupils engaged in regular paid-employment during term time grew from 34% in year nine to 42% in year ten. Moreover, among those engaged in regular paid-employment the average weekly pay increased by around 25% between year nine and year ten.

Regarding sport and fitness, little change took place in basic attitudes between year nine and year ten. For example, 32% of pupils in year nine regarded themselves as active or very active, and so did 31% in year ten. Similarly, 27% of pupils in year nine regarded themselves as fit or very fit, and so did 26% in year ten.

Regarding social and personal attitudes, the following main developments occurred between year nine and year ten. The proportion of pupils who nominated both parents as the adults with whom they got on best fell from 43% to 33%. The proportion of pupils who felt at ease when meeting people of their own age and opposite sex for the first time rose from 35% to 38%. The proportion of pupils who felt that they were in charge of their health rose from 55% to 61%.

The 1996 report from the Schools Health Education Unit (Balding, 1997) and the 1997 report (Balding, 1998) also allow comparisons to be made between pupils in year nine and pupils in year ten, although the 1998 report presented comprehensive information only for year eight and year ten (Balding, 1999). The 1996 report, based on the responses of 22,067 pupils between the ages of 12 and 15, enabled comparisons to be made between pupils in year nine and pupils in year ten on the following issues: cycling and safety helmets, favourite television programmes, engagement with the national lottery, and aerobic exercises.

The section on health and safety included several questions on cycling. The data demonstrated a decrease in the proportions of pupils who used a cycle from 80% in year nine to 73% in year ten. Among those who used a cycle there was an increase in the proportion who never or hardly ever used a safety helmet, from 63% in year nine to 72% in year ten.

The section on home included a question about favourite television programmes. The data demonstrated shifts in the proportion of pupils claiming to be regular viewers of specific soaps. Regular viewers of *Neighbours* dropped from 38% in year nine to 33% in year ten. On the other hand, regular viewers of *EastEnders* rose from 27% in year nine to 33% in year ten.

The section on money included questions on the national lottery. The data demonstrated a slight increase over the two age groups. While 11% of the year-nine pupils had bought a National Lottery draw ticket during the previous seven days the proportion rose to 13% among year-ten pupils. While 10% of the year-nine pupils had bought an instant scratch card during the previous seven days, the proportion rose to 11% among year-ten pupils.

The section on sport included a question about aerobic exercise. The data demonstrated a slight decrease in the proportion of pupils who had exercised and had to breathe harder three times or more during the previous seven days from 34% in year nine to 31% in year ten.

The 1997 report, based on the responses of 37,538 pupils between the ages of 9 and 16, enabled comparison to be made between pupils in year nine and pupils in year ten on a number of themes not included in the 1992 report, including bullying, computer games, cigarette advertising, savings, enjoyment of physical activities and availability of contraceptives.

The section on health and safety included a question on bullying. The data demonstrated that there was a slight decline in the proportion of pupils who felt afraid of going to school because of bullying from 29% in year nine to 24% in year ten.

The section on family and home included a question on playing computer games after school. The data demonstrated that there was a slight decline in the proportion of pupils who had engaged in this activity during the previous day from 37% in year nine to 34% in year ten.

The section on drugs included a question regarding the

influence of cigarette advertising. The data demonstrated that there was a slight decline in the proportion of pupils who considered that cigarette advertising had a lot or quite a lot of influence on young people starting smoking from 49% in year nine to 41% in year ten.

The section on money included a question on saving. The data demonstrated that there was a slight increase in the proportion of pupils who had put some of their own money into a savings scheme within the previous seven days from 32% in year nine to 35% in year ten.

The section on sport included a question about enjoyment of physical activities. The data demonstrated that there was a slight decrease in the proportion of pupils who said that they enjoyed physical activities a lot from 46% in year nine to 44% in year ten.

The section on social and personal attitudes included a question on the availability of contraceptives. The data demonstrated that there was an increase in the proportion of pupils who claimed to know that there was a special birth control service available for young people locally from 14% in year nine to 33% in year ten.

Several studies, including Kay and Francis (1996), have demonstrated that a positive attitude toward religion declines significantly between year nine and year ten as part of a progressive drift from religion which persists through the years of secondary schooling. There are two main theories in psychology advanced to account for this movement away from religion. Goldman's (1964) classic study drew on developmental psychology to argue that the movement away from religion is part of the developmental process away from concrete modes of thinking to abstract modes of thinking. Kay, Francis and Gibson (1996) considered that the evidence failed to support Goldman's classic theory and drew on psychology of social learning to argue that the movement away from religion is part of the social learning process in societies where adults are not generally taking religion seriously.

Clearly there is sufficient empirical evidence from previous studies to suggest that considerable change takes place in the worldview of young people between year nine and year ten and that the examination of age differences in spiritual health is worth exploring further.

Method

In order to examine the relationship between growing older and spiritual health, the dataset was simply divided between year-nine and year-ten pupils and the chi square test was employed to examine the statistical significance of differences between the two groups.

Personal domain

The statistics presented in table 5.1 demonstrate that there is very little significant shift in the level of spiritual health experienced in the personal domain between year nine and year ten of the secondary school. Looking at the indicators of positive affect first, in year nine 69% of the young people found life really worth living, and so did 70% in year ten. In year nine 56% of the young people felt that their life had a sense of purpose, and so did 55% in year ten.

Looking at the indicators of negative affect, in year nine 52% of the young people often felt depressed, and so did 52% in year ten. In year nine 27% of the young people had sometimes considered taking their own life, and so had 27% in year ten. In year nine 14% of the young people felt that they were not worth much as a person, and so did 13% in year ten. In year nine 35% of the young people often longed for someone to whom to turn for advice, and so did 35% in year ten.

Only one of the seven indicators in this section revealed a statistically significant shift between years nine and ten and this was by a mere two percentage points. In year nine 72% of the young people reported that they were happy in their school. In year ten this had dropped to 70%.

Communal domain

The statistics presented in table 5.2 demonstrate that a few small but significant developments are taking place in the communal domain of spiritual health between year nine and year ten. During this period there is a growing tendency for young people to seek less support from their parents and to seek more support from their peers. While 52% of the young people found it helpful to talk about their problems with their mother during year nine, the proportion fell to 48% during year ten. While 33% of the young people found it helpful to talk about their problems with their father during year nine, the proportion fell to 31% during year ten. On the other hand, while 62% of the young people found it helpful to talk about their problems with close friends during year nine, the proportion rose to 65% during year ten.

During the transition between year nine and year ten there is a significant amelioration in the problem of school bullying. In year nine 31% of the young people were worried about being bullied at school. In year ten the proportion fell to 25%. At the same time, 90% of the young people in both year nine and year ten said that they like the people with whom they go to school.

During the transition between year nine and year ten there is, however, no amelioration in the anxieties which young people report regarding relationships. In year nine 51% of the young people were worried about how they get on with other people, and so were 51% in year ten. In year nine 34% of the young people were worried about their attractiveness to the opposite sex, and so were 34% in year ten.

Environmental domain

The statistics presented in table 5.3 demonstrate some important ways in which spiritual health in the environmental domain deteriorates between year nine and year ten. During this period racist attitudes strengthen in ways which may be disruptive of healthy urban living. While in year nine 16% of the young people felt that there were too many black people living in this country, the proportion rose to 19% in year ten. While in year nine 29% of the young people thought that immigration into Britain should be restricted, the proportion rose to 35% in year ten.

At the same time, concerns about violence on global and local levels lessen between year nine and year ten. In year nine 57% of the young people were concerned about the risk of nuclear war, but the proportion fell slightly to 54% in year ten. In year nine 21% of the young people felt that there was too much violence on television, but the proportion fell slightly to 19% in year ten.

Concern for the global environment remains quite static between year nine and year ten, neither gaining nor losing in significance. In year nine 64% of the young people were concerned about the risk of pollution to the environment, and so were 64% in year ten. In year nine 59% of the young people were concerned about the poverty of the third world, and so were 60% in year ten.

There is one significant sign of hope regarding development in spiritual health in the environmental domain between year nine and year ten, as young people claim a greater sense of ownership over their world. In year nine 27% of the young people felt that there is nothing they can do to help solve the world's problems. In year ten the proportion fell slightly, but significantly, to 25%.

Transcendental domain

The statistics presented in table 5.4 demonstrate that traditional religion loses the goodwill of a significant number of young people between year nine and year ten. In year nine 44% of the young people believed in God, but in year ten the figure had fallen to 41%. In year nine 26% of the young people considered the Church to be irrelevant to life today but in year ten the figure had risen to 29%. In year nine 29% of the young people considered the Bible to be irrelevant to life today, but in year ten the figure had risen to 32%.

Over the same period of time, however, there was no similar decline in non-traditional religious beliefs, like horoscopes and fortune-telling. In year nine 34% of the young people believed in their horoscope, and in year ten the figure stood at 36%. In year nine 20% of the young people believed that fortune-tellers could tell the future, and in year ten the figure also stood at 20%. In year nine 30% of the young people believed it is possible to contact the spirits of the dead, and in year ten the figure stood at 32%.

What may be of particular interest in the statistics in this section concerns the way in which belief in life after death does not follow the same trajectory of decline as belief in God. In year nine 44% of the young people believed in God and 45% believed in life after death. In year ten belief in God had fallen from 44% to 41%, but belief in life after death had risen from 45% to 46%.

Conclusion

The growth, development and change that takes place during adolescence is so rapid that significant changes in spiritual health can be detected by snapshots taken just one year apart in year nine and in year ten. Some of these changes may bring hope to the urban environment by highlighting the positive effects which the developmental process and the educational process may be having on young lives. In the communal domain hope is generated by declining anxiety in school over bullying. In the environmental domain hope is generated by the increasing sense of responsibility and ownership being taken by young people for solving the problems of this world. At the same time, disappointment might be registered over the lack of development in other areas. In the personal domain there is no greater sense of purpose in life. In the communal domain there is no diminution of anxiety over relationships. In the environmental domain there is no substantive change in promoting greater concern for global citizenship or sustainable development. In the transcendental domain there is no sign of growing rationality over non-traditional religious beliefs. Moreover, there are other changes which actually erode hope for the urban environment. In the personal domain pupils are growing less positive about and less happy in their school. In the environmental domain there is an increase in racism and racist attitudes. In the transcendental domain the drift from traditional religion continues.

Urban planners may need to recognise the implications of the changes that are taking place in the spiritual health of young people as the maturation and socialisation processes take them through the years of secondary schooling. By no means all of the observed changes are inevitable consequences of aging and, consequently, well-planned intervention strategies during school-time and during leisure-time may help to improve the trajectory of spiritual health during the years of compulsory schooling.

6

North and south

Setting the context

This chapter poses the question regarding whether there is any significant difference in the levels of spiritual health across the four domains proposed by Fisher between young people living and growing up in the north of England and young people living and growing up in the south of England. The question makes sense in the light of a long debate regarding the differences between the two halves of England.

During the 1980s it became increasingly fashionable to talk of Britain being divided, commercially and politically, between north and south. The recession of the early 1980s had hit manufacturing industry in the north of England hard. Then the subsequent boom of the mid 1980s centred on the financial and service industries of London and the south east. As a result, differences in economic indicators such as house prices and unemployment rates widened considerably throughout Britain (Smith, 1989). Meanwhile, although they were comfortably re-elected in 1983 and in 1987, support for the Conservative Party became increasingly concentrated in the economically successful and suburban shires of the southern half of England (Curtice and Stead, 1986, 1988). The recession of the late 1980s, however, transformed the economic geography of England once again (Spencer, Beange and Curtice, 1992). This recession hit the southern half of the country much harder than it hit the northern half, while the north began enjoying the fruits of the subsequent recovery. Yet the differences

between north and south may go much deeper than the fluctuat-
ing and fragile influences of the economy.

Surprisingly few attempts have been made to profile differences in the psychology and human characteristics of the people
living in the north and south of England. One notable exception
has been the three studies reported by Curtice (1988, 1992, 1996)
drawing on the British Social Attitudes Survey dataset. Even here,
however, Curtice has focused largely on indicators directly relevant to economic wellbeing, leaving the real riches of that dataset to examine the differences between north and south largely
unexplored.

In his first study, which drew on aggregated data for the five
British Social Attitudes Surveys conducted in 1983, 1984, 1985,
1986, and 1987, Curtice (1988) reported some highly interesting
differences in economic evaluations made by people living in the
north and the south. While 34% of those living in the north expected prices to go up a lot in the next year, the proportion fell to
25% in the south. While 31% of those living in the north expected
unemployment to go up a lot in the next year, the proportion
fell to 21% in the south. While 49% of those living in the north
expected household income to fall behind prices in the next year,
the proportion fell to 37% in the south. While 29% of those living
in the north expected living on a household income to be difficult
or very difficult, the proportion fell to 20% in the south.

A different kind of question reported by Curtice (1988) invited
respondents to assess whether certain specified aspects of life were
better in the north or in the south. Half the respondents (51%)
considered that there were better chances in the north for young
people to buy their first home, 20% thought the chances were
better in the south, and the remaining 27% thought there were
no real differences. Regarding setting up their own business, 54%
considered the opportunities better in the south, 5% considered
the opportunities better in the north, and the remaining 39%
thought there were no real differences. Employment prospects

were considered to be better in the south by 84%, and better in the north by 1%, with the remaining 14% considering there to be no real difference.

Turning to ideological issues, Curtice (1988) found north and south quite sharply divided on items which stress the need for greater economic equality in society or which focus on unemployment as a major source of economic inequality. While 36% of those living in the south argued that unemployment benefit is too low and causes hardship, the proportion rose to 55% in the north. While 37% of those living in the south argued that income should be redistributed from the better-off to the less well-off, the proportion rose to 50% in the north. While 57% of those in the south argued that ordinary people do not get a fair share of the nation's wealth, the proportion rose to 70% in the north.

The final section of Curtice's (1988) analysis turned to moral attitudes and found no real differences between north and south. Agreement that homosexuality is not at all wrong was given by 14% in the north and by 16% in the south. Agreement to allow abortion if the woman does not want the child was given by 41% in the north and by 43% in the south. Agreement that divorce should be made easier was given by 11% in the north and by 9% in the south.

In his third study, Curtice (1996) drew on the three British Social Attitudes Surveys conducted in 1993, 1994, and 1995, so that a comparison could be made between the two periods of time: 1983–1987 and 1993–1995. He found that any differences between north and south remained but that they were less clear cut in the early 1990s. In the mid 1980s a clear majority believed that both employment prospects and business opportunities were better in the south than in the north. In the early 1990s there were still relatively few people who believed that either employment or business opportunities were better in the north than in the south. However, the proportion of people who thought that employment prospects were better in the south had dropped from

81% in the mid 1980s to 58% in the early 1990s. The proportion believing that business opportunities were better in the south also fell from 54% to 41%. However, what was once the more positive side of the northern economy had become less convincing. The proportion of people who considered that there was 'no real difference' in buying a first home in the north and in the south rose from 27% in the mid 1980s to 40% in the early 1990s.

Curtice (1996) also demonstrated significant changes in personal economic evaluation between the mid 1980s and the early 1990s. In the mid 1980s those living in the north were consistently more pessimistic in their evaluation of their personal economic circumstances than those living in the south. Subsequently, however, the northern half of the country became more optimistic and the southern more pessimistic. For example, the proportion of people who agreed that unemployment was of greater concern to them and to their families than inflation decreased by 8% in the north, but rose by 22% in the south.

The final section of Curtice's (1996) analysis turned attention to attitudes toward the European Union and found no real differences between the north and the south. Agreement that Britain's relationship with the European Union should be closer was given by 30% in the north and by 29% in the south. Agreement that Britain's policy should be to increase EU powers or form a single EU government was given by 31% in the north and by 33% in the south. Agreement that the pound should be kept as the only currency for Britain was given by 67% in the north and by 63% in the south.

The continuing differences between the north and the south of England into the twenty-first century have been confirmed by a number of independent studies. For example, Anyadike-Danes (2004) concentrated on profiling the differences in levels of male non-employment in the north and in the south. He demonstrates that in 'the relatively depressed north east of England, the proportion of working-age males without a job is twice as large as in the relatively prosperous south east'. Even sharper contrasts, however, are highlighted by focusing on those closer to retirement age. Almost half of all 60- to 64-year-old males living in the north east are not working by reason of sickness or disability, three times the proportion in the south east.

Doran, Drever and Whitehead (2004) drew on the 2001 population census data to explore whether there was a north-south divide in social class inequalities in health in Britain. They concluded that a geographical divide in social class inequalities existed at the start of the twenty-first century, with each of the seven social classes having higher rates of poor health in Wales, and in the north east and north west regions of England than elsewhere.

In calculating his figures Curtice (1988, 1992, 1996) agreed on a broad division of the country between the Humber on the east and the Mersey on the west. Clearly there is sufficient empirical evidence based on this division from previous analyses to suggest that north-south differences are worth taking seriously and that the examination of north-south differences in spiritual health is worth exploring further.

Method

In order to examine the relationship between spiritual health and geographical location the dataset was divided into three groups: Wales, the north of England and the south of England. The division between north and south was made on the basis of the geographical division employed for similar analyses using the British Social Attitudes Survey as reported by Curtice (1988, 1992, 1996). The chi square test was employed to examine the statistical significance of differences between the north of England and the south of England. Wales was excluded from this particular analysis.

Personal domain

The statistics presented in table 6.1 suggest that within the personal domain the majority of indicators reveal no significant differences in the level of spiritual health experienced in the north of England and in the south of England. Thus on the positive side of things, 55% of the young people living in the north felt that their life has a sense of purpose and so did 55% living in the south. In the north 72% of the young people were happy in their school, and so were 71% in the south.

On the negative side, 52% of the young people living in the north often felt depressed, and so did 53% living in the south. In the north 13% of the young people felt they were not worth much as a person, and so did 13% in the south. In the north 35% of the young people often longed for someone to whom to turn for advice, and so did 36% in the south.

There are, however, two indicators in this section which may suggest that spiritual health in the personal domain is somewhat stronger in the south than in the north. The first indicator relates to the overall positive affect generated by life. In the south 72% of the young people found life really worth living, but in the north the figure was significantly lower at 69%. The second indicator relates to the overall negative affect generated by life. In the south 26% of the young people have sometimes considered taking their own life, but in the north this figure was significantly higher at 28%.

Communal domain

The statistics presented in table 6.2 indicate that in some ways spiritual health in the communal domain is significantly lower in the north of England than in the south of England. This point is made by the following three indicators. More of the young people in the north than in the south were worried about how they get on with other people (51% compared with 49%). More of the young people in the north than in the south were worried about their attractiveness to the opposite sex (36% compared with 33%). More of the young people in the north than in the south were worried about being bullied at school (31% compared with 24%).

According to other indicators in this section there were no substantive differences in the experiences of the young people living in the north of England and the young people living in the south. In the north 50% of the young people found it helpful to talk about their problems with their mother, and so did 50% in the south. In the north 32% of the young people found it helpful to talk about their problems with their father, and so did 32% in the south. In the north 63% of the young people found it helpful to talk about their problems with their friends, and so did 64% in the south. In the north 90% of the young people liked the people they go to school with, and so did 89% in the south.

Environmental domain

The statistics presented in table 6.3 demonstrate that some significant differences are identified by the seven indicators concerned with the environmental domain of spiritual health between those living in the north and those living in the south. These differences can be summarised under three headings.

First, racism and racist attitudes are significantly stronger in the south of England than in the north of England. In the south 21% of the young people said that there were too many black people living in this country, compared with 16% in the north. In the south 36% of the young people thought that immigration into Britain should be restricted, compared with 31% in the north.

Second, priorities given to sustainable development issues and to world development issues are given different weight in the north and in the south. More concern was shown by the young people living in the north than by the young people living in the south regarding the risk of pollution to the environment (64% compared with 60%). Less concern was shown by the young people living in the north than by the young people living in the south regarding the poverty of the third world (57% compared with 61%).

Third, the young people living and growing up in the north were significantly less concerned about global violence. In the north 51% of the young people were concerned about the risk of nuclear war, compared with 60% in the south.

The two remaining indicators in this section reveal little substantive difference between north and south. In the north 20% of the young people considered that there was too much violence on television, and so did 19% in the south. In the north 26% of the young people considered that there was nothing they could do to help solve the world's problems, and so did 27% in the south.

Transcendental domain

The statistics presented in table 6.4 indicate that young people living and growing up in the north of England are more open to a transcendental interpretation of life than young people in the south. In the north young people are more likely to believe both in aspects of traditional religion and in aspects of non-traditional religion.

In terms of traditional religion, in the north 43% of the young people believed in God, while in the south the figure was significantly lower at 41%. In the north 47% of the young people believed in life after death, while in the south the figure was significantly lower at 41%. In the north 28% of the young people dismissed the Bible as irrelevant to life today, while in the south the figure was significantly higher at 31%. However, similar proportions of young people in the north and in the south took the view that the Church seems irrelevant to life today (26% and 27% respectively).

In terms of non-traditional religion, in the north 37% of the young people believed in their horoscope, compared with 32% in the south. In the north 22% of the young people believed that fortune-tellers can tell the future, compared with 15% in the south. In the north 31% of the young people believed that it is possible to contact the spirits of the dead, compared with 29% in the south.

Conclusion

This analysis has confirmed that there are significant differences between north and south across the four domains of spiritual health proposed by Fisher. Some of these indicators point to greater hope for the urban future in the north, and others of these indicators point to greater hope for the urban future in the south.

Within two of the domains young people living in the south record better overall indicators of spiritual health compared with young people living in the north. Both domains carry implications for urban hope. In the personal domain, young people in the south record a lower level of suicidal ideation. This carries signs of hope for the south. In the communal domain, young people in the south display lower levels of anxiety about relationships in general and lower levels of fear about being bullied in school. This carries signs of hope for the south.

Within the other two domains, however, young people living in the north record better overall indicators of spiritual health compared with young people living in the south. Both domains carry implications for urban hope. In the environmental domain, young people in the north record lower levels of racism. This carries signs of hope for the north. In the transcendental domain, young people in the north record higher levels of traditional religiosity. Certainly, as far as the faith communities are concerned, this carries signs of hope for the north.

Urban planners may need to recognise the importance of persisting differences between the north and the south in shaping hope for the urban future. Broadly-based differences calculated on such a crude measure of the macro division between north and south may well be indicative of even sharper differences calculated on the meso and micro divisions of regions and of local neighbourhoods. Geographical location may lead to significant differences in spiritual health and in urban hope.

7

Employed fathers

Setting the context

This chapter poses the question whether there is any significant difference in the levels of spiritual health across the four domains proposed by Fisher between young people living and growing up in homes where the father figure was engaged in full-time employment and in homes where this was not the case. This question makes sense in the light of a long tradition of research concerned with the relationship between paternal employment status and values and behaviour during childhood, adolescence and adulthood. The following review provides an introduction to this literature.

Rona and Chinn (1991) examined the relationship between the height of primary school children and father's employment status among three samples in England and Scotland. Their data found that children with an unemployed father were shorter, especially if the father had been unemployed for more than a year, in comparison alongside children with a currently employed father. After adjustment for parents' height, child's weight at birth, father's social class and family size, the difference was reduced but remained statistically significant.

Monck, Graham, Richman and Dobbs (1994) examined self-reported mood disturbance in a community population sample of 529 15- to 20-year-old females in England. Employing the Great Ormond Street Mood Questionnaire they found that one in five of the respondents (21%) scored over the cut-off point previously established to indicate risk of psychiatric disorder. Scoring over the cut-off point was associated neither with age nor with parental social class. It was, however, associated with parental unemployment.

O'Neill and Sweetman (1998) examined the relationship between sons' employment history and fathers' employment history in Britain, using a working sample of 987 father-son pairs generated from the March 1958 birth cohort. They found that a son whose father was unemployed twenty years earlier was almost twice as likely to be unemployed as a son whose father was not unemployed twenty years earlier. Furthermore, this discrepancy remained significant after controlling for a range of son's characteristics, including education, ability and family composition.

De Goede, Spruijt, Maas and Duindam (2000) examined the relationship between a range of family background variables and youth unemployment in a national survey of 955 non-school-going 18- to 27-year-old males and females in the Netherlands. For males, parental unemployment demonstrated the strongest correlation with youth employment. For females, affective relationships with parents provided stronger prediction than parental employment status. Overall the results suggested that family factors were better predictors of youth unemployment than individual or personal factors.

Pedersen (2001) examined the experience of victimisation among 10,812 13- to 18-year-old school pupils in Oslo. From the total sample, 6% reported that they had been victims of violent victimisation during the past year. The data demonstrated that demographic indicators associated with victimisation risk included immigrant status, working-class background, and parents who were unemployed or on social welfare.

Berntsson, Kohler and Gustafsson (2001) examined the nature and level of psychosomatic complaints among a representative sample of 3,760 7- to 12-year-old pupils in the Nordic countries. They found that headaches and stomach complaints were the most common. They also found that there were significantly higher levels of such complaints in families with low education, blue-collar work, low income, and unemployed fathers.

Pedersen, Mastekaasa and Wichstrøm (2001) examined early cannabis intake among a national sample of 2,436 12- to 16-year-old adolescents in Norway. They found a significantly higher level of parental unemployment among early cannabis users.

Kuhlthau and Perrin (2001) examined the relationship between the health status of children and the employment status of their parents, using data from a cross-sectional survey in the United States of America. Their data demonstrated that having a child with poor health status, as measured by general reported health, hospitalisation, activity limitations and chronic condition or disability, was associated with reduced employment of mothers or fathers.

Lundborg (2002) examined the predictors of alcohol use among a Swedish cross-sectional sample of 833 12- to 18-year-old adolescents, with focus on participation in drinking, frequency of drinking, intensity of drinking, and binge drinking. Separate analyses were conducted for beer, wine and spirits. Having a father who was currently unemployed was associated with an increased probability of binge drinking, but a reduced frequency of wine consumption.

Vance, Bowen, Fernandez and Thompson (2002) examined a range of risk and protective factors as predicting behavioural outcomes in a sample of 337 high-risk adolescents with aggression and serious emotional disturbance. Better behavioural outcomes were predicted by a history of consistent parental employment, as well as by positive parent-child relations, higher levels of current family support, contact with pro-social peers, higher reading levels, good problem-solving abilities, and superior interpersonal skills.

Gunther, Slavenburg, Feron and van Os (2003) examined childhood social and early developmental factors associated with mental health service use among children by comparing the profile of 80 6- to 13-year-old children referred to the Community Mental Health Centre in Maastricht with 320 matched controls who had not accessed mental health services. They found that the children referred to the mental health service were more likely to be living in a one parent family, having a divorced mother or having an unemployed father.

Sund, Larsson and Wichstrøm (2003) examined the relationships between various psychosocial factors and depressive symptoms in early adolescence among a representative sample of 12- to 14-year-old adolescents in two counties in Norway. They found significantly higher mean scores of depressive symptoms among adolescents having unemployed parents.

Clearly there is sufficient empirical evidence from previous studies to suggest that differences between living and growing up in homes where the father figure was engaged in full-time employment and in homes where this was not the case are worth taking seriously and that the examination of such differences in spiritual health is worth exploring further.

Method

In order to examine the relationship between spiritual health and living in a home with a father figure in full-time employment the dataset was divided into two groups distinguishing between those homes in which a father figure was engaged in full-time employment and those homes in which this was not the case. This second category combined homes in which there was no father figure and homes in which the father figure was retired, sick, unemployed, or employed part-time. The chi square test was employed to examine the statistical significance of differences between the two groups. For simplicity of comparison the two groups will be referred to as homes with employed fathers and homes without employed fathers.

Personal domain

The statistics presented in table 7.1 demonstrate that the presence of an employed father figure in the household is a significant predictor of higher levels of spiritual health in the personal domain. All the seven indicators point in the same direction.

The young people in homes where the father figure is in employment recorded higher scores on the indicators of positive affect. Thus, 73% of the young people from homes with employed fathers were happy in their school, compared with 63% from homes without employed fathers; 71% of the young people from homes with employed fathers found life really worth living, compared with 64% from homes without employed fathers; and 57% of the young people from homes with employed fathers felt that their life has a sense of purpose, compared with 51% from homes without employed fathers.

The young people in homes where the father figure is in employment recorded lower scores on the indicators of negative affect. Thus, 13% of the young people from homes with employed fathers felt that they were not worth much as a person, compared with 16% from homes without employed fathers; 51% of the young people from homes with employed fathers often felt depressed, compared with 57% from homes without employed fathers; and 26% of the young people from homes with employed fathers have sometimes considered taking their own life, compared with 31% from homes without employed fathers.

The young people from homes without employed fathers were more likely than the young people from homes with employed fathers often to long for someone to whom to turn for advice (37% compared with 35%).

Communal domain

The statistics presented in table 7.2 demonstrate that the presence of an employed father figure in the household is a significant predictor of some aspects of spiritual health in the communal domain. The main difference between the two groups is that the young people from homes without employed fathers show less successful relationships at school. Thus, 31% of the young people from homes without employed fathers were worried about being bullied at school, compared with 27% of those from homes with employed fathers. Fewer young people from homes without employed fathers found it helpful to discuss their problems with close friends (61%), compared with 64% from homes with employed fathers. Fewer young people from homes without employed fathers said that they like the people with whom they go to school (87%), compared with 90% from homes with employed fathers.

In other ways, however, the two groups show no substantive differences. Thus, between 33% and 34% of both groups were worried about their attractiveness to the opposite sex; between 50% and 51% of both groups were worried about how they get on with other people; and between 49% and 50% of both groups found it helpful to talk about their problems with their mother. Since there was no father figure present in some of the homes identified for the present analysis, it is unhelpful to compare relationships with fathers between the two groups.

Environmental domain

The statistics presented in table 7.3 demonstrate that the young people from homes without employed fathers are less likely to feel engagement with the social, economic and political issues confronting the world. From homes without employed fathers 60% of the young people were concerned about the risk of pollution to the environment, compared with 64% from homes with employed fathers. From homes without employed fathers 53% of the young people were concerned about the poverty of the third world, compared with 61% from homes with employed fathers. From homes without employed fathers, 50% of the young people were concerned about the risk of nuclear war, compared with 56% from homes with employed fathers. Consistent with this general trend is the finding that the young people from homes without employed fathers were more likely to feel that there is nothing they can do to help solve the world's problems (29%), compared with 25% from homes with employed fathers.

The two questions designed to access attitudes toward racism produce slightly different findings. The two groups do not differ significantly in response to the first question: 18% of the young people from homes without employed fathers and 17% from homes with employed fathers argued that there are too many black people living in this country. However, fewer young people from homes without employed fathers argued that immigration into Britain should be restricted (27%), compared with 33% from homes with employed fathers.

Young people from homes without employed fathers were significantly more likely than young people from homes with employed fathers to argue that there is too much violence on television (23% compared with 19%).

Transcendental domain

The statistics presented in table 7.4 suggest that young people from homes without employed fathers are more open both to traditional religion and to non-traditional religion.

In terms of traditional religion, the young people from homes without employed fathers were less likely than the young people from homes with employed fathers to dismiss the Bible as irrelevant for life today (28% compared with 31%) or to dismiss the

Church as irrelevant for life today (25% compared with 28%). The young people from homes without employed fathers were also more likely than the young people from homes with employed fathers to believe in life after death (48% compared with 45%). Belief in God, however, did not differ significantly between the two groups (44% and 43%).

In terms of non-traditional religion, young people from homes without employed fathers were more likely than young people from homes with employed fathers to believe in their horoscope (37% compared with 35%), to believe fortune-tellers can tell the future (25% compared with 19%), and to believe it is possible to contact the spirits of the dead (33% compared with 31%).

Conclusion

This analysis has confirmed that there are significant differences between young people living in homes with employed fathers and young people living in homes without employed fathers across the four domains of spiritual health proposed by Fisher. Young people living in homes where there is no father figure in full-time employment record significantly poorer levels of spiritual health in the personal domain (having a lower sense of purpose in life and suffering from more suicidal ideation), in the communal domain (forming poorer relationships with their peers at school) and in the environmental domain (showing less engagement with world issues). On the other hand, they record greater openness to the transcendental domain (showing greater traditional and non-traditional religious beliefs).

Urban planners may need to recognise that as traditional patterns of employment change in some urban areas there may be significant implications not only for those of working age, but for whole families and for young people in particular.

8

Broken homes

Setting the context

This chapter poses the question regarding whether there is any significant difference in the levels of spiritual health across the four domains proposed by Fisher between young people living and growing up in intact families and young people living and growing up in broken families. The question makes sense in the light of a long tradition of research concerned with the relationship between family disintegration or parental separation and divorce and the worldviews of school children and students.

One group of studies has looked at the relationship between parental divorce and differences in young people's behaviour, attitude or achievement during the school years. For example, Douglas (1970) studied bed-wetting among 15-year-old adolescents. He reported that adolescents whose parents had either separated or divorced during their first five years of life were twice as likely to be bed-wetting as those whose parents were together.

Ferri (1976) looked at school behaviour among 11-year-old children. His analysis of the National Child Development Study data found that children whose parents had divorced had poorer behaviour at school and were considered less well adjusted, although this relationship disappeared after controlling for other indices of deprivation.

Elliott and Richards (1991) explored disruptive behaviour and self-reported worry and unhappiness among 16-year-old adolescents in the National Child Development Study. Their data showed two findings. If parents divorced when children were between the ages of 7 and 16, the children had higher scores of unhappiness and worry and displayed more disruptive behaviour at the age of 16. They also scored higher on both indices at the age of 7, before their parents divorced. Elliott and Richards (1991) also looked at the relationship between marital disruption and educational achievement in maths and reading at the ages of 11 and 16 respectively. Again, significant differences among those whose parents had divorced and those continuing to live in intact families were reduced by controlling for other background variables.

Clark and Barber (1994) compared adolescent self-esteem in post-divorce, mother-headed families, and two-parent, always married families. No difference in self-esteem by family structure was found. On the other hand, the study by Martin-Lebrun, Poussin, Barumandzadeh and Bost (1997) among first-year secondary pupils found that pupils from intact homes recorded higher self-esteem scores than pupils where parents had separated or divorced.

Suh, Schutz and Johanson (1996) examined the relationship between family structure and initiating non-medical drug use among adolescents. They found that 12- to 17-year-old adolescents from intact families were less likely to initiate non-medical drug use. Similarly, Jenkins and Zunguze (1998) examined the relationship of family structure to adolescent drug use and peer-related factors. They found that pupils from intact families reported less frequent drug use, fewer drug-using friends, and perceptions of more peer disapproval of drug use. Neher and Short (1998) also found that children of divorced parents reported significantly more substance-using friends and less use of coping and social skills than children from intact families.

Borkhuis and Patalano (1997) compared the personality profiles of 52 adolescents from divorced families and 55 adolescents from intact families. They found that the adolescents from divorced families demonstrated greater signs of overall emotional distress, depression, pessimism about the future, anxiety, somatic symptomatology, agitation, irritability, aggression and alienation. They also demonstrated lower levels of impulse control and lower self-esteem.

Max, Brokaw and McQueen (1997) investigated the relationship between adolescent religiosity and parental religiosity in intact families and in families disrupted by separation or divorce. They found that adolescents from disrupted families were less religious than adolescents from intact families. This finding is consistent with the results of an earlier study by Ambert and Saucier (1986) who found in a sample of 275 adolescents that those from separated or divorced families were less likely to attend church than those from intact families.

Giuliani, Iafrate and Rosnati (1998) examined the relationship between family structure and adolescents' friendships and romantic relationships. They found that compared with adolescents from intact homes, adolescents from homes which had experienced separation or divorce displayed a higher level of distrust of others, were less likely to see marriage as a certain step in their own lives and showed a higher degree of fear toward marriage.

Aseltine (1996) found a positive correlation between depression and parental separation and divorce. Rubenstein, Halton, Kasten, Rubin and Stechler (1998) reported a positive correlation between suicidal behaviour and parental separation and divorce among high school students.

Ely, Richards, Wadsworth and Elliott (1999) re-analysed data from the three British birth cohorts which studied children born in 1946, 1958 and 1970. They found lower educational attainment associated with parental divorce in all three cohorts.

Guijarro, Naranjo, Padilla, Gutierez, Lammers and Blum (1999) found a significant relationship between adolescent pregnancy and parental separation in a study conducted among 135 females between the ages of 12 and 19 years.

Kierkus and Baer (2002) examined the relationship between

family structure and delinquent behaviour among a representative sample of 1,891 children in Ontario, Canada. The findings suggested that family structure was a significant predictor of most self-reported delinquent behaviours. In a national probability sample of 1,725 adolescents Rebellon (2002) also confirmed the link between delinquency and parental separation or divorce early in life.

Quensel, McArdle, Brinkley, Wiegersma, Blom, Fitzgerald, Johnson, Kolte, Michels, Pierolini, Pos and Stoekel (2002) examined the relationship between broken homes and drug use among representative samples of 3,386 school pupils around the age of 15 years residing in five European cities. Their data found small but statistically significant correlations between family structure and five forms of deviant behaviour: tobacco smoking, cannabis use, delinquency, general drug use, and a composite risk behaviour scale.

A second group of studies has looked at the relationship between parental divorce and differences in the behaviour, attitudes, personality or achievement of university and college students. For example, Crossman, Shea and Adams (1980) compared the level of ego development, locus of control, and identity achievement in 294 college students who came from intact, divorced, and divorced-remarried family backgrounds. Divorced backgrounds were not predictive of lower scores on any of the three measures. Similarly, Parish (1981) examined the self-concept of 1,409 college students in the United States of America. He found no significant differences in self-concept between students from divorced families and students from intact families. Phillips and Asbury (1990) examined several indicators of self-concept and mental health among a sample of 900 black freshmen students, of whom 356 came from divorced or separated backgrounds. They found no significant differences on any of the measures. Garber (1991) also failed to find a relationship between parental divorce and self-concept in his sample of 324 undergraduates. Heyer and Nelson

(1993) found no difference in autonomy scores in a sample of 388 college students between those whose parents were divorced and those from intact families, although those from divorced backgrounds recorded higher confidence and sexual identity scores.

Vess, Schwebel and Moreland (1983) compared the sex role orientation and sex role preference of two groups of college students, 84 students who had experienced parental divorce before the age of 10 and 135 students whose parents had never divorced or separated. No significant differences were found between the two groups.

Lopez, Campbell and Watkins (1988) examined aspects of adjustment to college among 255 students from intact homes and 112 students from non-intact homes in the United States of America. They found no significant differences between the two groups.

Gabardi and Rosén (1991) explored the relationship between several measures of adjustment and parental divorce among a sample of 500 college students in the United States of America. Multivariate analyses of variance indicated that students from divorced families had significantly more sexual partners and more negative attitudes toward marriage than students from intact families.

Jennings, Salts and Smith (1991) employed the Favourableness of Attitudes Towards Marriage Scale among 340 college freshmen, 67 of whom came from divorced families. They found a significantly less favourable attitude toward marriage among those whose parents had separated or divorced. Similarly, Greenberg and Nay (1982) studied attitudes toward divorce among college students. They found that those from broken homes were more favourable toward divorce than other young people. On the other hand, Livingston and Kordinak (1990) examined the relationship between parental divorce and marital role expectations among a sample of 80 college students. They found no simple relationship between these two variables.

A third group of studies has looked at the relationship between parental divorce and differences in behaviour, attitudes and experiences of adults throughout their life stages, including recent work by Spruijt and de Goede (1997), Gahler (1998), Wolfinger (1998), Nurco, Kinlock, O'Grady and Hanlon (1998), O'Connor, Thorpe, Dunn and Golding (1999), Kiernan and Cherlin (1999), Wallerstein and Lewis (2004), Barrett and Turner (2005), Modestin, Furrer and Malti (2005), Segrin, Taylor and Altman (2005). The recent study by Amato and Cheadle (2005) looked for the effects of divorce one step further by examining the link between divorce in the grandparent generation and outcomes in the grandchild generation across a sample of 691 individuals in the third generation. The data demonstrated that divorce in the grandparent generation was associated in the grandchild generation with lower education, more marital discord, weaker ties with mothers, and weaker ties with fathers, but there was no association with general wellbeing in the grandchild generation.

Clearly there is sufficient empirical evidence from previous studies to suggest that differences between living and growing up in intact homes or in broken homes are worth taking seriously and that the examination of such differences in spiritual health is worth exploring further.

Method

In order to examine the relationship between family structure and spiritual health, the dataset was divided into two groups distinguishing between those young people who continued to live with their original parents and those young people whose family structure had been disrupted by parental separation, divorce, or other form of restructuring. The chi square test was employed to examine the statistical significance of differences between the two groups. For simplicity of comparison the two groups will be referred to as intact homes and broken homes.

Personal domain

The statistics presented in table 8.1 demonstrate that family structure is highly significant in predicting spiritual health in the personal domain. According to all seven indicators in this section young people from broken homes experience a lower level of spiritual health compared with young people from intact homes.

The young people from broken homes recorded lower scores on the indicators of positive affect. Thus, 65% of the young people from broken homes found life really worth living, compared with 71% from intact homes. Similarly, 65% of the young people from broken homes liked the people with whom they go to school, compared with 73% from intact homes. Fewer young people from broken homes felt their life has a sense of purpose (52%), compared with 57% from intact homes.

The young people from broken homes also recorded higher scores on the indicators of negative affect. Thus, 16% of young people from broken homes felt that they were not worth much as a person, compared with 13% from intact homes. Nearly three-fifths of the young people from broken homes often felt depressed (58%), compared with 51% from intact homes. A third of the young people from broken homes have sometimes considered taking their own life (33%), compared with 25% from intact homes.

The young people from broken homes were more likely than the young people from intact homes often to long for someone to whom to turn for advice (39% compared with 34%).

Communal domain

The statistics presented in table 8.2 demonstrate that family structure is significant for one key aspect of spiritual health in the communal domain, but not for the whole of this domain. Predictably, the young people from broken homes reported somewhat less healthy relationships with both of their parents. While 51% of the young people from intact homes found it helpful to talk about their problems with their mother, the proportion fell significantly to 48% among those from broken homes. While 33% of the young people from intact homes found it helpful to talk about their problems with their father, the proportion fell to 28% among those from broken homes. Finding less help from their parents, the young people from broken homes were more likely to turn to their friends. While 63% of the young people from intact homes found it helpful to talk about their problems with close friends, the proportion rose to 66% among those from broken homes.

In other ways the responses between the two groups are very close. Half of the young people from intact homes were worried about how they get on with other people (50%), and so were 52% from broken homes. A third of the young people from intact homes were worried about their attractiveness to the opposite sex (34%), and so were 35% from broken homes. Just over a quarter of the young people from intact homes were worried about being bullied at school (28%), and so were 28% from broken homes. Nine out of ten of the young people from intact homes liked the people with whom they go to school (90%), and so did 89% from broken homes.

Environmental domain

The statistics presented in table 8.3 demonstrate that family structure functions as a significant predictor of the way in which young people view their engagement with world issues of social, political and economic concern. Young people from broken homes show less engagement with such matters and feel less empowered to have an influence on the world around them. This point is made by the following figures.

While 65% of the young people from intact homes were

concerned about the risk of pollution to the environment, the proportion fell to 60% among those from broken homes. While 61% of the young people from intact homes were concerned about the poverty of the third world, the proportion fell to 55% among those from broken homes. While 56% of the young people from intact homes were concerned about the risk of nuclear war, the proportion fell to 53% among those from broken homes. While 25% of the young people from intact homes said there was nothing they could do to help solve the world's problems, the proportion rose to 28% among those from broken homes.

In other ways the responses between the two groups are very close. Between 17% and 18% of both groups argued that there are too many black people living in this country. Between 31% and 32% of both groups argued that immigration into Britain should be restricted. Between 19% and 20% of both groups argued that there is too much violence on television.

Transcendental domain

The statistics presented in table 8.4 demonstrate that family structure functions as a significant predictor of spiritual health in the transcendental domain. Young people from broken homes show less engagement with traditional religiosity and more engagement with non-traditional religiosity.

In terms of traditional religiosity, belief in God fell from 44% among the young people in intact homes to 37% among those in broken homes. The view that the Church seems irrelevant for life today rose from 27% among the young people in intact homes to 29% among those in broken homes. The view that the Bible seems irrelevant for life today rose from 30% among the young people in intact homes to 32% among those in broken homes. Between 45% and 46% of both groups believed in life after death.

In terms of non-traditional religion, belief in their horoscope rose from 33% among the young people in intact homes to 41%

among those in broken homes. Belief in fortune-tellers being able to tell the future rose from 18% among the young people in intact homes to 25% among those in broken homes. Belief in the possibility of contacting the spirits of the dead rose from 29% among the young people in intact homes to 37% among those in broken homes.

Conclusion

This analysis has confirmed that there are significant differences between young people living in intact homes and young people living in broken homes across the four domains of spiritual health proposed by Fisher. Young people living in broken homes record significantly poorer levels of spiritual health in the personal domain (having a lower sense of purpose in life), in the communal domain (having less satisfactory relationships with their parents), in the environmental domain (showing less engagement with world issues), and in the transcendental domain (showing less commitment to traditional religiosity, and giving greater credence to horoscopes and fortune-tellers).

Urban planners may need to recognise that as traditional patterns of family life become increasingly eroded in contemporary society the spiritual health of young people living in urban areas may also become increasingly fragile and vulnerable.

9

Anglican schools

Setting the context

This chapter turns attention away from personal individual differences (like sex and age) and away from family individual differences (like living in the north or south, employed fathers, and broken homes) to begin to examine whether there are differences between different types of schools. Specifically this chapter poses the question regarding the relationship between attending an Anglican voluntary school within the state-maintained sector and levels of spiritual health across the four domains proposed by Fisher. This question is posed against the background of previous research concerned with the differences between pupils educated in non-denominational state-maintained schools and pupils educated in Anglican voluntary schools within the state-maintained sector in England and Wales. First, however, attention needs to be given to the history and to the theological and educational principles underpinning the involvement of the Church of England (and Church in Wales) in church schools.

Historically the initiative for building schools in England and Wales came not from the state but from the churches. The Church of England played a crucial part in this initiative, largely through the National Society founded in 1811. Between 1833 and 1870 government monies were made available to help the National Society and other church-related societies, like the British and Foreign School Society, to build new schools, but not until the 1870 Education Act was there machinery to build government-funded schools apart from through the voluntary societies. At the time of the 1870 Education Act the Church of England was responsible for the largest part of the nation's schools (Cruickshank, 1963).

From 1870 to 1944 board schools and local education authority schools developed alongside church schools. Most of these schools provided an elementary education for children between the ages of 5 and 14. In 1944 this dual system was encapsulated within a new law of education, which provided for a partnership in the provision of schooling between the church authorities and the state. The 1944 Education Act made provision for the development of two types of church schools: voluntary aided schools where the church retained both control and ongoing financial liability, and voluntary controlled schools where the church gave more control to the local education authority but was absolved from ongoing financial liability. The choice was left largely in the hands of individual governing bodies as far as the Church of England and Church in Wales were concerned. From the implementation of the 1944 Education Act schooling was to be divided into a primary phase, usually from 5 to 11, and a secondary phase, usually from 11 to at least 15 (subsequently raised to 16 in 1972). The Anglican Church, following the 1944 Education Act, faced a considerable challenge in the provision of schools, and individual schools had to make a decision as to whether they would opt for primary or secondary status. In the event the vast majority of Anglican schools opted for status as primary schools, which led directly to the current imbalance of provision. In September 1999, almost 25% of state-maintained primary schools were Anglican, compared with 5.6% of state-maintained secondary schools.

The general impression is that the demand for pupil admissions to Anglican secondary schools remains strong (Chadwick, 2001). In some areas of the country the Anglican secondary schools tend to be in great demand from church-affiliated families and are heavily over-subscribed. In other areas of the country, as a result of the historic location of these schools, they tend to concentrate more on serving the local community, regardless of the faith position of individual parents, and reflect their original trust deeds, which usually define their purpose as the provision of education for the children of the poor and manufacturing classes. The imbalance in provision between the primary and secondary sectors, combined with the historic commitment to serving the local community, means that the current position with regard to Anglican secondary schools in England and Wales is complex and quite distinct from schools run by other faiths or denominations. The Anglican Church, in its own writings and reports, encapsulates this complexity by referring to a dynamic tension that exists in all its secondary and some of its primary schools, between the task of providing an Anglican education for the children of Anglican parents and the task of providing an education for all children from the community immediately around the school. This has been a subject of continuing discussion and development of thinking over the last thirty years and is encapsulated in *The Fourth R* (Ramsey, 1970), *A Future in Partnership* (Waddington, 1984) and, most recently, in *The Way Ahead* (Dearing, 2001).

In seeking to establish the implications for the Church of England of the attitudes of pupils in church schools on matters of personal, moral and religious values, it is very important to bear in mind this dynamic tension in diversity within the admissions and to understand as far as possible how this might impact on the views of pupils within an individual school.

Given the tradition of opening a proportion of the places in Anglican schools to pupils who are being brought up in homes affiliated to a variety of faiths or to none, it is important to understand how the Anglican Church expects its schools to respond to the situation while being true to their foundation. All Anglican schools within the state-maintained sector must include within their Instrument of Government an ethos statement which provides the basis from which school policy and strategy are developed. In 1999 the Anglican Church adopted the following model ethos statement for its schools, which was in turn adopted by most Anglican schools without variation.

Recognising its historic foundation, the school will preserve and develop its religious character in accordance with the principles of the Church of England/Church in Wales and in partnership with the churches at parish and diocesan level.

The school aims to serve its community by providing an education of the highest quality within the context of Christian belief and practice. It encourages an understanding of the meaning and significance of faith, and promotes Christian values through the experience it offers to all its pupils (Brown and Lankshear, 2000).

Relatively little research has been undertaken to examine the differences between pupils educated in Anglican state-maintained schools in England and Wales and pupils educated in non-denominational state-maintained schools. In a foundational study, Francis (1986a) administered a scale of attitude toward Christianity to all year-five and year-six pupils within ten Church of England voluntary aided primary schools and fifteen non-denominational state-maintained schools in East Anglia in 1974, 1978, and again in 1982. After using multiple regression to control for a range of other influences on the pupils' attitude toward Christianity, these data indicated that the Church of England schools exercised a small negative influence on their pupils' attitude toward Christianity. The direction of the school influence on pupils' attitude was consistent for all three samples taken in 1974, 1978, and 1982.

Francis (1987) set out to replicate this earlier study among year-six pupils throughout all the Church of England voluntary aided, Church of England voluntary controlled, and non-denominational state-maintained schools in Gloucestershire. These data attributed neither positive nor negative influence to

Church of England voluntary aided schools, but demonstrated a significant negative influence exercised by Church of England voluntary controlled schools.

Three studies set out to compare pupils in Church of England and non-denominational state-maintained secondary schools. In the first study, Francis and Carter (1980) compared the attitude toward Christianity of year-eleven pupils attending Church of England voluntary aided secondary schools and non-denominational state-maintained secondary schools. These data provided no support for the notion that Church of England secondary schools exert either a positive or a negative influence on their pupils' attitude toward Christianity.

In the second study, Francis and Jewell (1992) compared the attitude toward the church of year-ten pupils attending the four non-denominational secondary schools and the one Church of England voluntary secondary school serving the area around the same town. The data demonstrated that the Church of England school recruited a higher proportion of pupils from churchgoing homes and that churchgoing homes tended to represent the higher social classes. After taking into account the influence of sex, social class, and parental religiosity, path analysis indicated that the Church of England school exerted neither a positive nor a negative influence on its pupils' religious practice, belief, or attitude.

In the third study, Lankshear (2005) compared the personal, moral and religious values of 957 pupils attending Anglican voluntary aided secondary schools with the values of 24,027 pupils attending non-denominational state-maintained schools. In the analysis further comparisons were made between males and females and between three religious groups: non-affiliates, Anglicans and those affiliated with other Christian denominations. The data demonstrated that Anglicans attending Anglican schools recorded higher levels of religious values and comparable levels of moral values, in comparison with Anglicans attending non-denominational schools. Non-affiliates attending Anglican schools recorded higher levels of personal dissatisfaction, lower levels of moral values and comparable levels of religious values, in comparison with non-affiliates attending non-denominational schools.

Clearly there is sufficient empirical evidence from previous studies to suggest that attending an Anglican school is worth taking seriously as predictive of individual differences in areas of personal, social and religious values and that examination of the relationship between attending an Anglican school and spiritual health is worth exploring further.

Method

Since about 5% of the year-nine and year-ten pupils currently educated in the state-maintained sector of schools in England and Wales are in schools founded by the Anglican Church, the sample of pupils in the survey was designed to reflect this distribution. In order, then, to examine the relationships between spiritual health and attending an Anglican school, the present chapter makes a direct comparison between two groups of pupils: those educated in non-denominational state-maintained secondary schools and those educated in Anglican state-maintained secondary schools. The chi square test was employed to examine the statistical significance of differences between the two groups. For simplicity of comparison the two groups will be referred to as Anglican schools and non-denominational schools.

Personal domain

The statistics presented in table 9.1 demonstrate that within the personal domain there are a number of ways in which young people attending Anglican schools enjoy the same level of spiritual health as young people attending non-denominational schools. There were no significant differences between the proportions of the young people in the two sectors who were happy in their school (70% in non-denominational schools and 69% in Anglican schools), who felt that their lives had a sense of purpose (54% in non-denominational schools and 51% in Anglican schools) or who had sometimes considered taking their own life (28% in non-denominational schools and 30% in Anglican schools).

In respect of some other indicators of spiritual health in the personal domain, however, the young people attending Anglican schools recorded significantly lower scores than young people in non-denominational schools. In Anglican schools 64% of the young people found life really worth living, compared with 69% in non-denominational schools. In Anglican schools 58% of the young people reported that they often felt depressed, compared with 52% in non-denominational schools. In Anglican schools 17% of the young people felt that they were not worth much as a person, compared with 14% in non-denominational schools. These reported higher levels of negative affect among the young people in Anglican schools are also reflected in the fact that 39% of the young people in Anglican schools often longed for someone to whom to turn for advice, compared with 34% of those in non-denominational schools.

Communal domain

The statistics presented in table 9.2 demonstrate that within the communal domain there are a number of ways in which young people attending Anglican schools enjoy the same level of spiritual health as young people attending non-denominational schools. There were no significant differences between the proportions of young people in the sectors who found it helpful to talk about their problems with their mother (50% in non-denominational schools and 52% in Anglican schools), who found it helpful to talk about their problems with their father (31% in non-denominational schools and 31% in Anglican schools), who found it helpful to talk about their problems with close friends (63% in non-denominational schools and 64% in Anglican schools), or who liked the people with whom they attended school (90% in non-denominational schools and 90% in Anglican schools).

In respect of some other indicators of spiritual health in the communal domain, however, the young people attending Anglican schools recorded significantly lower scores of spiritual health than the young people in non-denominational schools. In Anglican schools 37% of the young people were worried about their attractiveness to the opposite sex, compared with 33% in non-denominational schools. In Anglican schools 54% of the young people were worried about how they get on with other people, compared with 49% in non-denominational schools. In Anglican schools 34% of the young people were worried about being bullied at school, compared with 28% in non-denominational schools.

Environmental domain

The statistics presented in table 9.3 demonstrate that within the environmental domain there are a number of ways in which the young people attending Anglican schools enjoy the same level of spiritual health as the young people attending non-denominational schools. There were no significant differences between the proportions of the young people in the two sectors who considered that there were too many black people living in this country (18% in non-denominational schools and 19% in Anglican schools), who argued that immigration into Britain should be restricted (31% in non-denominational schools and 32% in Anglican schools), who were concerned about the risk of nuclear war (55% in non-denominational schools and 56% in Anglican schools), or who felt that there was nothing they could do to help solve the world's problems (27% in non-denominational schools and 24% in Anglican schools).

In respect of some other indicators of spiritual health in the environmental domain, however, the young people attending Anglican schools recorded significantly higher scores than the young people in non-denominational schools. In Anglican schools 68% of the young people expressed concern about the risk of pollution to the environment, compared with 63% in non-denominational schools. In Anglican schools 62% of the young people expressed concern about the poverty of the third world, compared with 57% in non-denominational schools. In Anglican schools 26% of the young people considered that there was too much violence on television, compared with 20% in non-denominational schools.

Transcendental domain

The statistics presented in table 9.4 demonstrate that within the transcendental domain there are a number of ways in which young people attending Anglican schools enjoy the same level of spiritual health as young people attending non-denominational schools. There were no significant differences between the proportions of the young people in the two sectors who regarded the Church as irrelevant for life today (28% in non-denominational schools and 28% in Anglican schools), who regarded the Bible as irrelevant for life today (31% in non-denominational schools and 29% in Anglican schools), who believed in their horoscope (36% in non-denominational schools and 36% in Anglican schools), and who believed that it is possible to contact the spirits of the dead (32% in non-denominational schools and 33% in Anglican schools).

In respect of some other indicators of spiritual health in the transcendental domain, however, the young people attending Anglican schools recorded significantly different scores in comparison with the young people attending non-denominational schools. They were more likely to believe in God and to believe in life after death. In Anglican schools 51% of the young people believed in

God, compared with 37% in non-denominational schools. In Anglican schools 54% of the young people believed in life after death, compared with 43% in non-denominational schools. The young people in Anglican schools also recorded a higher level of belief in fortune-tellers, compared with the young people in non-denominational schools (24% compared with 20%).

Conclusion

This analysis has demonstrated that, although young people attending Anglican schools share a number of indicators of spiritual health in common with young people in non-denominational schools, there are significant differences between the two groups in respect of all four of Fisher's domains of spiritual health. In comparison with young people in non-denominational schools, young people in Anglican schools record signs of lower spiritual health in the personal domain (less likely to find life really worth living) and in the communal domain (less confident in relationships with others), and signs of better spiritual health in the environmental domain (more concern about world poverty) and in the transcendental domain (more likely to believe in God, although they are also more likely to believe in fortune-tellers).

The positive interpretation of these findings is that Anglican secondary schools may be working with less advantaged young people in the urban environment (as indicated by the lower spiritual health in the personal and communal domains) and nonetheless adding value to their spiritual health (as indicated by better spiritual health in the environmental and transcendental domains). According to this account Anglican schools add hope to the urban environment.

Urban planners may need to recognise and to value the distinctive contribution made to urban living by the continuing involvement of the Anglican Church within the state-maintained sector of education.

10

Catholic Schools

Setting the context

In England and Wales the two denominations which retained a significant investment with the state-maintained sector of education following the 1944 Education Act were the Church of England (and the Church in Wales) and the Roman Catholic Church. This chapter focuses specifically on Roman Catholic schools and poses the question regarding the relationship between attending a Roman Catholic school within the state-maintained sector and levels of spiritual health across the four domains proposed by Fisher. This question is posed against the background of previous research concerned with the differences between pupils educated in non-denominational state-maintained schools and pupils educated in Roman Catholic voluntary schools within the state-maintained sector in England and Wales. First, however, attention needs to be given to the historical differences between Anglican and Catholic investment in education in England and Wales (see Chadwick, 1997).

When the National Society was established in 1811 its aim was to work with the established Church of England to provide a network of schools to educate the children of the nation in the principles of the established religion. When the Catholic Poor School Committee was established in 1847 the aim was very different: the aim was to provide an alternative network of schools for a religious minority which stood outside the established Church of the nation. At the time of the 1944 Education Act the Catholic community stood committed to two costly principles: to seek voluntary aided status for a national network of primary schools and to finance and build a parallel national network of secondary schools. By the beginning of the twenty-first century the Roman Catholic Church provided about one in ten primary places and one in ten secondary places within the state-maintained sector. The changing demographic profile of the Catholic population has, however, meant that the original aim of staffing Catholic schools with Catholic teachers to teach Catholic pupils has been diluted by recruiting numbers of non-Catholic staff and non-Catholic pupils into some schools (Francis, 1986b).

Gerald Grace's (2001) paper on 'The state and Catholic schools in England and Wales: politics, ideology and mission integrity' provides a good overview of the way in which the Catholic Church responded to educational developments during the 1990s and into the twenty-first century. He comments as follows.

Contemporary Catholic schooling in England and Wales is in many ways a success story. Catholic schools are strongly represented in the top sections of published academic league tables and of test score results. An increasing number of Catholic schools are oversubscribed by parents anxious to obtain admission for their children and young people to schools frequently described in the mass media as 'star performers' (Grace, 2001: 497).

Since the early 1960s there have been four main strands of research concerned with pupils attending Catholic schools in England and Wales. The first phase occurred during the 1960s and comprises the three original and independent studies conducted by Brothers (1964), Lawlor (1965) and Spencer (1968) as part of an initial attempt to discover something about the distinctiveness and effectiveness of Catholic schools. For example, in a study of Catholic school children and students, Lawlor (1965) found what she described as evidence of an impressive, real and deep religious commitment. At the same time, she found their religion to emphasise the other wordly, to be associated with a tendency to opt out of this world and the human community, and to reflect a lower level of concern for others.

The second phase occurred during the 1970s and was stimulated by the initiatives of Michael Hornsby-Smith and his associates, as summarised by Hornsby-Smith (1978). For example, a study carried out with Ann Thomas compared the attitudes of girls educated in an Anglican school and in a Catholic convent school. The data demonstrated that the girls in the Catholic school were more likely to aspire to outstanding scholarship or sporting achievement, were more preoccupied with the state of family life, and were more critical toward television, modern art and modern drama.

The third phase occurred during the late 1970s and 1980s and was stimulated by the initiatives of Leslie J. Francis and his associates. One set of studies in this strand concentrated on the relationship between Catholic schools and pupils' attitude toward Christianity. For example, Francis (1979, 1986a, 1987) examined the influence of Catholic primary schools on pupils' attitude toward Christianity. After taking into account factors like social class, intelligence, and parental religiosity, path analysis identified a unique contribution made by Catholic primary schools to the development of a positive attitude toward Christianity among 10- to-11-year-old pupils. Boyle and Francis (1986) explored the comparative influence of Catholic secondary and Catholic middle schools on the attitude toward Christianity of 12- to 13-year-old pupils. They found no significant difference between these two types of schools. Francis and Carter (1980) compared pupils attending Catholic, Anglican and county secondary schools. After taking into account other influences, the data demonstrated neither positive nor negative influence exerted by Catholic secondary schools on the pupils' attitude toward Christianity.

A second set of studies in this strand by Egan and Francis

among pupils attending Catholic secondary schools in England and Wales drew attention to the important interaction between the Catholic school and the pupils' home backgrounds. Francis (1986b) assessed attitude toward Christianity among pupils between the ages of eleven and sixteen attending Catholic comprehensive schools in two Midland conurbations. The data demonstrated that non-Catholic pupils attending Catholic schools recorded a less sympathetic attitude toward Christianity than Catholic pupils. He concluded that, if one of the aims of the Catholic Church in maintaining Catholic schools in England is to provide a faith community in which Catholic pupils are supported by a positive attitude toward Christianity among their peers, these findings place a caveat on a policy of recruiting a significant proportion of non-Catholic pupils, even from church-going backgrounds.

Egan (1985, 1988), and Egan and Francis (1986) developed a set of three instruments to assess attitudes toward attending Catholic schools. The scales measured 'attitude toward the traditional method of the Catholic school system', 'attitude toward religious education in the Catholic school system', and 'attitude toward attending the Catholic school'. These studies explored the differences in attitudes held by practising Catholics, non-practising Catholics, and non-Catholic pupils attending Catholic secondary schools in Wales. The data demonstrated that the most serious disaffection with the Catholic school is attributable not so much to the non-Catholic pupils as to the non-practising Catholic pupils. This is a much larger problem for the Catholic Church in Wales. While less than 9% of the Welsh sample were non-Catholics, less than half of the girls and only slightly more than two-fifths of the boys were weekly mass attenders, while only two-fifths of both sexes were supported by weekly mass attending mothers and only one-quarter by weekly mass attending fathers.

The fourth phase occurred during the late 1980s, the 1990s and the early 2000s when a number of independent initiatives emerged. For example, Cuttance (1989) employed measures of cognitive outcomes in English, in mathematics and in overall attainment across all subjects derived from the Scottish school leavers survey of 1981. These data demonstrated a clear perform- ance advantage associated with the Catholic sector of schools in Scotland.

Tritter (1992) developed a set of four scales to assess general religious attitudes, specific Catholic beliefs, specific Jewish beliefs and secular morality. These scales were used to compare pupils attending a county school, a Catholic school and a Jewish school. The data suggested that religious schools produced students with stronger and more uniform attitudes toward morality than county schools.

Curran and Francis (1996) developed a twelve item scale to measure Catholic identity and employed this scale among 11- to 12-year-old pupils attending Catholic secondary schools. The re- sponses indicated a basically positive view of being Catholic. Half (50%) of the pupils reported that they find going to mass *very* helpful and nearly two-thirds (63%) reported that they find go- ing to confession *very* helpful. Over two-thirds (68%) sometimes pray to 'Our Lady'. The correlations with other indices of religios- ity indicated the importance of a Catholic background, a Catholic home and church involvement in promoting Catholic identity, in addition to attendance of a Catholic secondary school.

In a series of studies examining academic performance, examin- ation results at GCSE, and performance at key stage two and key stage four, Morris (1994, 1995, 1997, 1998a, 1998b, 2001, 2005) drew attention to the apparent success of Catholic schools in engendering a positive attitude toward learning among their pupils.

Scholefield (2001) examined the spiritual, moral, social and cultural values of 29 sixth-form students attending a voluntary aided Catholic secondary school. She found that the church's teaching on social justice received a more positive response from students than its teaching on sexual morality. These students did not see material success or status as their primary goal; they valued their own integrity and their relationships more highly than material success.

Francis (2002) drew attention to four distinct communities of values within the Catholic school as defined by pupils who are active Catholics, sliding Catholics, lapsed Catholics, and non-Catholics. The straight comparison between all pupils in Catholic schools and pupils in non-denominational schools demonstrated significant differences in the overall moral and religious climate among the two groups of pupils. Overall within the Catholic schools there was a higher level of commitment to religious values and a higher level of commitment to moral values. In this sense, parents who send their children to Catholic schools can expect their children to be part of a community in which the pupils display a higher level of commitment to Christian moral values and religious values than would be the case in non-denominational schools. However, closer analysis of the moral values and of the religious values of pupils educated within Catholic schools confirms that it is necessary to consider the pupil body attending these schools not as a homogeneous faith community but as four intersecting but highly distinctive faith communities.

Clearly there is sufficient empirical evidence from previous studies to suggest that attending a Catholic school is worth taking seriously as predictive of individual differences across a wide range of areas and that examination of the relationship between attending a Catholic school and spiritual health is worth exploring further.

Method

Since about 10% of the year-nine and year-ten pupils currently educated in the state-maintained sector of schools in England and Wales are attending schools founded by the Catholic Church, the sample of pupils in the survey was designed to reflect this distribution. In order, then, to examine the relationships between spiritual health and attending a Catholic school, the present chapter makes a direct comparison between two groups of pupils: those educated in non-denominational state-maintained secondary schools and those educated in Catholic state-maintained secondary schools. The chi square test was employed to examine the statistical significance of differences between the two groups. For simplicity of comparison the two groups will be referred to as Catholic schools and non-denominational schools.

Personal domain

The statistics presented in table 10.1 demonstrate that within the personal domain there are a number of ways in which young people attending Catholic schools enjoy the same level of spiritual health as young people attending non-denominational schools. In terms of indicators of positive affect, there are no significant differences between the proportions of the young people in the two sectors who found life really worth living (69% in non-denominational schools and 69% in Catholic schools) and who were happy in their school (70% in non-denominational schools and 69% in Catholic schools). In terms of indicators of negative affect there are no significant differences between the proportions of the young people in the two sectors who felt they were not worth much as a person (14% in non-denominational schools and 13% in Catholic schools), who often felt depressed (52% in non-denominational schools and 52% in Catholic schools), and who have sometimes considered taking their own life (28% in non-denominational schools and 26% in Catholic schools).

The striking difference between the two groups concerned the way in which pupils in Catholic schools were so much more likely than pupils in non-denominational schools to report a sense of purpose in life. Almost two-thirds of the young people attending Catholic schools felt their lives had a sense of purpose (64%), compared with 54% in non-denominational schools.

The young people attending Catholic schools were also slightly more likely than the young people attending non-denominational schools often to long for someone to whom to turn for advice (37% compared with 34%).

Communal domain

The statistics presented in table 10.2 demonstrate that within the communal domain there are a number of ways in which young people attending Catholic schools enjoy the same level of spiritual health as young people attending non-denominational schools. In terms of indicators of positive affect, there were no significant differences between the proportions of the young people in the two sectors who found it helpful to talk about their problems with their mothers (50% in non-denominational schools and 49% in Catholic schools), who found it helpful to talk about their problems with their fathers (31% in non-denominational schools and 33% in Catholic schools), who found it helpful to talk about their problems with close friends (63% in non-denominational schools and 63% in Catholic schools), and who liked the people with whom they go to school (90% in non-denominational schools and 89% in Catholic schools). In terms of indicators of negative affect, there were no significant differences between the proportions of the young people in the two sectors who were worried about their attractiveness to the opposite sex (33% in non-denominational schools and 33% in Catholic schools).

Where, however, significant differences emerged between the two groups, the young people in Catholic schools recorded significantly lower scores of spiritual health than the young people in non-denominational schools. In Catholic schools 31% of the young people were worried about being bullied at school, compared with 28% in non-denominational schools. In

119

Catholic schools 54% of the young people were worried about how they get on with other people, compared with 49% in non-denominational schools.

Environmental domain

The statistics presented in table 10.3 demonstrate that within the environmental domain there are a number of ways in which young people attending Catholic schools enjoy the same level of spiritual health as young people attending non-denominational schools. There were no significant differences between the proportions of the young people in the two sectors who considered that there were too many black people living in this country (18% in non-denominational schools and 17% in Catholic schools), who argued that immigration into Britain should be restricted (31% in non-denominational schools and 33% in Catholic schools), who considered that there was too much violence on television (20% in non-denominational schools and 20% in Catholic schools), who were concerned about the risk of pollution to the environment (63% in non-denominational schools and 61% in Catholic schools), or who felt that there was nothing they could do to help solve the world's problems (27% in non-denominational schools and 27% in Catholic schools).

There were, however, two indicators in this section which revealed different priorities among the young people educated within the two sectors of schools. The young people in Catholic schools were more likely than the young people in non-denominational schools to be concerned about the poverty of the third world (64% compared with 57%) and less likely to be concerned about the risk of nuclear war (51% compared with 55%).

Transcendental domain

The statistics presented in table 10.4 demonstrate that within the transcendental domain the young people attending Catholic schools displayed a much higher attachment to traditional religion compared with young people in non-denominational schools. In Catholic schools 71% of the young people believed in God, compared with 37% in non-denominational schools. In Catholic schools 56% of the young people believed in life after death, compared with 43% in non-denominational schools. In spite of these large differences in belief, the differences in levels of negativity toward traditional religion are only marginally lower in the Catholic sector. In Catholic schools 25% of the young people considered the Church to be irrelevant to life today compared with 28% in non-denominational schools. In Catholic schools 29% of the young people considered that the Bible seemed irrelevant for life today compared with 31% in non-denominational schools.

Not only are young people in Catholic schools more supportive of traditional religion, they are also more supportive of non-traditional religion. While 36% of the young people in non-denominational schools believed in their horoscope, the proportion rose to 39% in Catholic schools. While 20% of the young people in non-denominational schools believed fortune-tellers can tell the future, the proportion rose to 24% in Catholic schools. While 32% of the young people in non-denominational schools believed that it is possible to contact the spirits of the dead, the proportion rose to 34% in Catholic schools.

Conclusion

This analysis has demonstrated that, although young people attending Catholic schools share a number of indicators of spiritual health in common with young people in non-denominational schools, there are significant differences between the two groups in respect of all four of Fisher's domains of spiritual health. In the personal domain young people in Catholic schools show better spiritual health in terms of enjoying more sense of purpose in life. In the communal domain young people in Catholic schools show poorer spiritual health in terms of greater anxiety about relationships and bullying. In the environmental domain young people in Catholic schools show better spiritual health in terms of greater concern for world development. In the transcendental domain young people in Catholic schools show better spiritual health in terms of greater commitment to traditional religion, but poorer spiritual health in terms of commitment to non-traditional religious beliefs.

The positive interpretation of these findings is that Catholic secondary schools bring to the urban environment communities in which belief in God is the norm. Pupils educated in this environment develop a greater sense of purpose in their own lives, hold a greater commitment to world development, and are as open in their attitudes to other groups as young people educated in non-denominational schools. According to this account Catholic schools contribute greatly to the common good and add hope to the urban environment.

Urban planners may need to recognise and to value the distinctive contribution made to urban living by the continuing involvement of the Catholic Church within the state-maintained sector of education.

11

Christian schools

Setting the context

Church schools are a well established feature of the educational landscape in England and Wales. Long before the 1870 Education Act established machinery through which schools could be built directly by the state, the National Society, the British and Foreign School Society, and the Catholic Poor School Committee were well established in the field to build Anglican, Free Church, and Catholic Schools (Cruickshank, 1963; Murphy, 1971; Chadwick, 1997). The 1944 Education Act both consolidated and changed this partnership between the state and the churches in the provision of schools. As a consequence of this Act the Free Churches largely withdrew from church schools, the Roman Catholic Church set about building more church schools, and the Anglican Church adopted different approaches in different dioceses (Francis, 1987). By way of comparison, the independent Christian school movement is a newcomer to the educational scene in England and Wales. The present chapter poses the question regarding the relationship between attending an independent Christian school and levels of spiritual health across the four domains proposed by Fisher. This question is posed against the background of the development of this sector of schools and the limited research already conducted into pupils attending this sector.

Since there is no national organisation overseeing the development of independent Christian schools in England and Wales, it is no easy task to trace their development. The early history has been told by Deakin (1989), who maintains that the first school of this type was opened in Rochester in 1969. A few more new Christian schools followed in the early 1970s, but it was not until the early 1980s that substantial growth occurred. According to Walford (2002: 410) there were about ten such schools. According to Deakin (1989: 4) by 1988 the Christian Schools' Trust was in contact with 53 schools. From the beginning, the major objectives of the Christian Schools' Trust were to provide assistance with the development of curriculum materials, provide in-service training for teachers, and organise conferences. It was recognised that opening a Christian school might mean more than just having a Christian ethos, and might require specially written curriculum materials that contained the Christian messages. The subsequent development of Christian schools in England and Wales has been chronicled in a series of studies by Poyntz and Walford (1994), by Watson and MacKenzie (1996), and by Walford (1994, 1995a, 1995b, 1995c, 2000, 2001a, 2001b, 2001c, 2001d, 2002, 2003).

In 1993 Walford (1995a) conducted an enquiry among the 65 schools then included in the address list of the Christian Schools' Trust. Semi-structured interviews were conducted with the headteachers in 11 of these schools. Information was obtained on the curriculum, discipline, governance, and policy matters, as well as basic information on the school's pupils and staff. Headteachers were encouraged to talk at length about the educational philosophy of the school, the reasons why the school was established, and the links between the school's philosophy and the curriculum and teaching methods used. Questionnaires were then sent to the remaining 54 schools. Overall detailed information was received from 53 of the 65 schools. Walford's data demonstrate considerable diversity in these schools, but also clear underlying themes which unite them. The following profile is offered by Walford.

These schools share an ideology of biblically-based evangelical Christianity that seeks to relate the message of the Bible to all aspects of present day life whether personal, spiritual or educational. These schools have usually been set up by parents or a church group to deal with a growing dissatisfaction with what is seen as the increased secularism of the great majority of schools. The schools aim to provide a distinctive Christian approach to every part of school life and the curriculum and, usually, parents have a continuing role in the management and organisation of the schools (Walford, 1995a: 7).

While the Roman Catholic Church and the Anglican Church saw many advantages in collaboration with the state in order to receive public funding for church-related schools, those involved in the Christian school movement have been much more ambivalent about opportunities to receive public funding. The 1993 legislation for England and Wales allowed schools like independent Christian schools to apply to the Secretary of State for Education and Employment to become sponsored grant-maintained schools, and a similar process was available following the 1998 School Standards and Framework Act. While two Muslim primary schools and one Seventh-day Adventist secondary school took advantage of the 1993 Act, followed by a Sikh secondary school and a Greek Orthodox school, no independent Christian school has received state support. One Christian school made application to become grant-maintained, but the application was ultimately rejected. According to Walford's (2001a) analysis of interviews with headteachers, many would be reluctant to sacrifice independence. The main concerns of these headteachers:

focus round the degree of control that government might exert on the school and the limitations to freedom of action . . . . Private schools still do not have to cover the National Curriculum or deal with central government initiatives such as the Literacy Hour or Numeracy Hour. Other headteachers have specifically mentioned sex education as something they would wish to have complete control over, and the ability to select teachers. They are concerned that if they take funding from the state, they might eventually have to take teachers who are not evangelical Christians. A particular fear here is that of homosexual teachers (Walford, 2001a: 539).

As yet there is little empirical research regarding the pupils who attend independent Christian schools. In a pioneering study in this area, O'Keeffe (1992) administered the same scale of attitude toward Christianity, which had been used in earlier studies among pupils in Anglican and Roman Catholic schools by Francis (1987), to 439 pupils between the ages of 8 and 16 attending six independent Christian schools. O'Keeffe (1992: 105) drew the following conclusion from her data.

> The main conclusion to emerge from this study is that schools are exercising a positive influence on their pupils' attitudes toward Christianity. The responses of pupils demonstrate that the majority of pupils hold positive attitudes toward God, Jesus, the Bible and personal prayer.

In a second study Francis (2005d) profiled the values of 136 13- to 15-year-old boys attending independent Christian schools alongside the profile of 12,823 boys attending non-denominational state-maintained schools. This study revealed some very strong differences between boys educated in the two sectors.

Regarding religious beliefs, 89% of boys in the independent Christian schools believed that Jesus really rose from the dead, compared with 28% in the state-maintained sector. Four-fifths of boys in the independent Christian schools believed that God made the world in six days and rested on the seventh (82%), compared with 19% in the state-maintained sector. Two-thirds of boys in the independent Christian schools considered that Christianity was the only true religion (67%), compared with 13% in the state-maintained sector.

Regarding sexual morality, 70% of boys in independent Christian schools believed that homosexuality is wrong, compared with 21% in the state-maintained sector. Three-quarters of boys in independent Christian schools believed that abortion is wrong (73%), compared with 39% in the state-maintained sector. Two-thirds of boys in independent Christian schools believed that it is wrong to have sexual intercourse outside marriage (64%), compared with 13% in the state-maintained sector.

Regarding substance use, 47% of boys in independent Christian schools believed that it is wrong to become drunk, compared with 38% in the state-maintained sector. Half of boys in independent Christian schools believed that it is wrong to smoke cigarettes (50%), compared with 38% in the state-maintained sector. Three-fifths of boys in independent Christian schools believed that it is wrong to use marijuana (60%), compared with 53% in the state-maintained sector.

Clearly there is sufficient empirical evidence from previous studies to suggest that attending an independent Christian school is worth taking seriously as a predictor of individual differences in values and beliefs and that examination of the relationship between attending an independent Christian school and spiritual health is worth exploring further.

Method

The number of independent Christian schools in England and Wales offering places to year-nine and year-ten pupils remains quite small and the number of pupils within these year groups within any one school is also small. An over-sample of this sector provided a reasonable number of pupils to ensure generalisable findings. In order, then, to examine the relationship between spiritual health and attending an independent Christian school, the present chapter makes a direct comparison between two groups of pupils: those educated in non-denominational state-maintained schools and those educated in independent Christian schools. The chi square test was employed to examine the statistical significance of differences between the two groups. For simplicity of comparison, the two groups will be referred to as Christian schools and non-denominational schools.

Personal domain

The statistics presented in table 11.1 demonstrate that within the personal domain some of the indicators signal a much better level of spiritual health among young people in Christian schools compared with young people in non-denominational schools. While in the non-denominational schools 54% of the young people felt their life had a sense of purpose, the proportion rose to 75% in the Christian schools. While 52% of the young people in the non-denominational schools often felt depressed, the proportion fell to 38% in the Christian schools. While 28% of the young people in the non-denominational schools have sometimes considered taking their own life, the proportion fell to 15% in Christian schools.

In respect of the other four indicators of spiritual health in the personal domain there were no significant differences between the two sectors. In non-denominational schools 69% of the young people found life really worth living, and so did 74% in Christian schools. In the non-denominational schools 14% of the young people felt they were not worth much as a person, and so did 12% in Christian schools. In the non-denominational schools 34% of the young people often longed for someone to whom to turn for advice, and so did 33% in Christian schools. In non-denominational schools 70% of the young people were happy in their school, and so were 66% in Christian schools.

Communal domain

The statistics presented in table 11.2 demonstrate that within the communal domain there are some key differences in the levels of spiritual health experienced by the young people in Christian schools and in non-denominational schools. Some of these differences are to the advantage of the Christian school sector and some are to the disadvantage of the Christian school sector. On the positive side, the young people in Christian schools were less likely to be worried about being bullied at school (19% compared with 28% in non-denominational schools) and more likely to derive help from talking about their problems with close friends (75% compared with 63% in non-denominational schools). On the negative side, the young people in Christian schools were more likely to be worried about how they get on with other people (58% compared with 49% in non-denominational schools) and less likely to like the people with whom they go to school (84% compared with 90% in non-denominational schools).

In respect of the other three indicators within the communal domain there were no significant differences between the responses of the young people in the two sectors. In Christian schools, 38% of the young people were worried about their attractiveness to the opposite sex, and so were 33% in non-denominational schools. In Christian schools 51% of the young people found it helpful to talk about their problems with their mother, and so did 50% in non-denominational schools. In Christian schools 37% of the young people found it helpful to talk about their problems with their father, and so did 31% in non-denominational schools.

Environmental domain

The statistics presented in table 11.3 demonstrate that within the environmental domain young people within the Christian school sector enjoy a significantly higher level of spiritual health in comparison with young people in non-denominational schools. To begin with they were much more likely to feel empowered to exercise a beneficial influence on the world in which they live. While 27% of the young people in non-denominational schools felt that there was nothing they could do to help solve the world's problems, the proportion fell to 17% in Christian schools.

The young people in Christian schools were much less likely to hold racist attitudes. In non-denominational schools 18% of the young people maintained that there are too many black people living in this country, but the proportion fell to 6% in Christian schools. On the other hand, similar proportions of the young people in Christian schools (29%) and in non-denominational schools (31%) considered that immigration into Britain should be restricted.

The young people in Christian schools are much more likely to hold positive attitudes toward world development. In non-denominational schools 57% of the young people expressed concern regarding the poverty of the third world, but the proportion rose to 71% in Christian schools. On the other hand, similar proportions of the young people in Christian schools (61%) and in non-denominational schools (63%) were concerned about the risk of pollution to the environment.

The young people in Christian schools are much more likely to be concerned about violence on television and less likely to be concerned about the risk of nuclear war. While 20% of the young people in non-denominational schools considered that there is too much violence on television, the proportion rose to 35% in Christian schools. While 55% of the young people in non-denominational schools were concerned about the risk of nuclear war, the proportion fell to 32% in Christian schools.

Transcendental domain

The statistics presented in table 11.4 demonstrate that young people in Christian schools enjoy a significantly higher level of spiritual health in the transcendental domain compared with young people in non-denominational schools. This difference is reflected in two main ways. First, the young people in Christian schools held traditional religion in much higher regard. Four-fifths of the young people in Christian schools expressed belief in God (83%), compared with 37% in non-denominational schools. Three-quarters of the young people in Christian schools expressed belief in life after death (74%), compared with 43% in non-denominational schools. These beliefs were accompanied by a more positive attitude toward religious institutions. Just 13% of the young people in Christian schools considered the Church to be irrelevant to life today, compared with 28% in non-denominational schools. Just 14% of the young people in Christian schools considered the Bible to be irrelevant to life today, compared with 31% in non-denominational schools.

Second, the young people in Christian schools held non-traditional religious beliefs in much lower regard. Just 8% of the young people in Christian schools believed in their horoscope, compared with 36% in non-denominational schools. In Christian schools 13% of the young people believed that fortune-tellers can tell the future, compared with 20% in non-denominational schools. In Christian schools 21% of the young people believed in the possibility of contacting the spirits of the dead, compared with 32% in non-denominational schools.

Conclusion

This analysis has demonstrated that there are significant ways across all of Fisher's four domains in which young people in Christian schools enjoy a higher level of spiritual health compared

131

with young people in non-denominational schools. Within the personal domain young people in Christian schools benefit from a greater sense of purpose in life. Within the communal domain young people in Christian schools benefit from closer relationships with friends and from less fear of being bullied. Within the environmental domain young people in Christian schools are less racist in their attitudes and more concerned about world development issues. Within the transcendental domain young people in Christian schools are better rooted in traditional religious beliefs and less susceptible to non-traditional beliefs.

The positive interpretation of these findings is that Christian schools bring to the urban environment communities committed to shaping purposive young lives capable of contributing to the common good on both local and global levels. Such communities are constructive rather than divisive of urban hope for the future.

Urban planners may need to recognise and to value the distinctive contribution made to urban living by the relatively recent movement to develop independent Christian schools. This initiative by sectors of the Christian community is being replicated within other faith communities.

12

Social engagement

Setting the context

This chapter poses the question regarding relationships between social engagement in general and sport participation in particular and levels of spiritual health across the four domains proposed by Fisher. The question makes sense against a research tradition concerned with the broader social and psychological correlates of social engagement and sport participation during childhood and adolescence. The recent review of this field presented by Bailey (2005) distinguishes between three areas in which such research has concentrated: physical health, cognitive and academic development, and mental health.

Participation in sport may influence the physical health of children and young people in two ways. First, it could affect the causes of diseases during childhood. For example, Bailey (1999) highlights evidence suggesting a favourable relationship between physical activity and a host of factors affecting children's physical health, including diabetes, blood pressure, the ability to use fat for energy and bone health. In a recent study, Papaioannou, Karastogiannidou and Theodorakis (2004) examined the relationships between participation in sport and health-related behaviours among 5,991 11- to 16-year-old adolescents in Greece. They found that participation was associated with higher fruit consumption and lower tobacco consumption. Second, participation in sport could reduce the risk of chronic diseases later in life. For example, Freedman, Khan, Dietz, Srinivasan and Berenson

(2001) highlight the relationship of childhood obesity to coronary heart disease risk factors in adulthood.

It has been hypothesised that participation in sport could enhance academic performance by increasing the flow of blood to the brain, enhancing arousal levels, changing hormonal secretions, mental alertness and improving self-esteem, but the empirical basis for such claims remains varied (Shephard, 1997; Hills, 1998). For example, Hanks and Eckland (1976) considered a nationally representative sample of 2,077 high school students in the United States of America, tested in 1955 and again fifteen years later. The major outcome variables were school grades and academic track in the senior year of high school and subsequent educational aspirations. Control variables included socioeconomic status, school grades, and performance on a battery of standardised tests. The data demonstrated that participation in sport was not significantly related to senior academic track or subsequent achievement.

On the other hand, Otto and Alwin (1977) and Otto (1982) found that participation in sport had a positive effect on educational achievement, occupational status, and income in a follow-up study of 442 males who had been studied in high school fifteen years earlier. Braddock (1981) examined the effects of participation in sport by black and white males using the 1972 national Longitudinal Survey in the United Sates of America. He found sport participation was positively and significantly related to school grades and educational plans. Also using a national representative sample in the United States of America, Snyder and Spreitzer (1990) found that sport participation was associated with an increased likelihood of going to college for whites, blacks and Hispanics. Using the same dataset Marsh (1993) found positive correlations between sport participation and educational aspirations, homework, reduced absenteeism and subsequent college attendance. Drawing on three longitudinal studies, Shephard (1997: 113) concludes that 'academic performance is maintained or even enhanced by an increase in a student's level of habitual physical activity, despite a reduction in curriculum or free time for the study of academic material'.

Reviewing the literature in the area, Mutrie and Parfitt (1998) concluded that prolonged activity was positively associated with good mental health. The case is particularly strong with regard to good self-esteem. For example, Marsh (1993) examined the effects of participation in sport during the last two years of high school in a nationally representative study of American adolescents. A positive relationship was found between self-concept and participation, after controlling for race, socio-economic status, sex and ability level.

Delaney and Lee (1995) examined the relationship between self-esteem and participation in exercise and sport in a cross sectional study of Australian adolescents. A positive relationship between self-esteem and participation was found both among males and among females. Taylor (1995) examined the relationship between athletic participation and self-esteem among a sample of 651 undergraduate students. The study concluded that athletic participation was one of a number of college experiences that cumulatively contribute to increases in self-esteem. Steptoe and Butler (1996) examined the relationship between emotional wellbeing and participation among 5,061 16-year-old adolescents assessed as a follow-up to a birth cohort from April 1970 in England, Scotland and Wales. They found that sport and vigorous recreational activity was positively associated with emotional wellbeing, independent of sex, social class, health status, and use of hospital services. Yeung and Hemsley (1997) examined the relationship between exercise, personality and psychological health in a sample of 204 women recruited from health clubs and adult educational classes by postal survey. The data demonstrated that participation in physical exercise made a small but significant contribution to positive affect. In a study of 89 17-year-old adolescents in the United States of America, Sanders, Field, Diego and

Kaplan (2000) found a significant positive relationship between sport participation and lower depression scores.

Another group of studies, however, have failed to find an association between participation and positive social and psychological outcomes. For example, Zaharopoulos and Hodge (1991) examined the relationship between sport participation and a multidimensional model of self-concept among 113 13- to 17-year-old pupils attending a Dunedin public high school in New Zealand. It was found that athletes differed significantly from non-athletes in physical ability self-concept, but not in global self-concept. They concluded that their findings supported the multidimensionality of self-concept and refuted the assumption that sport participation enhances self-concept in general. Choquet (1995) examined illicit drug consumption in a large epidemiological study conducted among 12,381 11- to 19-year-old school pupils in France. This study found that 15% of French adolescents experimented with illicit drugs, rising from 4% among 11- to 12-year-old pupils to 30% among 18- to 19-year-old pupils. Extra-curricular activities, including sport, were found to be unrelated to drug consumption.

There are, nevertheless, good theoretical reasons for linking social engagement and participation with positive social and psychological outcomes. The concept of *social capital* provides a very useful theoretical framework through which to explicate this link (see, for example, Baron, Field and Schuller, 2001; Office for National Statistics, 2001). Three seminal authors behind the concept are Pierre Bourdieu (1997), James Coleman (1988) and Robert Putnam (2000), although it is largely to Putnam's influence and his skilfully titled book, *Bowling Alone*, that the concept has attracted much recent attention. For Putnam, social capital is essentially about social networks, and these are effectively developed through participation in shared activities. He uses bowling as a metaphor for America's changing patterns of social networking: bowling was once the stereotypical associational activity, offering not just recreation but also regular sustained social interactions, but it has increasingly become a rather solitary affair.

A uniting theme for social capital theorists is that of 'social cohesion', which is addressed through creating and strengthening the physical, social and cultural infrastructure of communities. Since sports and recreational participation provide a focus for social activity, an opportunity to make friends, develop social networks and reduce social isolation, such participation seems well placed to support the development of social capital. In turn social capital should be reflected in positive social and psychological outcomes.

Clearly there are sufficient theoretical grounds and sufficient empirical evidence from previous studies to suggest that social engagement in general and sports participation in particular are worth taking seriously as predictors of individual differences across a range of outcomes and that the examination of the relationship between social engagement and spiritual health is worth exploring further.

Method

The questionnaire included a check list of social, cultural, recreational and sporting activities in which young people may engage. Their responses to this check list indicated that some young people engaged in hardly any of these activities, while others engaged in a wide number of activities. In order to examine the relationship between spiritual health and social participation, the dataset was divided into three equal segments representing low participation, middle-range participation and high participation. Chi square was then employed to examine the statistical significance of differences between the two extreme groups, omitting the middle group from the analysis. For simplicity of comparison the two groups retained in the analysis will be referred to as low social engagement and high social engagement.

137

Personal domain

The statistics presented in table 12.1 demonstrate that social engagement is a good predictor of spiritual health in the personal domain. Young people with high social engagement record higher levels of spiritual health across five of the seven indicators within the domain. This difference is reflected in indicators both of positive affect and of negative affect.

Regarding positive affect, 72% of the young people with high social engagement felt life to be really worth living, compared with 63% with low social engagement. Similarly, 71% of the young people with high social engagement were happy in their school, compared with 68% with low social engagement. Three-fifths of the young people with high social engagement felt that their life had a sense of purpose (60%), compared with 53% with low social engagement.

Regarding negative affect, 49% of the young people with high social engagement often felt depressed, compared with 54% with low social engagement. Similarly, 13% of the young people with high social engagement felt that they were not worth much as a person, compared with 15% with low social engagement.

Regarding the other two indicators in the section, however, there were no statistically significant differences between the two groups. A third of the young people with high social engagement (35%) and with low social engagement (35%) often longed for someone to whom to turn for advice. Just over a quarter of the young people with high social engagement (28%) and with low social engagement (27%) have sometimes considered taking their own life.

Communal domain

The statistics presented in table 12.2 demonstrate that in some ways young people with high social engagement enjoy a better level of spiritual health in the communal domain. The young people with high social engagement were significantly more likely than those with low social engagement to like the people with whom they go to school (90% compared with 88%). The young people with high social engagement were significantly less likely than those with low social engagement to be worried about being bullied at school (27% compared with 32%). The young people with high social engagement were significantly less likely than those with low social engagement to be worried about their attractiveness to the opposite sex (33% compared with 36%). However, there were no significant differences between the two groups regarding overall relational anxiety: 52% of those with high social engagement and 54% of those with low social engagement were worried about how they get on with other people.

Social engagement also functions as a predictor of the levels of support young people receive from others. Those with high social engagement were more likely to have found it helpful to talk about their problems with their father (38% compared with 27% among those with low social engagement) but less likely to have found it helpful to talk about their problems with close friends (60% compared with 66% among those with low social engagement). Between 50% and 51% of both groups found it helpful to talk about their problems with their mother.

Environmental domain

The statistics presented in table 12.3 demonstrate that in some ways young people with high social engagement display lower levels of spiritual health in the environmental domain. This point is made in particular by the indicators concerned with racist attitudes. Thus, 18% of the young people with high social engagement agreed that there are too many black people living in the country, compared with 13% of those with low social engagement. Similarly, 33% of the young people with high social engagement agreed that immigration into Britain should be restricted, compared with 27% of those with low social engagement. The young people with high social engagement were also more likely than those with low social engagement to have taken the view that there is nothing they can do to help solve the world's problems (26% and 24% respectively).

The young people with high social engagement were more concerned about the risk of nuclear war (58% compared with 54%), but less concerned that there is too much violence on television (19% compared with 21%). The young people with high social engagement were more concerned about the risk of pollution to the environment (69% compared with 66%), but neither more nor less concerned about the poverty of the third world (60% in both groups).

Transcendental domain

The figures presented in table 12.4 demonstrate that there is no clear pattern of relationship between social engagement and spiritual health in the transcendental domain. Regarding traditional religion, between 42% and 43% of both groups believed in God, and 30% of both groups considered that the Bible seems irrelevant for life today. The young people with high social engagement were more inclined to believe in life after death (48%), compared with those with low social engagement (45%). Yet the young people with high social engagement were also more inclined to judge the Church as irrelevant for life today (28%), compared with those with low social engagement (26%).

Regarding non-traditional religion, the young people with high social engagement were less inclined to believe in their horoscope (34% compared with 37%) and less inclined to believe that fortune-tellers could tell the future (20% compared with 23%). On the other hand, the young people with high social engagement were more inclined to believe in the possibility of contacting the spirits of the dead (33% compared with 31%).

Conclusion

This analysis has demonstrated that there is no clear-cut relationship between social engagement and spiritual health. Within the personal domain young people with high social engagement record better spiritual health, especially in terms of a greater sense of purpose in life and less susceptibility to feelings of depression. Within the communal domain young people with high social engagement enjoy better spiritual health on some indicators (less fear of being bullied) but poorer spiritual health on other indicators (less support from close friends). Within the environmental domain young people with high levels of social engagement record poorer spiritual health, especially in terms of holding more racist attitudes and in terms of feeling powerless in the face of the world's problems. Within the transcendental domain overall no clear pattern emerges between social engagement and spiritual health.

In terms of urban planning and development these findings present mixed messages regarding the contribution being made to the spiritual health of young people by the provision of facilities and resources designed to maximise social engagement. Perhaps more attention needs rather to be given to understanding how such provision can maximise the healthy responses of young people.

13

Personal prayer

Setting the context

This chapter poses the question regarding the relationship between personal prayer and levels of spiritual health across the four domains proposed by Fisher. The question makes sense against a very long tradition of research concerned with the empirical correlates of prayer among those who pray. The research tradition concerned with the *subjective* correlates of prayer has to be distinguished from a very different research tradition concerned with the *objective* correlates of prayer.

Research concerned with the objective correlates of prayer is perhaps best known and characterised by Byrd's (1988) now classic study of prayer in the context of coronary care reported in the *Southern Medical Journal* and conducted over a ten-month period during which 393 patients admitted to the coronary care unit at San Francisco General Hospital were randomised to an intercessory prayer group or to a control group. The patients, staff, doctors, and Byrd himself were all unaware which patients had been targeted for prayer. The prayer treatment was supplied by 'born again' Christians who prayed outside the hospital. Each intercessor was asked to pray daily for rapid recovery and for prevention of complications and death, in addition to other areas of prayer they believed to be beneficial to the named patients. At entry to the coronary care unit there was no significant statistical difference between the two groups. After admission, however, the intercessory prayer group had a statistically-significant lower severity score than the control group.

Byrd's pioneering study was developed and extended by Harris, Gowda, Kolb, Strychacz, Vacek, Jones, Forker, O'Keefe and McCallister (1999) as reported in the *Archives of Internal Medicine*. Over a period extending nearly one year 1,013 patients admitted to the coronary care unit at the Mid American Heart Institute, Kansas City, were randomised at the time of admission to receive remote intercessory prayer (prayer group) or not (usual care group). The first names of the patients in the prayer group were given to a team of outside intercessors who prayed for them daily for four weeks. Patients were unaware that they were being prayed for, and the intercessors did not know and never met the patients. In this study the medical course from the time of admission to hospital to the time of discharge from hospital was summarised in a 'coronary care unit course score' derived from blinded, retrospective chart review. The data demonstrated that, compared with the usual care group, the prayer group experienced a statistically-significant better outcome.

Concern with the subjective correlates of prayer stood at the heart of the emerging discipline of the psychology of religion at the beginning of the twentieth century. For example, William James (1902) in his classic study, *The Variety of Religious Experience*, claimed that prayer is the very soul and essence of religion. Then in his work, *The Psychology of Religion*, Coe (1916) wrote that a history and psychology of prayer would be almost equivalent to a history and psychology of religion. The case was put even more strongly by Hodge (1931) in his study, *Prayer and its Psychology*, that prayer is the centre and soul of all religion, and upon the question of its validity depends the trustworthiness of religious experience in general. Then, for some reason or another, psychologists largely lost interest in religion in general and in prayer in particular. In their review of the field in the mid 1980s, Finney and Malony (1985: 104) concluded that, 'Nowhere is the long standing breach between psychology and religion more evident than in the lack of research on prayer.' Only a few studies of prayer exist in spite of the fact that prayer is of central religious importance. Similar points were made during the following decade in reviews by Hood, Morris and Watson (1987, 1989), by Poloma and Pendleton (1989), by Janssen, de Hart and den Draak (1989), and by McCullough (1995). Renewed interest in the field from the early 1990s has been signalled, for example, by Brown's (1994) *The Human Side of Prayer: the psychology of praying* and by Francis and Astley's (2001) *Psychological Perspectives on Prayer: a reader.*

Two strands of research in Britain began in the 1990s to explore the psychological correlates of prayer during childhood and adolescence. The first strand focused on the relationship between personal prayer and school-related attitudes. An initial study by Francis (1992) drew attention to the somewhat surprising finding that frequency of personal prayer was a significant predictor of school-related attitudes among a sample of 3,762 11-year-old pupils in England. The pupils completed six semantic differential scales of attitudes toward school, lessons in English, music, mathematics, sports, and religious education. After controlling for the potential influences of sex and social class, frequency of personal prayer was a significant predictor of a more positive attitude toward school and toward lessons in English, music, mathematics, and religious education, but not toward sports lessons.

A replication of this original study was reported by Montgomery and Francis (1996) among a sample of 392 11- to 16-year-old girls attending a state-maintained single-sex Catholic secondary school in England. The pupils completed the same set of six semantic differential scales. After controlling for the potential influence of age and social class, frequency of personal prayer was a significant predictor of a more positive attitude toward school, and toward lessons in music, religion, and English, but not toward lessons in mathematics and sports.

The second, more significant, strand focused on the relationship between personal prayer and purpose in life. Purpose in life is a particularly rich concept explored both by theology (Tillich, 1952) and by psychology (Frankl, 1978). Purpose in life is understood to be central to the meaning-making process which counters meaninglessness. As such, purpose in life is a central component of psychological wellbeing. It is purpose in life which makes living worthwhile and which stands between despair and suicide. Moreover, it is precisely to this construct that religious traditions speak. Substantive analyses of religion point to the beliefs, teaching and rituals which explicitly address the fundamental questions concerning the meaning and purpose of life. Functional analyses of religion point to the meaning-making process as central to the *raison d'être* of religious and para-religious systems. There are clear grounds, therefore, for hypothesising a positive relationship between religiosity and purpose in life.

In an initial study, Francis and Burton (1994) explored the relationship between personal prayer and perceived purpose in life among a sample of 674 12- to 16-year-old pupils attending a Catholic school and who identified themselves as members of the Catholic Church. Two main conclusions emerged from these data. First, the data demonstrated a significant positive relationship between frequency of personal prayer and perceived purpose in life, even after controlling for individual differences in frequency of church attendance. Second, personal prayer was shown to be a stronger predictor of perceived purpose in life than church attendance.

Building on this initial study, Francis and Evans (1996) strengthened the research design in two ways. They obtained a larger sample of pupils from across a wider range of schools. Then they ensured that church attendance was not a contaminating variable in explaining the correlation between prayer and purpose in life by conducting their analyses on two discrete subsets of their data. One subset comprised 914 males and 726 females who never attended church. The other subset comprised 232 males and 437 females who attended church most weeks. The data demonstrated a significant positive relationship between frequency of personal prayer and perceived purpose in life both among those pupils who attended church most weeks and among those pupils who never attended church.

In a third study, Francis (2005a) replicated the study by Francis and Evans (1996) and strengthened that study in two ways. First, a larger and more representative dataset was employed. This time one sample comprised 7,083 males and 5,634 females who never attended church, and the other sample comprised 1,738 males and 2,006 females who attended church nearly every week. Second, further control variables were included in the research design to reduce the emergence of spurious relationships. Once again, however, these data demonstrated a significant positive relationship between frequency of personal prayer and perceived purpose in life among both churchgoers and nonchurchgoers.

These basic findings are consistent with the following psychological mechanism which links prayer with purpose in life. The practice of prayer implies both a cognitive and an affective component. The cognitive component assumes, at least, the possibility of a transcendental power. Such a belief system is likely to support a purposive view of the nature of the universe. The affective component assumes, at least, the possibility of that transcendental power being aware of and taking an interest in the individual engaged in prayer. Such an affective system is likely to support a sense of value for the individual. In other words, acknowledging a transcendent being and relating to that transcendence through prayer places the whole of life into a wider context of meaning and purpose.

Clearly there are sufficient theoretical grounds and sufficient empirical evidence from previous studies to suggest that personal prayer is worth taking seriously as predictive of individual differences in areas of personal and social wellbeing and that the examination of the relationship between personal prayer and spiritual health is worth exploring further.

Method

The questionnaire included an item designed to rate the frequency of personal prayer on a five point scale: never, once or twice a year, sometimes, weekly and daily. In order to examine the relationship between spiritual health and personal prayer the dataset was divided into three segments, collapsing once or twice a year and weekly into the middle category of 'sometimes'. Chi square was then employed to examine the statistical significance of differences between all three groups now classified as never, sometimes and daily. The middle category was preserved in this analysis because the data indicated that important additional information was conveyed by this category.

Personal domain

The statistics presented in table 13.1 demonstrate that personal prayer functions as a very powerful predictor of individual differences in spiritual health in the personal domain. Overall young people who pray enjoy a much higher level of spiritual health in the personal domain. The strongest difference is seen in respect of the indicator concerned with purpose in life. While 48% of the young people who never pray recorded a sense of purpose in life, the proportions rose to 60% among those who pray sometimes and to 73% among those who pray daily. In respect of the other indicators of positive affect, 74% of the young people who pray daily found life really worth living, compared with 69% of those who never pray. Similarly, 74% of the young people who pray daily were happy in their school, compared with 67% of those who never pray.

In terms of indicators of negative affect, however, prayer

147

predicts somewhat less healthy outcomes. Thus, 14% of the young people who pray daily felt that they were not worth much as a person, compared with 13% who never pray. Slightly more of the young people who pray daily often felt depressed (51% compared with 49% who never pray). More of the young people who pray daily often longed for someone to whom to turn for advice (39% compared with 30% who never pray). However, there was no significant relationship between prayer and suicidal ideation: 27% of the young people who never pray, 28% who pray sometimes and 26% who pray daily have sometimes considered taking their own life.

Communal domain

The statistics presented in table 13.2 demonstrate that according to some indicators personal prayer predicts better spiritual health in the communal domain, but that according to other indicators personal prayer predicts poorer spiritual health in the communal domain.

Better spiritual health is indicated by the way in which the young people who pray feel better supported by family and by close friends. Three-fifths of the young people who pray daily found it helpful to talk about their problems with their mother (59%), compared with 45% who never pray. Two-fifths of the young people who pray daily found it helpful to talk about their problems with their father (39%), compared with 30% who never pray. Over two-thirds of the young people who pray daily found it helpful to talk about their problems with close friends (70%), compared with 58% who never pray.

Poorer spiritual health, however, is indicated by the way in which young people who pray feel more anxious about relationships and about inter-personal matters. A third of the young people who pray daily were concerned about being bullied at school (33%), compared with 23% who never pray. Two-fifths of the young people who pray daily were worried about their attractiveness to the opposite sex (40%), compared with 29% who never pray; and 57% of the young people who pray daily were worried about how they get on with other people, compared with 45% who never pray. While 90% of the young people who never pray liked the people with whom they go to school, the proportion fell to 87% among those who pray daily.

Environmental domain

The statistics presented in table 13.3 demonstrate that personal prayer functions as a very powerful predictor of individual differences in spiritual health in the environmental domain. Overall young people who pray enjoy a much higher level of spiritual health in the environmental domain.

First and foremost, personal prayer is associated with the view that young people can make a difference to the world. The young people who never pray were twice as likely as the young people who pray daily to feel that there is nothing they can do to help solve the world's problems (32% compared with 18%).

Second, personal prayer is associated with more inclusive acceptance of other people and with less racist attitudes. The young people who pray daily were significantly less likely than the young people who never pray to argue that there are too many black people living in this country (13% compared with 21%) or to argue that immigration into Britain should be restricted (27% compared with 34%).

Third, personal prayer is associated with greater concern for global citizenship and sustainable development. The young people who pray daily were significantly more likely than the young people who never pray to be concerned about the risk of pollution to the environment (73% compared with 57%) or to be concerned about the poverty of the third world (77% compared with 48%).

Fourth, personal prayer is associated with greater concern about the escalation of violence in the world, both globally and nationally. The young people who pray daily were significantly more likely than the young people who never pray to be concerned about the risk of nuclear war (63% compared with 49%) or to be concerned that there is too much violence on television (34% compared with 15%).

Transcendental domain

The statistics presented in table 13.4 demonstrate that personal prayer functions as a very powerful predictor of individual differences in spiritual health in the transcendental domain. It is of course hardly surprising that personal prayer is strongly related to traditional religious beliefs. Thus, 92% of the young people who pray daily believed in God, compared with 17% who never pray; and 68% of the young people who pray daily believed in life after death, compared with 34% who never pray. Just 16% of the young people who pray daily deemed the Church irrelevant to life today, compared with 35% who never pray; and just 16% of the young people who pray daily deemed the Bible irrelevant to life today, compared with 40% who never pray.

It is the young people who pray sometimes, but not daily, who showed the greatest openness to non-traditional religious belief. Thus, 39% of the young people who pray sometimes believed in their horoscope, compared with 33% who never pray and 29% who pray daily; 22% of the young people who pray sometimes believed fortune-tellers could tell the future, compared with 19% who never pray and 20% who pray daily; and 32% of the young people who pray sometimes believed it is possible to contact the spirits of the dead, compared with 31% who never pray and 29% who pray daily.

Conclusion

This analysis has demonstrated that there is an overall clear relationship between personal prayer and spiritual health. Young people who pray have a clear profile of better spiritual health in the transcendental domain, but this strength is also reflected through the other three domains proposed by Fisher's model of spiritual health. Young people who pray enjoy better spiritual health in the personal domain (especially as reflected in a stronger sense of purpose in life), in the communal domain (especially as reflected in greater support from parents and close friends) and in the environmental domain (especially as reflected in more inclusive social attitudes and in greater concern for matters of global citizenship and sustainable development). There are, nevertheless, some important negative correlates of personal prayer. In the personal domain young people who pray are more likely to suffer from self-doubts. In the communal domain young people who pray are more likely to fall victim to bullying at school.

These findings should alert urban planners to the important role of religious faith in developing spiritual health among young people and consequently in generating hope for urban life. In other words, personal faith may carry very significant public consequences in terms of resourcing the social capital infrastructure of the urban environment. In this sense it may be both irresponsible and detrimental to the common good to ignore the hidden potential within religious practice for resourcing urban hope.

14

Christians

Setting the context

This chapter initiates a sequence of five chapters concerned with examining the power of self-identified religious affiliation in predicting individual differences in spiritual health across the four domains proposed by Fisher. This first chapter in the sequence sets the context for all five chapters by discussing the notion of self-assigned religious affiliation and its usefulness in predicting individual differences in the psychological and social domains.

The majority of research projects conducted in England and Wales during the past twenty years into the worldviews of adolescents have routinely chosen to ignore the potential role of religion in shaping values, attitudes and behaviours, as exampled by Department of Education and Science (1983), Furnham and Stacey (1991), Balding (1993; 1997; 1998; 1999), Hendry, Shucksmith, Love and Glendinning (1993), Woodroffe, Glickman, Barker and Power (1993), Roberts and Sachdev (1996) and Kremer, Trew and Ogle (1997). The implicit assumption is clearly that religion is both privatised and marginalised in the modern world to the point that information about religiosity is irrelevant in understanding and interpreting the social and public worldview of young people.

The first major empirical survey to challenge this assumption within England and Wales was a study based on over 13,000 adolescents reported by Francis and Kay (1995). According to this study, religion persists as an important predictor of adolescent values over a wide range of areas. A second more recent analysis, reported by Gill (1999), came to similar conclusions from data collected among adults in the British Social Attitudes Surveys. On this account, religion is neither fully privatised nor fully marginalised in the modern world of the adolescent.

Clearly in modern society there remains a place for religious belief, religious practice and religious affiliation. The key question concerns the extent to which these well established dimensions of religion function as predictors of social values, attitudes and behaviours and the value of using any one of these indicators in isolation from the others.

Historically, one of the most commonly used markers of religiosity in social surveys was self-assigned religious affiliation. More recently confidence in self-assigned religious affiliation as a socially useful indicator of religiosity has been undermined from three directions. First, one influential account of religion in contemporary society has emphasised the persistence of 'believing without belonging' (Davie, 1994). A misreading of this account seems to elevate the importance of religious believing over religious affiliation. This misreading is based on ambiguity in the word 'belonging' which is used somewhat oddly in the classic phrase 'believing without belonging' to refer to practice rather than to affiliation. Second, researchers who are more concerned with religious practice than with religious affiliation draw attention to the fact that affiliation is itself a relatively poor predictor of practice. While the majority of self-assigned Baptists may well be regular churchgoers, the majority of self-assigned Anglicans in England appear never to consider going to church. Herein is the problem of 'religious nominalism'. The mistake is to consider that religious affiliation is insignificant in its own right except as a surrogate for other religious measures. Third, a number of scholars, working particularly in the social psychology of religion, have refined instruments to distinguish carefully between finely nuanced dimensions of religiosity, as exampled by the distinction between intrinsic, extrinsic and quest orientations (Batson, Schoenrade and Ventis, 1993). The mistake is to consider that only a complex theoretical account of religion can provide an adequate basis for empirical enquiry.

Although self-assigned religious affiliation is currently neglected as a socially useful indicator of religiosity, this remains potentially the most publicly acceptable and the most generally available indicator in light of the routine inclusion of a religious affiliation question in many national censuses and in the census for England, Wales and Scotland for the first time in 2001.

An important and powerful attempt to rehabilitate self-assigned religious affiliation as a theoretically coherent and socially significant indicator has been advanced by Fane (1999). Fane draws on Bouma's (1992) sociological theory of religious identification, according to which he defines religious affiliation as a useful social category giving some indication of the cultural background and general orientating values of a person. Then Bouma posits a process through which 'cultural background' and 'general orientating values' are acquired. Importantly, this process of acquisition is exactly the same for religious identity as it is for political or sporting or philosophical identities, and consists of: first, 'meaning systems', which Bouma (1992: 106) describes as 'a set or collection of answers to questions about the meaning and purpose of life', and second, 'plausibility structures' (borrowed from Berger 1967, 1969), which Bouma (1992: 107) describes as 'social arrangements which serve to inculcate, celebrate, perpetuate and apply a meaning system'. He maintains that all of us possess meaning systems from which we derive our existential purpose. He cites a living church as being one example of a plausibility structure through which a meaning system is, literally, made plausible and then disseminated. Although a self-assigned religious identity might also imply commitment to a plausibility structure (practice) and adherence to its related meaning system (belief), Bouma (1992: 108) suggests that it might be equally, perhaps more, significant in terms of the exposure to the particular cultural background that it represents. Crucially, this alternative conceptualisation avoids the difficult terrain of religious affiliation as proxy for practice and belief by recognising that even non-churchgoers and non-believers 'may still show *the effect* of the meaning system and plausibility structure with which they identify' (Bouma, 1992: 108, emphasis added).

The value of Bouma's sociological theory of religious identification is that it allows us to perceive, and thus analyse, a self-assigned religious affiliation as a key component of social identity, in a way similar to age, gender, class location, political persuasion, nationality, ethnic group and others (see Zavalloni, 1975: 200). It informs our attitudes and, in turn, our modes of behaviour by contributing to our self-definition both of who we are, but equally importantly, of who we are not. This type of analysis is especially advantageous when interpreting census data, because it is inclusive of all those who claim a religious affiliation, not only of the minority who also attend church.

Alongside Bouma's theory of religious identification, Fane (1999) also draws on Bibby's (1985) theory of 'encasement' developed from his empirical surveys in Canada. Bibby argues that Canadian Christians are 'encased' within the Christian tradition. In other words, this tradition has a strong, influential hold over both its active and latent members from which affiliates find it extremely difficult to extricate themselves. Contrary to the claims of secularisation theorists that low levels of church attendance are indicative of the erosion of religion's social significance (see Wallis and Bruce, 1992), Bibby (1985, 1987) would argue that this trend is actually a manifestation of the re-packaging of religion in the context of late twentieth century consumer-orientated society. Consumers, as we all are, are free to select 'fragments' of faith, and we are encouraged to do this by the way in which the churches have simulated the marketing strategies of the wider society.

The central point to glean from Bibby's analysis is that the potential for religion, in this case Christianity, to be a socially significant attitudinal and behavioural determinant has not necessarily disappeared. If anything, the Christian 'casing' may have been strengthened, because the accommodationist stance adopted by the Christian churches has, according to Bibby, reduced the need for affiliates to look elsewhere.

A major debate during the shaping of the religious question for the 2001 census in England, Scotland and Wales concerned the desirability of subdividing the Christian category according to denomination. Such division is routinely the case in other countries and provides a much more useful level of information for social planning as demonstrated by Francis (2003). The Religious Affiliation Group established by the Census Content Working Group of the Office for National Statistics strongly recommended division of the Christian category, but this advice was ignored by those responsible for drafting the Census White Paper. The Scottish Parliament insisted on the division, but the Westminster Parliament accepted the steer of the White Paper. Against this background, the aim of the present chapter is to examine the usefulness of aggregating the Christian denominations into a single category for predicting individual differences in spiritual health across Fisher's four domains.

Because of the way that social research in England and Wales (when it takes religious affiliation into account) generally recognises the better sense of treating Christian denominations (or groups of denominations) separately, there is no real research tradition concerned with profiling Christian affiliates as one group. A paper published at the time of the 2001 census by Francis (2001b) found that, treated as a single category, Christian affiliates presented a distinctive psycho-social profile in comparison with non-affiliates.

In respect of alcohol consumption, Christian affiliates were slightly but significantly more likely than non-affiliates to consider that it is wrong to become drunk (20% compared with 16%). In respect of sexual ethics, Christian affiliates were slightly but significantly more likely than non-affiliates to consider that it is wrong to have sexual intercourse outside marriage (15% compared with 11%). Christian affiliates were less inclined to regard homosexuality as wrong (36% compared with 38%), but more inclined to regard divorce as wrong (20% compared with 17%) and more inclined to regard abortion as wrong (38% compared with 33%). Christian affiliates were also more inclined than non-affiliates to consider that pornography is too readily available (36% compared with 30%).

This small sample of statistics provides some evidence that self-assigned Christian religious affiliation is predictive of individual differences of a socio-psychological nature and that examination of the relationship between self-assigned Christian affiliation and spiritual health is worth exploring further.

Method

The questionnaire included an item concerned with religious affiliation. The check list of responses began with 'none', followed by a range of Christian denominations, other world faiths, and a write-in box for other categories. In order to examine the relation-ship between spiritual health and self-assigned affiliation with the Christian tradition all the separate Christian denominations were aggregated into one category. Chi square was then employed to examine the statistical significance of differences between the two groups identified as: no religious affiliation and Christian affilia-tion. For simplicity of comparison the two groups will be referred to as young non-affiliates and as young Christian affiliates.

Personal domain

The statistics presented in table 14.1 demonstrate that overall the young Christian affiliates enjoy a better level of spiritual health in the personal domain than is the case among the young non-affiliates. This view is supported by all three indicators concerned with positive affect and by two of the four indicators concerned with negative affect.

Regarding positive affect, the young Christian affiliates recorded a greater sense of purpose in life than the young non-affiliates (60% compared with 50%). The young Christian affiliates recorded a greater sense of life really being worth living than the young non-affiliates (71% compared with 68%). The young Christian affiliates recorded greater happiness in their school compared with the young non-affiliates (74% compared with 67%).

Regarding negative affect, the young Christian affiliates were slightly but significantly less likely to feel that they were not worth much as a person (13% compared with 14%). The young Christian affiliates were less likely to have considered taking their own life compared with the non-affiliates (26% compared with 28%).

On the other hand, the young Christian affiliates were more likely than the young non-affiliates to have often felt depressed (54% compared with 51%) and to have often longed for someone to whom to turn for advice (37% compared with 33%).

Communal domain

The statistics presented in table 14.2 demonstrate that in some ways young Christian affiliates enjoy better spiritual health in the communal domain in comparison with young non-affiliates, but that in other ways they experience poorer spiritual health.

Better spiritual health in the communal domain among the young Christian affiliates is indicated by the following statistics. While 48% of the young non-affiliates found it helpful to talk about their problems with their mother, the proportion rose to 52% among the young Christian affiliates. While 31% of the young non-affiliates found it helpful to talk about their problems with their father, the proportion rose to 33% among the young Christian affiliates. While 61% of the young non-affiliates found it helpful to talk about their problems with close friends, the proportion rose to 66% among the young Christian affiliates.

Poorer spiritual health in the communal domain among the young Christian affiliates is indicated by the following statistics. While 25% of the young non-affiliates were worried about being bullied at school, the proportion rose to 30% among the young Christian affiliates. While 31% of the young non-affiliates were worried about their attractiveness to the opposite sex, the proportion rose to 37% among the young Christian affiliates. While 48% of the young non-affiliates were worried about how they got on with other people, the proportion rose to 54% among the young Christian affiliates.

The same proportions of both groups liked the people with whom they go to school: 90% among the young non-affiliates and 90% among the young Christian affiliates.

Environmental domain

The statistics presented in table 14.3 demonstrate that Christian affiliation is a good predictor of better levels of spiritual health in the environmental domain. This view is supported by the following data.

First and foremost, the young Christian affiliates felt significantly more empowered to have an effect on the world in which they live. While 29% of the young non-affiliates maintained that there is nothing they can do to help solve the world's problems, the proportion fell to 23% among the young Christian affiliates.

Second, the young Christian affiliates held significantly less racist attitudes. While 19% of the young non-affiliates argued that there are too many black people living in this country, the proportion fell to 16% among the young Christian affiliates. On the other hand, between 32% and 33% of both groups maintained that immigration into Britain should be restricted.

Third, the young Christian affiliates held significantly more positive attitudes toward global citizenship and sustainable development. While 52% of the young non-affiliates were concerned about the poverty of the third world, the proportion rose to 66% among the young Christian affiliates. While 60% of the young non-affiliates were concerned about the risk of pollution to the environment, the proportion rose to 67% among the young Christian affiliates.

Fourth, the young Christian affiliates displayed a higher level of concern regarding violence on local and on global planes. While 53% of the young non-affiliates were concerned about the risk of nuclear war, the proportion rose to 58% among the young Christian affiliates. While 17% of the young non-affiliates were concerned about the level of violence on television, the proportion rose to 21% among the young Christian affiliates.

Transcendental domain

The statistics in table 14.4 demonstrate that self-assigned affiliation with the Christian tradition functions as a significant predictor of better spiritual health in the transcendental domain, with respect to the indicators of traditional religion. Well over half of the young Christian affiliates expressed belief in God (56%), compared with 24% of the young non-affiliates. Half the young Christian affiliates expressed belief in life after death (50%), compared with 38% of the non-affiliates. While 33% of the young non-affiliates dismissed the Church as irrelevant to life today, the proportion fell to 22% among the young Christian affiliates. While 36% of the young non-affiliates dismissed the Bible as irrelevant for life today, the proportion fell to 25% among the young Christian affiliates.

In terms of non-traditional religious beliefs, however, the young Christian affiliates shared a great deal in common with the young non-affiliates. Thus, one in three of the non-affiliates believed in their horoscope (35%), and so did 35% of the young Christian affiliates. One in five non-affiliates believed fortune-tellers could tell the future (20%), and so did 20% of the young Christian affiliates. On the other hand, while 33% of the young non-affiliates believed it was possible to contact the spirits of the dead, the proportion fell slightly but significantly to 31% among the young Christian affiliates.

Conclusion

This analysis has demonstrated that there is an overall clear relationship between self-assigned affiliation with the Christian tradition in England and Wales and spiritual health. Young people who regard themselves as Christian affiliates demonstrate better levels of spiritual health across all four domains proposed by Fisher's model. In the personal domain young Christian affiliates display better spiritual health in terms of enjoying a greater sense of purpose in life. In the communal domain young Christian affiliates display better spiritual health in terms of having better relationships with parents and with close friends. In the environmental domain young Christian affiliates display better spiritual health in terms of holding less racist attitudes and in terms of being more positive about the contribution which they could make to the world's future. In the transcendental domain, young Christian affiliates display better spiritual health in terms of displaying a more positive and confident attitude toward traditional religious beliefs.

This finding should alert urban planners to value the information provided by the 2001 census regarding the proportion of the population described as Christian in different areas. This description conveys important information about levels of spiritual health. In turn spiritual health helps to shape urban hope. Further erosion in the level of Christian affiliation in England and Wales could predict deterioration in spiritual health and undermine urban hope for the future.

15

Muslims

Setting the context

The intention of this chapter is to profile the levels of spiritual health experienced by young Muslims in England and Wales across the four domains proposed by Fisher. The profiling will be based on self-assigned religious affiliation alongside those young people with no affiliation to a religious group.

Several studies have provided insights into the values, attitudes, beliefs and identity of young Muslims in Britain, including the work by Anwar (1994), Basit (1997), Archer (2001), Sahin (2002), Sahin and Francis (2002) and Abbas (2003). Few studies, however, have enabled direct comparison to be made between young Muslims and young people affiliated with other religious groups or young people with no affiliation to a religious group, apart from the two pioneering studies by Francis (2001b) and by Smith (2002, 2006).

The study reported by Francis (2001b) among 13- to 15-year-old adolescents found some interesting differences between young Islamic affiliates and young people with no affiliation to a religious group. In respect of sexual ethics, young Muslims were more inclined than young non-affiliates to regard it as wrong to have sexual intercourse outside marriage (49% compared with 11%). Young Muslims were more inclined than young non-affiliates to regard homosexuality as wrong (55% compared with 38%). Young Muslims were more inclined than young non-affiliates to regard divorce as wrong (42% compared with 17%) and to regard abortion as wrong (58% compared with 33%). Young Muslims were also more inclined than young non-affiliates to consider that pornography is too readily available (40% compared with 30%).

The study reported by Smith (2002, 2006) included the following areas: substance use, attitude toward professional sources of support, attitude toward work, and attitude toward leisure. In respect of substance use, 70% of young Muslims regarded it as wrong to become drunk, compared with 15% of young non-affiliates. Young Muslims also held a more proscriptive attitude toward tobacco and heroin. Thus, 55% of young Muslims regarded it as wrong to smoke cigarettes, compared with 34% of young non-affiliates; 71% of young Muslims regarded it as wrong to use heroin, compared with 61% of young non-affiliates. The use of marijuana was regarded as wrong by 38% of young Muslims and 37% of young non-affiliates.

In respect of attitude toward professional sources of support, young Muslims were more open than young non-affiliates to discussing personal matters with school teachers and youth leaders, but not with doctors and social workers. While 42% of young non-affiliates were reluctant to discuss their problems with a school teacher, the proportion fell to 29% among young Muslims. While 41% of young non-affiliates were reluctant to discuss their problems with a youth leader, the proportion fell to 25% among young Muslims. On the other hand, 32% of young non-affiliates were reluctant to discuss their problems with a doctor, and so were 36% of young Muslims; 34% of young non-affiliates were reluctant to discuss their problems with a social worker, and so were 28% of young Muslims.

In respect of attitude toward work, young Muslims generally projected a more positive profile than young non-affiliates. While 71% of young non-affiliates considered that a job gives people a sense of purpose in life, the proportion rose to 79% among young Muslims. While 87% of young non-affiliates said that they want to get to the top in their work when they get a job, the proportion rose to 94% among young Muslims.

In respect of attitude toward leisure, compared with young non-affiliates, young Muslims felt that their parents exercised much greater control over their free time. Thus, 55% of young Muslims said that their parents prefer them to stay in as much as possible, compared with 22% of young non-affiliates. While 50% of young non-affiliates said that their parents allow them to do what they like in their leisure time, the proportion fell to 37% among young Muslims.

This sample of statistics provides some evidence that self-assigned religious affiliation as Muslim is predictive of individual differences of a socio-psychological nature and that examination of the relationship between self-assigned Islamic affiliation and spiritual health is worth exploring further.

Method

The questionnaire included an item concerned with religious affiliation. The check list began with 'none', followed by a range of Christian denominations and the other five main world faiths listed in the 2001 census for England and Wales. In order to examine the relationship between spiritual health and self-assigned affiliation with the Islamic tradition, a direct comparison was made between the young people who checked the following two categories: none and Muslim. Chi square was then employed to examine the statistical significance of differences between these two groups. For simplicity of comparison the two groups will be referred to as young non-affiliates and as young Islamic affili-ates. Since the dataset contained 509 young Islamic affiliates these findings are fairly secure.

Personal domain

The statistics presented in table 15.1 demonstrate that in terms of positive affect the young Islamic affiliates enjoy a better level of spiritual health in comparison with the young non-affiliates. While 50% of the young non-affiliates felt their life had a sense of purpose, the proportion rose to 66% among the young Islamic affiliates. While 67% of the young non-affiliates were happy in their school, the proportion rose to 77% among the young Islamic affiliates. There were, however, no significant differences between the two groups in terms of the proportions who found life really worth living: 68% of the young non-affiliates compared with 69% of the young Islamic affiliates.

In terms of two major indicators of negative affect, there were no significant differences in levels of spiritual health reported by the young non-affiliates and by the young Islamic affiliates. Thus, 51% of the young non-affiliates often felt depressed, and so did 48% of the young Islamic affiliates. Similarly, 28% of the young non-affiliates have sometimes considered taking their own life, and so have 30% of the young Islamic affiliates.

In terms of two other indicators of negative affect, the young Islamic affiliates reported somewhat poorer levels of spiritual health. While 14% of the young non-affiliates felt that they were not worth much as a person, the proportion rose to 17% among the young Islamic affiliates. While 33% of the young non-affiliates often longed for someone to whom to turn for advice, the proportion rose to 39% among the young Islamic affiliates.

Communal domain

The statistics presented in table 15.2 demonstrate that, according to the majority of indicators included within the communal domain, young Islamic affiliates experience neither better nor worse levels of spiritual health in comparison with young non-affiliates. Looking first at indicators concerned with positive affect, 90% of the young non-affiliates liked the people with whom they went to school, and so did 88% of the young Islamic affiliates. Nearly a third of the young non-affiliates found it helpful to talk about their problems with their father (31%), and so did 31% of the young Islamic affiliates. Three-fifths of the young non-affiliates found it helpful to talk about their problems with close friends (61%), and so did 62% of the young Islamic affiliates. Looking second at indicators of negative affect, 31% of the young non-affiliates were worried about their attractiveness to the opposite sex, and so were 28% of the young Islamic affiliates. Similarly, 48% of the young non-affiliates were worried about how they get on with other people, and so were 45% of the young Islamic affiliates.

The remaining two indicators within the communal domain, however, drew attention to ways in which the experiences of young Islamic affiliates differ from those of young non-affiliates. One difference is positive and the other difference is negative in terms of spiritual health. The positive difference is reflected in the way in which a higher proportion of the young Islamic affiliates found it helpful to talk about their problems with their mother (52%), compared with 48% among the young non-affiliates. The negative difference is reflected in the way in which a higher proportion of the young Islamic affiliates were worried about being bullied at school (34%), compared with 25% among the young non-affiliates.

Environmental domain

The statistics presented in table 15.3 demonstrate that, across several indicators in this section concerned with the environmental domain, young Islamic affiliates display the same levels of spiritual health as young non-affiliates. The same proportions of the young non-affiliates (29%) and of the young Islamic affiliates

(29%) took the view that there is nothing they can do to help solve the world's problems. Similar proportions of the young non-affiliates (60%) and the young Islamic affiliates (62%) were concerned about the risk of pollution to the environment. Similar proportions of the young non-affiliates (53%) and the young Islamic affiliates (50%) were concerned about the risk of nuclear war.

On the other hand, the young Islamic affiliates held more positive attitudes than the young non-affiliates to world development and citizenship issues both globally and locally. While 52% of the young non-affiliates were concerned about the poverty of the third world, the proportion rose to 62% among the young Islamic affiliates. While 32% of the young non-affiliates argued that immigration into Britain should be restricted, the proportion fell to 18% among the young Islamic affiliates. Although not statistically significant in light of the sample size, a similar trend is reflected in the indicator of racist attitudes. While 19% of the young non-affiliates maintained that there are too many black people living in this country, the proportion fell to 14% among the young Islamic affiliates.

The young Islamic affiliates were twice as likely as the young non-affiliates to take the view that there is too much violence on television (38% compared with 17%).

Transcendental domain

The statistics in table 15.4 demonstrate that self-assigned affiliation with the Islamic tradition functions as a significant predictor of better spiritual health in the transcendental domain, with respect to the indicators of both traditional religion and non-traditional religion.

In terms of traditional religion, almost all the young Islamic affiliates (91%) expressed belief in God, compared with 24% of the young non-affiliates. Two-thirds of the young Islamic affiliates (69%) expressed belief in life after death, compared with 38% of the young non-affiliates. The young Islamic affiliates displayed significantly more respect than young non-affiliates for the Bible and for the Church. While 36% of the young non-affiliates dismissed the Bible as irrelevant for life today, the proportion fell to 24% among the young Islamic affiliates. While 33% of the young non-affiliates dismissed the Church as irrelevant for life today, the proportion fell to 23% among the young Islamic affiliates.

In terms of non-traditional religion, the young Islamic affiliates were significantly less likely than the young non-affiliates to believe in spiritual forces shaping their lives. While 35% of the young non-affiliates believed in their horoscope, the proportion fell to 23% among the young Islamic affiliates. While 33% of the young non-affiliates believed that it is possible to contact the spirits of the dead, the proportion fell to 16% among the young Islamic affiliates. Although not statistically significant, a similar trend is reflected in belief in fortune-tellers. While 20% of the young non-affiliates believed that fortune-tellers can tell the future, the proportion fell to 17% among the young Islamic affiliates.

Conclusion

This analysis has demonstrated that there are significant ways in which young people affiliated with the Islamic tradition enjoy higher levels of spiritual health in comparison with young people who belong to no religious tradition. This difference is reflected most strongly in the transcendental domain where young Islamic affiliates demonstrate high commitment to traditional religion and greater rejection of non-traditional religious beliefs. In the environmental domain young Islamic affiliates display greater concern for world development issues. In the communal domain young Islamic affiliates experience greater support from their mothers. In the personal domain young Islamic affiliates express a greater sense of purpose in life.

There are, however, some significant warning signs in these data. In spite of enjoying overall better spiritual health, young Islamic affiliates are as likely as young non-affiliates to feel disempowered to influence world events. They are more likely to experience low self-esteem and much more likely to be worried about being bullied at school.

These findings demonstrate the significant contribution to urban hope which can be generated by the good spiritual health nurtured within the Islamic community. They also demonstrate how this contribution may be dissipated through issues of social exclusion as reflected in low self-esteem and in high victimisation. These are crucial issues which need to be taken into account by urban planners.

16

Jews

Setting the context

The intention of this chapter is to profile the levels of spiritual health experienced by young Jews in England and Wales across the four domains proposed by Fisher. The profiling will be based on self-assigned religious affiliation alongside those young people with no affiliation to a religious group.

Smith's (2002, 2006) study comparing the attitudes and values of young people from different faith backgrounds included Christians, Hindus, Muslims and Sikhs, but not Jews. The more limited study reported by Francis (2001b), however, included young Jews alongside Christians, Hindus, Muslims and Sikhs, and is, therefore, able to test to some extent the distinctiveness of the worldview of young Jews living and growing up in England and Wales.

The study reported by Francis (2001b) among 13- to 15-year-old adolescents found some interesting differences between young Jewish affiliates and young people with no affiliation to a religious group. Regarding alcohol consumption, young Jews were marginally more inclined to regard it as wrong to become drunk (20%), compared with 16% of young non-affiliates. In respect of sexual ethics, young Jews were somewhat more inclined than young non-affiliates to regard it as wrong to have sexual intercourse outside marriage (23% compared with 11%). Young Jews were also marginally more inclined than young non-affiliates to regard divorce as wrong (21% compared with 17%) and to regard pornography as too readily available (36% compared with 30%).

On the other hand, young Jews took a more liberal view than young non-affiliates on the issues of homosexuality and abortion. While 38% of young non-affiliates regarded homosexuality as wrong, the proportion fell to 24% among young Jews. While 33% of young non-affiliates regarded abortion as wrong, the proportion fell to 27% among young Jews.

This small sample of statistics provides some evidence that self-assigned religious affiliation as Jewish is predictive of individual differences of a socio-psychological nature and that examination of the relationship between self-assigned Jewish affiliation and spiritual health is worth exploring further.

Method

The questionnaire included an item concerned with religious affiliation. The check list began with 'none', followed by a range of Christian denominations and the other five main world faiths listed in the 2001 census for England and Wales. In order to examine the relationship between spiritual health and self-assigned affiliation with the Jewish tradition, a direct comparison was made between the young people who checked the following two categories: none and Jewish. Chi square was then employed to examine the statistical significance of differences between the two groups. For simplicity of comparison the two groups will be referred to as young non-affiliates and young Jewish affiliates. Since the dataset contained only 53 young Jewish affiliates considerable difference is required in the percentage responses before statistical significance is reached.

Personal domain

The statistics presented in table 16.1 demonstrate that overall young Jewish affiliates enjoy a better level of spiritual health in the personal domain than is the case among young non-affiliates. Differences recorded on three of the seven indicators reached statistical significance and point to large substantive differences. While 67% of the young non-affiliates were happy in their school, the proportion rose to 83% among the young Jewish affiliates. While 68% of the young non-affiliates found life really worth living, the proportion rose to 87% among the young Jewish affiliates. While 50% of the young non-affiliates felt their life had a sense of purpose, the proportion rose to 67% among the young Jewish affiliates.

While not reaching statistical significance due to the sample size, three of the remaining four indicators point consistently in the same direction. While 51% of the young non-affiliates often felt depressed, the proportion fell to 43% among the young Jewish affiliates. While 14% of the young non-affiliates felt that they were not worth much as a person, the proportion fell to 11% among the young Jewish affiliates. While 28% of the young non-affiliates have sometimes considered taking their own lives, the proportion fell to 19% among the young Jewish affiliates.

Slightly more young Jewish affiliates than young non-affiliates often longed for someone to whom to turn for advice (39% compared with 33%), although this difference does not reach statistical significance.

Communal domain

The statistics presented in table 16.2 demonstrate that in some ways young Jewish affiliates enjoy a better level of spiritual health in the communal domain than is the case among young non-affiliates. The really striking difference concerns the place of the mother in the Jewish family. Three-quarters of the young Jewish affiliates found it helpful to talk about their problems with their mother (76%), compared with 48% of the young non-affiliates. Although not reaching statistical significance due to the sample size, the young Jewish affiliates also seemed to derive more support from their father and from close friends. Thus, 41% of the young Jewish affiliates found it helpful to talk about their problems with their father, compared with 31% of the young non-affiliates. Similarly, 68% of the young Jewish affiliates found it helpful to talk about their problems with close friends, compared with 61% of the young non-affiliates.

While differences recorded on none of the indicators of negative affect in this section reached statistical significance due to the sample size, the clear impression is given that in some ways young Jewish affiliates experience a poorer level of spiritual health in the communal domain. While 25% of the young non-affiliates were worried about being bullied at school, the proportion rose to 34% among the young Jewish affiliates. While 31% of the young non-affiliates were worried about their attractiveness to the opposite sex, the proportion rose to 37% among the young Jewish affiliates. While 48% of the young non-affiliates were worried about how they get on with other people, the proportion rose to 55% among the young Jewish affiliates.

Very close proportions of both groups (90% of young non-affiliates and 89% of young Jewish affiliates) liked the people with whom they go to school.

Environmental domain

The statistics presented in table 16.3 demonstrate that in one particular area young Jewish affiliates enjoy a better level of spiritual health in the environmental domain compared with young non-affiliates. The young Jewish affiliates showed a significantly higher level of concern for matters relevant to global citizenship and sustainable development. While 60% of the young non-affiliates were concerned about the risk of pollution to the environment, the proportion rose to 76% among the young Jewish affiliates. While 52% of the young non-affiliates were concerned about the poverty of the third world, the proportion rose to 66% among the young Jewish affiliates.

Differences on none of the other five indicators in this section reached statistical significance. One in five of the young non-affiliates argued that there are too many black people living in this country (19%), and so did 17% of the young Jewish affiliates. A third of the young non-affiliates argued that immigration into Britain should be restricted (32%) and so did 40% of the young Jewish affiliates. Similar proportions of both groups were concerned about the risk of nuclear war (53% of the young non-affiliates and 57% of the young Jewish affiliates). Similar proportions of both groups were concerned that there is too much violence on television (17% of the young non-affiliates and 20% of the young Jewish affiliates). Similar proportions of both groups felt that there was nothing they could do to help solve the world's problems (29% of the young non-affiliates and 26% of the young Jewish affiliates).

Transcendental domain

The statistics presented in table 16.4 demonstrate that young Jewish affiliates enjoy a higher level of spiritual health in the transcendental domain as reflected through traditional religion. Two-thirds of the young Jewish affiliates believed in God (64%), compared with one-quarter of the young non-affiliates (24%). The young Jewish affiliates were significantly less likely than the young non-affiliates to have rejected the Bible as irrelevant for life today (23% compared with 36%). Although the differences recorded by the other two indicators concerned with traditional religion fail to reach statistical significance, these differences also point in the same direction. The young Jewish affiliates were somewhat more likely than the young non-affiliates to believe in life after death (43% compared with 38%). The young Jewish affiliates were somewhat less likely than the young non-affiliates to have rejected the Church as irrelevant for life today (27% compared with 33%).

In terms of non-traditional religious beliefs, there is very little difference between the two groups. A third of the young non-affiliates believed in their horoscope (35%), and so did 35% of the young Jewish affiliates. A third of the young non-affiliates believed in the possibility of contacting the spirits of the dead (33%) and so did 31% of the young Jewish affiliates. A fifth of the young non-affiliates (20%) believed fortune-tellers can tell the future, and so did 17% of the young Jewish affiliates.

Conclusion

This analysis has demonstrated that there are significant ways in which young people affiliated with the Jewish tradition enjoy higher levels of spiritual health in comparison with young people who belong to no religious tradition. Moreover, this finding holds true across all four domains of spiritual health proposed by Fisher. In the personal domain young Jewish affiliates enjoy a significantly greater sense of purpose in life. In the communal domain young Jewish affiliates enjoy better and closer relationships with family and with friends, and especially with their mother. In the environmental domain young Jewish affiliates display higher levels of concern for matters relevant to global citizenship and sustainable development. In the transcendental domain young Jewish affiliates display greater commitment to belief in God and greater respect for religious traditions.

The one significant warning sign highlighted by these data concern the vulnerability of young Jewish affiliates to higher risks of bullying at school.

These findings demonstrate the significant contribution to urban hope which can be generated by the good spiritual health nurtured within the Jewish community, not least through the significant role of the mother recognised and respected by the young

Jewish affiliates themselves. This contribution may, nonetheless, be undervalued and submerged in a culture of victimisation and bullying at schools. This is a crucial issue which needs to be taken seriously by urban schools and by urban communities if religious difference is to strengthen and not undermine urban hope.

17

Hindus

Setting the context

The intention of this chapter is to profile the levels of spiritual health experienced by young Hindus in England and Wales across the four domains proposed by Fisher. The profiling will be based on self-assigned religious affiliation alongside those young people with no affiliation to a religious group.

Several studies have provided insights into the values, attitudes, beliefs and identity of young Hindus in Britain, including the work by Jackson (1989, 1996), Nesbitt and Jackson (1992), Jackson and Nesbitt (1993), Nesbitt (1998, 1999, 2001), Abbas (2003), and Bhanot and Santosh (2003). Few studies, however, have enabled direct comparison to be made between young Hindus and young people affiliated with other religious groups or young people with no affiliation to a religious group, apart from the two pioneering studies by Francis (2001b) and by Smith (2002, 2006).

The study reported by Francis (2001b) among 13- to 15-year-old adolescents found some interesting differences between young Hindu affiliates and young people with no affiliation to a religious group. In respect of sexual ethics, young Hindus were more inclined than young non-affiliates to regard it as wrong to have sexual intercourse outside marriage (29% compared with 11%). Young Hindus were also more inclined than young non-affiliates to regard pornography as too readily available (45% compared with 30%). On the other hand, young Hindus took a more liberal attitude toward homosexuality. While 38% of young non-affiliates regarded homosexuality as wrong, the proportion fell to 28% among young Hindus. Views on abortion and divorce were quite similar among young Hindus and young non-affiliates. Thus, 33% of young non-affiliates considered abortion to be wrong, and so did 31% of young Hindus. Similarly, 17% of young non-affiliates considered divorce to be wrong, and so did 20% of young Hindus.

The study reported by Smith (2002, 2006) included the following areas: substance use, attitude toward professional sources of support, attitude toward work, and attitude toward leisure. In respect of substance use, 53% of young Hindus regarded it as wrong to become drunk, compared with 15% of young non-affiliates. Young Hindus also held a more proscriptive attitude toward tobacco, marijuana and heroin. Thus, 53% of young Hindus regarded it as wrong to smoke cigarettes, compared with 34% of young non-affiliates; 51% of young Hindus regarded it as wrong to use marijuana, compared with 37% of young non-affiliates; 73% of young Hindus regarded it as wrong to use heroin, compared with 61% of young non-affiliates.

In respect of attitude toward professional sources of support, young Hindus were less open than young non-affiliates to discussing personal matters with all the professional groups identified in the survey. While 42% of young non-affiliates were reluctant to discuss their problems with a school teacher, the proportion rose to 46% among young Hindus. While 41% of young non-affiliates were reluctant to discuss their problems with a youth leader, the proportion rose to 45% among young Hindus. While 32% of young non-affiliates were reluctant to discuss their problems with a doctor, the proportion rose to 45% among young Hindus. While 34% of young non-affiliates were reluctant to discuss their problems with a social worker, the proportion rose to 40% among young Hindus.

In respect of attitude toward work, young Hindus generally presented a more positive profile than young non-affiliates. While

71% of young non-affiliates considered that a job gives people a sense of purpose in life, the proportion rose to 79% among young Hindus. While 87% of young non-affiliates said that they want to get to the top in their work when they get a job, the proportion rose to 96% among young Hindus.

In respect of attitudes toward leisure, compared with young non-affiliates, young Hindus felt that their parents exercised much greater control over their free time. Thus, 46% of young Hindus said that their parents prefer them to stay in as much as possible, compared with 22% of young non-affiliates. While 50% of young non-affiliates said that their parents allow them to do what they like in their leisure time, the proportion fell to 37% among young Hindus.

This sample of statistics provides some evidence that self-assigned religious affiliation as Hindu is predictive of individual differences of a socio-psychological nature and that examination of the relationship between self-assigned Hindu affiliation and spiritual health is worth exploring further.

Method

The questionnaire included an item concerned with religious affiliation. The check list began with 'none', followed by a range of Christian denominations and the other five main world faiths listed in the 2001 census for England and Wales. In order to examine the relationship between spiritual health and self-assigned affiliation with the Hindu tradition, a direct comparison was made between the young people who checked the following two categories: none or Hindu. Chi square was then employed to examine the statistical significance of differences between the two groups. For simplicity of comparison the two groups will be referred to as young non-affiliates and as young Hindu affiliates. Since the dataset contained only 153 young Hindu affiliates considerable difference is required in the percentage responses before statistical significance is reached.

Personal domain

The statistics presented in table 17.1 demonstrate that there are some key ways within the personal domain that young Hindu affiliates enjoy better spiritual health than young non-affiliates. The young Hindu affiliates were more likely to have a sense of purpose in life and more likely to be happy in their school. While 50% of the young non-affiliates felt that their life has a sense of purpose, the proportion rose to 62% among the young Hindu affiliates. While 67% of the young non-affiliates felt happy in their school, the proportion rose to 80% among the young Hindu affiliates. On the other hand, the young Hindu affiliates were significantly more likely than young non-affiliates often to long for someone to whom to turn for advice (44% compared with 33%), suggesting some vulnerability to their spiritual health in the personal domain.

In respect of the other four indicators of spiritual health in the personal domain there were no significant differences between the two groups. Two-thirds of the young non-affiliates found life really worth living (68%), and so did 64% of the young Hindu affiliates. Regarding indicators of negative affect, 14% of the young non-affiliates felt that they were not worth much as a person, and so did 10% of the young Hindu affiliates. Half of the young non-affiliates often felt depressed (51%), and so did 49% of the young Hindu affiliates. Over a quarter of the young non-affiliates have sometimes considered taking their own life (28%), and so have 27% of the young Hindu affiliates.

Communal domain

The statistics in table 17.2 demonstrate that there are some key ways within the communal domain that young Hindu affiliates experience poorer spiritual health than young non-affiliates. Key to this observation is that young Hindu affiliates live under significantly greater fear of bullying: 34% of the young Hindu affiliates were worried about being bullied at school, compared with 25% of the young non-affiliates. The young Hindu affiliates were also significantly more anxious about relationships in general. While 48% of the young non-affiliates were worried about how they get on with other people, the proportion rose to 60% among the young Hindu affiliates. While 31% of the young non-affiliates were worried about their attractiveness to the opposite sex, the proportion rose to 40% among the young Hindu affiliates.

Across the other four indicators within the communal domain the differences between the two groups fail to reach statistical significance due in part to the size of the sample. In spite of living under greater fear of bullying at school, the young Hindu affiliates were as likely to like the people with whom they go to school: 93% of the young Hindu affiliates liked the people with whom they go to school, and so did 90% of the young non-affiliates. Nearly half of the young non-affiliates found it helpful to talk about their problems with their mother (48%), and so did 41% of the young Hindu affiliates. Nearly a third of the young non-affiliates found it helpful to talk about their problems with their father (31%), and so did 28% of the young Hindu affiliates. Three-fifths of the young non-affiliates found it helpful to talk about their problems with close friends (61%), and so did 68% of the young Hindu affiliates.

Environmental domain

The statistics presented in table 17.3 demonstrate that overall in the environmental domain young Hindu affiliates enjoy a better level of spiritual health than young non-affiliates. In particular the young Hindu affiliates held a more positive and more hopeful attitude toward the contribution which they can make to the future of the world. While 29% of the young non-affiliates said that there is nothing they can do to help solve the world's problems, the proportion taking this view fell to 20% among the young Hindu affiliates.

The young Hindu affiliates showed greater concern for world development. Three-quarters of the young Hindu affiliates expressed concern about the poverty of the third world (74%), compared with 52% of the young non-affiliates. Although the difference did not reach statistical significance due to the sample size, the young Hindu affiliates tended to show greater concern about the risk of pollution to the environment (67% compared with 60% among the young non-affiliates).

The young Hindu affiliates were less likely to display racist attitudes. While 19% of the young non-affiliates argued that there are too many black people living in this country, the proportion fell to 9% among the young Hindu affiliates. While 32% of the young non-affiliates argued that immigration into Britain should be restricted, the proportion fell to 14% among the young Hindu affiliates.

The young Hindu affiliates were more concerned than the young non-affiliates regarding the amount of violence on television (23% compared with 17%). There were no statistically significant differences between the proportions of the two groups who were concerned about the risk of nuclear war (53% of the young non-affiliates and 45% of the young Hindu affiliates).

Transcendental domain

The statistics presented in table 17.4 demonstrate that young Hindu affiliates enjoy a significantly better level of spiritual health in the transcendental domain than is the case among young non-affiliates. In terms of traditional religion, the young Hindu affiliates were more inclined to hold religious beliefs and to value religious institutions. Four-fifths of the young Hindu affiliates believed in God (80%), compared with 24% of the young non-affiliates. Three-quarters of the young Hindu affiliates believed in life after death (73%), compared with 38% of the young non-affiliates. While 33% of the young non-affiliates dismissed the Church as irrelevant to life today, the proportion fell to 19% among the young Hindu affiliates. While 36% of the young non-affiliates dismissed the Bible as irrelevant to life today, the proportion fell to 23% among the young Hindu affiliates.

In terms of non-traditional religious beliefs, the young Hindu affiliates were significantly less likely than the young non-affiliates to believe that it is possible to contact the spirits of the dead (21% compared with 33%). Regarding the other two indicators in this section, however, there were no significant differences between the two groups. A third of the young non-affiliates believed in their horoscope (35%), and so did 40% of the young Hindu affiliates. A fifth of the young non-affiliates believed fortune-tellers could tell the future (20%), and so did 21% of the young Hindu affiliates.

Conclusion

This analysis has demonstrated that young people affiliated with the Hindu tradition enjoy higher levels of spiritual health compared with young people who belong to no religious tradition across three of the four domains defined by Fisher. In the personal domain young Hindu affiliates enjoy a significantly greater sense of purpose in life. In the environmental domain young Hindu affiliates demonstrate a more positive attitude to matters of global development and hold a more hopeful view of the contribution which they themselves can make to the world's future. In the transcendental domain young Hindu affiliates affirm belief in God and value the contribution of other religious traditions.

It is in the communal domain, however, that this positive view of the spiritual health of young Hindu affiliates is questioned. Young Hindu affiliates are significantly more likely than young non-affiliates to live under the fear of being bullied at school, and they are more likely to be anxious about their relationships with other people.

These findings demonstrate the significant contribution to urban hope which can be generated by the good spiritual health nurtured within the Hindu community. This contribution may, nonetheless, be undervalued and submerged in a culture of victimisation and bullying in schools which may damage the self-image and confidence of young Hindu affiliates. This is a crucial issue which needs to be taken seriously by urban schools and by urban communities if religious difference is to strengthen and not undermine urban hope.

18

Sikhs

Setting the context

The intention of this chapter is to profile the level of spiritual health experienced by young Sikhs in England and Wales across the four domains proposed by Fisher. The profiling will be based on self-assigned religious affiliation alongside those young people with no affiliation to a religious group.

Several studies have provided insights into the values, attitudes, beliefs and identity of young Sikhs in Britain, including the work by Drury (1991), Nesbitt and Jackson (1993, 1995), Nesbitt (1995, 1997a, 1997b, 2005) and Abbas (2003). Few studies, however, have enabled direct comparisons to be made between young Sikhs and young people affiliated with other religious groups or young people with no affiliation to a religious group, apart from the two pioneering studies by Francis (2001b) and by Smith (2002, 2006).

The study reported by Francis (2001b) among 13- to 15-year-old adolescents found some interesting differences between young Sikh affiliates and young people with no affiliation to a religious group. In respect of sexual ethics, young Sikhs were more inclined than young non-affiliates to regard it as wrong to have sexual intercourse outside marriage (27% compared with 11%). Young Sikhs also took a more conservative stand than young non-affiliates on the issues of abortion, divorce and pornography. While 33% of young non-affiliates regarded abortion as wrong, the proportion rose to 40% among young Sikhs. While

17% of young non-affiliates regarded divorce as wrong, the proportion rose to 28% among young Sikhs. While 30% of young non-affiliates regarded pornography as too readily available, the proportion rose to 40% among young Sikhs. On the other hand, young Sikhs took a more liberal attitude toward homosexuality. While 38% of young non-affiliates regarded homosexuality as wrong, the proportion fell to 31% among young Sikhs.

The study reported by Smith (2002, 2006) included the following areas: substance use, attitude toward professional sources of support, attitude toward work, and attitude toward leisure. In respect of substance use, 30% of young Sikhs regarded it as wrong to become drunk, compared with 15% of young non-affiliates. Young Sikhs also held a more proscriptive attitude toward tobacco, but not toward marijuana and heroin. Thus 42% of young Sikhs regarded it as wrong to smoke cigarettes, compared with 34% of young non-affiliates. On the other hand, the use of marijuana was regarded as wrong by 35% of young Sikhs and by 37% of young non-affiliates. The use of heroin was regarded as wrong by 60% of young Sikhs and 61% of young non-affiliates.

In respect of attitude toward professional sources of support, young Sikhs were more open than young non-affiliates to discussing personal matters with school teachers, youth leaders and social workers, but less open with doctors. While 42% of young non-affiliates were reluctant to discuss their problems with a school teacher, the proportion dropped to 34% among young Sikhs. While 41% of young non-affiliates were reluctant to discuss their problems with a youth leader, the proportion fell to 35% among young Sikhs. While 34% of young non-affiliates were reluctant to discuss their problems with a social worker, the proportion fell to 28% among young Sikhs. On the other hand, 32% of young non-affiliates and 36% of young Sikhs were reluctant to discuss their problems with a doctor.

In respect of attitude toward work, young Sikhs generally presented a more positive profile than young non-affiliates. While

71% of young non-affiliates considered that a job gives people a sense of purpose in life, the proportion rose to 79% among young Sikhs. While 87% of young non-affiliates said that they want to get to the top in their work when they get a job, the proportion rose to 95% among young Sikhs.

In respect of attitude toward leisure, compared with young non-affiliates, young Sikhs felt that their parents exercised much greater control over their free time. Thus, 55% of young Sikhs said that their parents prefer them to stay in as much as possible, compared with 22% of young non-affiliates. While 50% of young non-affiliates said that their parents allow them to do what they like in their leisure time, the proportion fell to 32% among young Sikhs.

This sample of statistics provides some evidence that self-assigned religious affiliation as Sikh is predictive of individual differences of a socio-psychological nature and that examination of the relationship between self-assigned Sikh affiliation and spiritual health is worth exploring further.

Method

The questionnaire included an item concerned with religious affiliation. The check list began with 'none', followed by a range of Christian denominations and the other five main world faiths listed in the 2001 census for England and Wales. In order to examine the relationship between spiritual health and self-assigned affiliation with the Sikh tradition, a direct comparison was made between the young people who checked the following two categories: none and Sikh. Chi square was then employed to examine the statistical significance of differences between the two groups. For simplicity of comparison the two groups will be referred to as young non-affiliates and as young Sikh affiliates. Since the dataset contained 253 young Sikh affiliates these findings are fairly secure.

Personal domain

The statistics presented in table 18.1 demonstrate that within the personal domain of spiritual health only one of the seven indicators identified a significant difference between young Sikh affiliates and young non-affiliates. The young Sikh affiliates were significantly more likely to long for someone to whom to turn for advice than was the case among the young non-affiliates (40% compared with 33%).

Regarding the other indicators of negative affect within the personal domain, 14% of the young non-affiliates felt that they were not worth much as a person, and so did 16% of the young Sikh affiliates. Half of the young non-affiliates often felt depressed (51%), and so did 56% of the young Sikh affiliates. Over a quarter of the young non-affiliates (28%) have sometimes considered taking their own life, and so have 29% of the young Sikh affiliates.

Regarding the indicators of positive affect within the personal domain, 68% of the young non-affiliates found life really worth living, and so did 65% of the young Sikh affiliates. Two-thirds of the young non-affiliates were happy in their school (67%), and so were 71% of the young Sikh affiliates. Half of the young non-affiliates felt their life had a sense of purpose (50%), and so did 52% of the young Sikh affiliates.

Communal domain

The statistics presented in table 18.2 demonstrate that within the communal domain of spiritual health only one of the seven indicators identified a significant difference between young Sikh affiliates and young non-affiliates. The young Sikh affiliates were significantly more likely to be worried about being bullied at school than was the case among the young non-affiliates (36% compared with 25%).

Regarding the other indicators of negative affect within the communal domain, 31% of the young non-affiliates were worried about their attractiveness to the opposite sex, and so were 34% of the young Sikh affiliates. Half of the young non-affiliates were worried about how they get on with other people (48%), and so were 51% of the young Sikh affiliates.

Regarding the indicators of positive affect within the communal domain, 48% of the young non-affiliates found it helpful to talk about their problems with their mother, and so did 45% of the young Sikh affiliates. A third of the young non-affiliates found it helpful to talk about their problems with their father (31%), and so did 27% of the young Sikh affiliates. Three-fifths of the young non-affiliates found it helpful to talk about their problems with close friends (61%), and so did 63% of the young Sikh affiliates. Nine out of ten young non-affiliates liked the people with whom they go to school (90%), and so did 87% of the young Sikh affiliates.

Environmental domain

The statistics presented in table 18.3 demonstrate that within the environmental domain of spiritual health only three of the seven indicators identified a significant difference between young Sikh affiliates and young non-affiliates. The young Sikh affiliates have a more open attitude toward racial integration in England and Wales and a more concerned attitude toward world development. While 19% of the young non-affiliates argued that there are too many black people living in this country, the proportion fell to 7% among the young Sikh affiliates. While 32% of the young non-affiliates argued that immigration into Britain should be restricted, the proportion fell to 16% among the young Sikh affiliates. While 52% of the young non-affiliates were concerned about the poverty of the third world, the proportion rose to 63% among the young Sikh affiliates.

Regarding the other indicators within the environmental domain, 17% of the young non-affiliates considered there is too much violence on television, and so did 20% of the young Sikh affiliates. Three-fifths of the young non-affiliates were concerned about the risk of pollution to the environment (60%), and so were 62% of the young Sikh affiliates. Just over half of the young non-affiliates were concerned about the risk of nuclear war (53%), and so were 52% of the young Sikh affiliates.

Similar proportions of the young non-affiliates (29%) and the young Sikh affiliates (25%) considered that there was nothing they could do to help solve the world's problems.

Transcendental domain

The statistics presented in table 18.4 demonstrate that young Sikh affiliates enjoy a significantly better level of spiritual health in the transcendental domain than is the case among young non-affiliates. In terms of traditional religion, the young Sikh affiliates were more inclined to hold religious beliefs and to value religious institutions. Three-quarters of the young Sikh affiliates believed in God (75%), compared with 24% of the young non-affiliates. Three-fifths of the young Sikh affiliates believed in life after death (58%), compared with 38% of the young non-affiliates. While 33% of the young non-affiliates dismissed the Church as irrelevant for life today, the proportion fell to 22% among the young Sikh affiliates. While 36% of the young non-affiliates dismissed the Bible as irrelevant to life today, the proportion fell to 20% among the young Sikh affiliates.

In terms of non-traditional religious beliefs, the young Sikh affiliates were less inclined to believe in contacting the spirits of the dead, but more inclined to believe in horoscopes and in fortune-tellers. While 33% of the young non-affiliates believed that it is possible to contact the spirits of the dead, the proportion fell to 23% among the young Sikh affiliates. While 35% of the young non-affiliates believed in their horoscope, the proportion rose to 42% among the young Sikh affiliates. While 20% of the young non-affiliates believed that fortune-tellers can tell the future, the proportion rose to 32% among the young Sikh affiliates.

Conclusion

This analysis has demonstrated that young people affiliated with the Sikh tradition follow a somewhat different profile of spiritual health from that followed by young people affiliated with the other religious traditions examined in the preceding chapters. A few key statistics draw attention to this difference in the personal domain and in the communal domain.

Within the personal domain of spiritual health, there is a general tendency for religious affiliates to enjoy a greater sense of purpose in life. While 50% of the young non-affiliates felt their life has a sense of purpose, the proportions rose to 60% among the young Christian affiliates, to 66% among the young Islamic affiliates, to 67% among the young Jewish affiliates, and to 62% among the young Hindu affiliates. Among the young Sikh affiliates the proportion stood at 52%, very close to the non-affiliates.

Within the communal domain of spiritual health, there is a general tendency for religious affiliates to enjoy a closer relationship with their parents. While 48% of the young non-affiliates found it helpful to talk about their problems with their mother, the proportions rose to 52% among the young Christian affiliates, to 52% among the young Islamic affiliates, and to 76% among the young Jewish affiliates. Among the young Hindu affiliates the proportion fell to 41% and among the young Sikh affiliates to 45%.

In the environmental domain and in the transcendental domain, however, young Sikh affiliates share more in common with the profile of spiritual health shaped by young people affiliated with the other religious traditions examined in the preceding chapters. A few key statistics draw attention to these similarities.

Within the environmental domain of spiritual health, there is a general tendency for religious affiliates to show greater commitment to world development. While 52% of the young non-affiliates are concerned about the poverty of the third world, the proportions rose to 66% among the young Christian affiliates, to 62% among the young Islamic affiliates, to 66% among the young Jewish affiliates, to 74% among the young Hindu affiliates and to 63% among the young Sikh affiliates.

Within the transcendental domain of spiritual health, young religious affiliates tend to have a worldview shaped by belief in life after death. While 38% of the young non-affiliates believed in life after death, the proportions rose to 50% among the young Christian affiliates, to 69% among the young Islamic affiliates, to 43% among the young Jewish affiliates, to 73% among the young Hindu affiliates, and to 58% among the young Sikh affiliates.

There remains one aspect of poor spiritual health which the young Sikh affiliates share in common with the young affiliates of other religious traditions, namely a higher level of anxiety regarding victimisation. While 25% of the young non-affiliates were worried about being bullied at school, the proportions rose to 30% among the young Christian affiliates, to 34% among the young Islamic affiliates, to 34% among the young Jewish affiliates, to 34% among the young Hindu affiliates, and to 36% among the young Sikh affiliates.

For urban hope to thrive in an age of religious diversity schools and local communities must face up to the hidden damage inflicted by bullying on young lives, on community development, and on urban hope.

19

Theological reflection

John Fisher's model of spiritual health has provided a powerful tool through which to hear and to analyse the voices of young people living and growing up in the urban areas of England and Wales. Throughout this analysis the argument has been that spiritual health holds the key to urban hope and to the future of urban living. The intention of this concluding chapter is to examine two key theological issues raised by the study: the connection between Fisher's model of spiritual health and the Christian theological tradition, and the sense in which an individual differences approach to spiritual health can be regarded as theologically valid.

Christian doctrine and spiritual health

While Fisher's model of spiritual health was developed to articulate and to give expression to a broadly-based understanding of spirituality, intelligible to those who hold a non-religious world-view as well as to those who have been shaped by a range of religious traditions, the model itself can be viewed helpfully and creatively from the perspective of the Christian tradition and in the light of Christian theological principles. The pivotal starting point for Fisher's model is grounded in the notion of relationships. It is at heart a relational model. The Christian tradition itself has a great deal to say about the centrality of a relational model, beginning with the doctrine of God, reflected in the doctrine of creation, developed in the doctrine of the fall, and reaching culmination in the doctrine of salvation through the person of Christ.

The Christian doctrine of God is given voice in the ancient creeds of the Church which formulate and develop teaching about the Trinity. This ancient doctrine of the Trinity has been revitalised in several strands of contemporary Christian theological thought and interpreted to illuminate the ways in which relationships stand at the very centre of the nature of God. The doctrine of God as Father, Son and Holy Spirit proclaims dynamic and relational being.

The Christian doctrine of creation is able to draw on the inspirational language of Genesis 1.27:

God created human beings in God's own image;
in the image of God, God created them;
male and female God created them.

Two profound insights follow from this view of creation relevant to the present argument (and a third will be deduced later). The first insight is that even in the monotheistically-shaped mind of the Hebrew writer of this part of Genesis, the richness and diversity of God requires a plural noun (*elohim*). The second insight is that human beings created in the divine image are capable of sustaining relationships both one with another (male and female God created them) and with their creator God. The doctrine of creation proclaims relational potential.

In the Christian tradition the implications of the doctrine of creation need always to be filtered through an understanding of the doctrine of the fall. According to the doctrine of the fall the image of God in God's creation became and remains damaged. The nature and extent of the damage varies from one theological perspective to another, but the main point of the doctrine of the fall is consistent. In the fall relationships are broken across all four of Fisher's domains. In this theological account of disrupted relationships, Fisher's four domains need to be read in reverse order, beginning with the transcendental and leading to the personal.

The biblically-grounded doctrine of the fall is clear about the priority of damage in the transcendental domain. Good relationships between creator and creature are broken. According to Genesis 3.21, the Lord God banished Adam from the Garden of Eden, and drove Adam out. The biblically-grounded doctrine of the fall is equally clear about damage in the environmental domain. Good relationships between human beings and the environment are broken. According to Genesis 3.15, the Lord God created division and discord between human beings and the world of the serpent:

> I shall put enmity between you and the woman,
> between your brood and hers.
> They will strike at your head,
> And you will strike at their heel.

According to Genesis 3.17–18, the Lord God created division between human beings and the natural environment:

> On your account the earth will be cursed.
> You will get your food from it only by labour
> all the days of your life;
> it will yield thorns and thistles for you.

The biblically-grounded doctrine of the fall is clear about damage in the communal domain. Good relationships are broken between one human being and another. According to Genesis 3.16 the Lord God created division and discord between Adam and Eve, between men and women. According to Genesis 4 division and discord between Cain and Abel leads to the ultimate disruption in the communal domain, in the act of murder. The biblically-grounded doctrine of the fall is equally clear about damage in the personal domain. Good relationships have been broken between an individual human being and his or her inner-self. According to Genesis 3.10, Adam experienced guilt, questioned his self-worth and lost his self-esteem. When Adam heard the sound of the Lord God in the garden, he was afraid and hid. According to Genesis 4.14 Cain assessed himself as 'a wanderer, a fugitive on the earth'.

The Christian doctrine of salvation through the person of Christ sets out to tackle and to reverse the fundamental relational problems posed by the doctrine of the fall. Precisely how the doctrine of salvation is expressed within different perspectives within the Christian tradition necessarily varies according to the different ways in which the problems of the fall are conceptualised. A thoroughly worked-through doctrine of salvation, however, needs to address the relational issues posed by all four of Fisher's domains. The work of Christ needs to be seen to be effective in restoring relationships in the transcendental domain (between creature and creator), in the environmental domain (between human beings and the world of which they are part), in the communal domain (between the sexes, between the ethnic groups, between the rich and the poor, between the oppressed and the oppressor, and so on), and in the personal domain (between an individual and his or her inner-self).

Just as the doctrine of the fall begins with the transcendental domain, so does the doctrine of redemption and salvation. At the heart of the Christian doctrine of salvation stands an understanding of the person of Christ. In more technical language soteriology builds on Christology. In the classic doctrines of the person of Christ, the tension between the transcendent and the immanent, and the disruption between God and humanity are healed. If, for example, the problem of the disruption between God and humanity is conceptualised in terms of the first Adam, then the Pauline discussion of the second Adam resolves the problem within the same terms. According to 1 Corinthians 15.21–22:

Since it was a man who brought death into the world, a man

also brought resurrection of the dead. As in Adam all die, so in Christ all will be brought to life.

At the heart of the Christian doctrine of salvation stands the good news that right relationships have been restored in the transcendent domain between humanity and the creator God in whose image humanity has been created. The challenge remains for those right relationships to be realised in the present context.

Flowing from the central concern of the Christian doctrine of salvation with the transcendental domain, there are profound implications for the other three domains (environmental, communal and personal). In classic Christian discussion it is generally the communal domain which seems to follow closely in the wake of the transcendental domain. Both the connection and the prioritisation seem to be clearly established in dominical teaching about the nature of living under the reign of God (or life in the kingdom of God). The point is illustrated, for example, in Mark 12.29–31 when Jesus replied to the question posed by one of the scribes, 'Which is the first of all the commandments?'

> The first is, 'Hear, O Israel: the Lord our God is the one Lord, and you must love the Lord your God with all your heart, with all your soul, with all your mind, and with all your strength.' The second is this: 'You must love your neighbour as yourself.'

In Luke 10.29–37 the point of the second commandment is illustrated through the story of the Good Samaritan. At the heart of the Christian doctrine of salvation stands the good news that right relationships have been restored in the communal domain between the individual and the individual's neighbour. The challenge remains for those right relationships to be realised in the present context.

The Christian doctrine of salvation, clearly established in the transcendental and communal domains, also has implications for the personal domain. The enigmatic emphasis of the second commandment needs to be fully explicated. If love of neighbour (communal domain) is to flow from love of self (personal domain), real theological reflection is needed on what is meant by love of self. Clearly if love of self is to inspire love of neighbour, love of self must be the very antithesis of selfishness. Within the context of the Christian doctrine of salvation, this love of self is nothing more nor less than an acceptance of the acceptance and love which God extends to the individual. If God finds us loveable, we are called to become loveable and to love ourselves. If God finds us acceptable, we are called to become acceptable and to accept ourselves. At the heart of the Christian doctrine of salvation stands the good news that right relationships have been restored in the personal domain between the individual and the individual's inner-being. The challenge remains for those right relationships to be realised in the present context.

The Christian doctrine of salvation also has implications for the environmental domain, in the sense of our connectedness with and our interdependence with the natural, physical and human global environment. In terms of the salvific work of Christ, the reversal of the disruptive consequences of the fall cannot stop with the transcendental, communal and personal domains. The salvific work of Christ needs to address the whole of the problem posed by the complexities of the doctrine of the fall. In this sense the battle between Adam and the soil needs to be resolved. The conflict between Cain and Abel needs to be reversed. The ethnic and linguistic barriers established by the destruction of Babel need themselves to be destroyed. At the heart of the Christian doctrine of salvation stands the good news that right relationships have been restored in the environmental domain not only between the peoples of the world, but between humanity and the rest of creation. The challenge remains for those right relationships to be realised in the present context.

Theology of individual differences

The notion of individual differences has been well-established in psychology over many decades and was given new prominence in the late 1970s by the formation of the International Society for the Study of Individual Differences and the associated journal *Personality and Individual Differences*. It is an extension of this approach which has shaped the analyses and chapter structure of the present book. The individual differences approach maintains that clear patterns exist in human values and behaviours which can be predicted by certain personal and contextual variables. The present study has focused in particular on five categories of individual difference: personal factors, defined as sex and age; home background factors, defined in terms of the north-south divide, paternal employment status, and family structure; school-related factors, defined in terms of Anglican schools, Catholic schools, and Christian schools; theoretical factors, defined in terms of social engagement and personal prayer; and religious identity factors, defined in terms of self-assigned religious affiliation as Christian, Muslim, Jew, Hindu, and Sikh.

There are problems with the implied determinism of the individual differences approach which may make the ideological basis of such research suspect within some theological circles. The tradition of empirical theology nurtured within the University of Wales, Bangor has begun to address these problems by developing a theology of individual differences grounded in the Christian doctrine of creation:

Attention has already been drawn in an earlier part of this chapter to the influence of Genesis 1.27 on shaping the Christian doctrine of creation:

God created human beings in God's own image;
in the image of God, God created them;
male and female God created them.

Earlier in this chapter two insights were articulated on the basis of this view of creation, and a third anticipated. The first insight was that even in the monotheistically-shaped mind of the Hebrew writer of this part of Genesis, the richness and diversity of God requires a plural noun. Alongside the later-developed doctrine of the Trinity, the creation narrative posits plurality (and the possibility of diversity) within the Godhead. The second insight is that human beings are created in the divine image and that, as a consequence, something important about the nature of being human can be derived from a properly-developed theology regarding the nature of God. Whatever plurality (and possibility of diversity) appertains to the nature of God should also appertain to the nature of humanity. The third insight follows from the remarkable suggestion that both male and female are created in the image of God. Empirically speaking male and female are distinguished one from the other in a variety of ways. The doctrine of creation in the image of God affirms that such differences are both intentional and worth understanding, and at the same time of equal standing and worth. Empirical observation of the individual difference known as sex should help to generate insight into the nature of the God in whose image both male and female were and are created.

A theology of individual differences which begins with sex differences can posit a range of other personal individual differences which may help to define what it is to be human created in the image of God. We have argued elsewhere that ethnicity and personality may function in similar ways to sex within a Christian theology of creation (Francis, 2005c). If male and female are both created in the image of God, it becomes a proper matter of theological enquiry to understand differences between the sexes and to examine the value of diversity and equality in sex and gender. If black and white are both created in the image of God, it becomes a proper matter of theological enquiry to understand differences between ethnic groups and to examine the value of diversity and equality in ethnicity. If introverts and extraverts are both created in the image of God, it becomes a proper matter of theological enquiry to understand differences between psychological types and to examine the value of diversity and equality in personality.

A theology of individual differences built on such a platform, based on the doctrine of creation, seeks not to submerge individuality but to rejoice in exploring the rich diversity and stable patterns within human individuality.

Conclusion

Introduction

Hope stands at the very heart of the Christian gospel. The good news of the resurrection of Christ proclaims the ultimate victory of life over death, the victory of good over evil, the victory of hope over despair. The good news of the resurrection of Christ proclaims the reign of God (the Kingdom of God) in which broken lives are made whole and the broken city restored. The good news of the resurrection of Christ proclaims urban hope.

The key thesis of the present study maintains that urban hope begins with close attention to the spiritual health of those who shape their lives in the urban environment, especially those who are living out their adolescent years there. In terms of the Christian tradition and Christian theology, spiritual health has been conceptualised in relational terms. Drawing on key Christian doctrines, especially doctrines concerning the nature of God, creation and redemption, good spiritual health has been conceptualised in terms of establishing and maintaining right relationships in four areas: the personal domain of right relationships with the self; the communal domain of right relationships with others; the environmental domain of right relationships with the physical and human world on the local and global levels; and the transcendental domain of right relationships with God.

Drawing on statistical analyses shaped by a theological and psychological approach to individual differences, the present study set out both to provide an overview of the spiritual health of the young people living and growing up in urban areas of England and Wales at the beginning of the twenty-first century, and to identify factors which predict better or poorer levels of spiritual health. In developing the individual differences approach attention has been given to five different kinds of factors: key personal factors included age and sex; key family background factors included geographical location, family structure and father's employment status; key school factors included attendance at Anglican schools within the state-maintained sector, attendance at Catholic schools within the state-maintained sector, and attendance at independent Christian schools; key attitudinal factors included the role of social engagement and the contribution made by personal prayer; and key religious factors included affiliation with the Christian, Islamic, Jewish, Hindu and Sikh traditions. The findings from these analyses help to position the Christian theology of hope within a realistic assessment of the empirical context, and thereby help to focus opportunities and challenges facing the realisation of the Christian vocation to ministry and mission in the urban environments.

Personal differences

The *overview* presented in chapter three gave some good grounds for hope in the spiritual health of the young people living and growing up in urban areas of England and Wales at the beginning of the twenty-first century. Perhaps more importantly, however, chapter three also identified flaws in the spiritual health of these young people which could significantly threaten the quality of life in urban England and Wales. For example, the data drew attention to the following issues: in the personal domain an unacceptably high level of suicidal ideation; in the communal domain an unacceptably high level of racist attitudes; in the environmental domain an unacceptably high level of political powerlessness; and in the transcendental domain a range of beliefs which may damage aspects of human growth and development. Each of these issues tests the power of the Christian theology of hope to transform all that detracts from healthy living and from good spiritual health. In the personal domain the Christian theology of hope offers the sense of purpose and meaning to life, a view which stands so powerfully between human pain and suicidal ideation. In the communal domain the Christian theology of hope offers a view of humankind united in the image of the creator God, a view which stands so powerfully against ethnic, social and economic differences and against racist attitudes. In the environmental domain the Christian theology of hope offers the view of human partnership and collaboration alongside the creator God with full and proper responsibility for shaping and for sharing the physical and human resources of the created order, a view which stands so powerfully against accepting powerlessness in the face of even the greatest political challenges. In the transcendental domain the Christian theology of hope offers a view of positive potential between the transcendental and the human realms, a view which stands so powerfully against unhealthy and damaging perspectives regarding the transcendental forces considered to interact with human destiny.

The analysis regarding *sex differences* presented in chapter four has confirmed the importance of sex in shaping spiritual health. In terms of Fisher's four ideal types, males are more likely than females to be personalists, having better spiritual health in the personal domain with a greater sense of self-worth. Males are also more likely than females to be communalists, having better spiritual health in the communal domain with fewer anxieties on relational matters. On the other hand, females are more likely to be environmentalists, having better spiritual health in the environmental domain with a greater sense of connectedness with local and global issues of citizenship and sustainable development. Females are also more likely than males to be religionists, having better spiritual health in the transcendental domain defined in

205

traditional theistic terms. In these ways males and females may be offering different insights into hope for the urban future. The Christian theology of hope offers two important insights into these empirically identified differences between the sexes, both derived from the doctrine of creation which affirms the creation of men and women in the divine image. On the one hand, this doctrine affirms and respects the fundamental differences between men and women. On the other hand, this doctrine also affirms the equality of opportunity extended to men and to women to grow into the fullness of the divine image. In the personal and communal domains the Christian theology of hope extends the invitation to young women to grasp confidence in their self-worth and in their interpersonal relationships. In the environmental and transcendental domains the Christian theology of hope extends the invitation to young men to grasp their responsibility for local and global issues of citizenship and sustainable development, and to recognise the claims of religious faith upon their individual lives.

The analysis regarding *age differences* presented in chapter five demonstrates that the growth and development taking place during adolescence is so rapid that significant changes in spiritual health can be detected by snapshots taken just one year apart in year nine and in year ten. Some of these changes may bring hope to the urban environment by highlighting the positive effects which the developmental process and the educational process may be having on young lives. In the communal domain hope is generated by declining anxiety in school over bullying. In the environmental domain hope is generated by the increasing sense of responsibility and ownership being taken by young people for solving the problems of this world. At the same time, disappointment might be registered over the lack of development in other areas. In the personal domain there is no greater sense of purpose in life. In the communal domain there is no diminution of anxiety over relationships. In the environmental domain there is no substantive change in promoting greater concern for global citizenship or sustainable development. In the transcendental domain there is no sign of growing rationality over non-traditional religious beliefs. Moreover, there are other changes which actually erode hope for the urban environment. In the personal domain pupils are growing less positive about and less happy in their school. In the environmental domain there is an increase in racism and racist attitudes. In the transcendental domain the drift from traditional religion continues. The Christian theology of hope recognises the potential for human growth and development into the fullness of Christ, as well as acknowledging the distractions impeding such growth and development. Throughout the stages of life the Christian theology of hope continues to present the image of Christ as inspiration and as challenge for human growth and development.

Home background differences

The analysis regarding *geographical differences* presented in chapter six has confirmed that there are significant differences between north and south across the four domains of spiritual health proposed by Fisher. Some of these indicators point to greater hope for the urban future in the north, and others of these indicators point to greater hope for the urban future in the south. Within two of the domains young people living in the south record better overall indicators of spiritual health compared with young people living in the north. Both domains carry implications for urban hope. In the personal domain, young people in the south record a lower level of suicidal ideation. This carries signs of hope for the south. In the communal domain, young people in the south display lower levels of anxiety about relationships in general and lower levels of fear about being bullied in school. This carries signs of hope for the south. Within the other two domains, however, young people living in the north record better overall indicators of spiritual health compared with young people living in the south. Both domains carry implications for urban hope. In the environmental domain, young people in the north record lower levels of racism. This carries signs of hope for the north. In the transcendental domain, young people in the north record higher levels of traditional religiosity. Certainly, as far as the faith communities are concerned, this carries signs of hope for the north. The Christian theology of hope recognises the equality of opportunities extended to all created in the image of the creator God. Taking seriously the empirical differences identified in levels of spiritual health expressed by young people living and growing up in the north and in the south, the Christian theology of hope will appreciate how slightly different emphases within ministry and mission in the north and in the south may be needed to redress imbalances in spiritual health. In the north more emphasis needs to be placed on developing spiritual health in the personal domain and in the communal domain. In the south more emphasis needs to be placed on developing spiritual health in the environmental domain and in the transcendental domain.

The analysis regarding *paternal employment status* presented in chapter seven has confirmed that there are significant differences between young people living in homes with employed fathers and young people living in homes without employed fathers across the four domains of spiritual health proposed by Fisher. Young people living in homes where there is no father figure in full-time employment record significantly poorer levels of spiritual health in the personal domain (having a lower sense of purpose in life and suffering from more suicidal ideation), in the communal domain (forming poorer relationships with their peers at school) and in the environmental domain (showing less engagement with world issues). On the other hand, they record greater openness to the transcendental domain (showing greater traditional and non-traditional religious beliefs). The Christian theology of hope appreciates and affirms the value of work within human life and the Christian churches have played a proper and vigorous role both in job-creation and in supporting the unemployed. The Christian theology of hope must, however, go well beyond the palliative measures of compensating for the inequalities generated within a capitalist economy. In its commitment to equality of opportunity for all those created in the image of the creator and creative God, the Christian theology of hope must also remain committed to examining and to critiquing the economic bases on which current inequalities in employment opportunities are grounded.

The analysis regarding *family structure* presented in chapter eight has confirmed that there are significant differences between young people living in intact homes and young people living in broken homes across the four domains of spiritual health proposed by Fisher. Young people living in broken homes record significantly poorer levels of spiritual health in the personal domain (having a lower sense of purpose in life), in the communal domain (having less satisfactory relationships with their parents), in the environmental domain (showing less engagement with world issues), and in the transcendental domain (showing less commitment to traditional religiosity, and giving greater credence to horoscopes and fortune-tellers). The Christian theology of hope affirms the importance of family life and grounds the stability of family life within the doctrine of creation. There remains every reason for the Christian Church to support a view of marital stability and to engage in vigorous programmes of marriage preparation and marriage support. At the same time, the Christian theology of hope would be failing in its commitment to the individual not to affirm and to support those individuals who choose to live in other forms of committed relationships or those whose marriage has failed. The Christian theology of hope rejoices in the God who forgives, and in the God who enables men and women to forgive each other and to forgive themselves. The Christian theology of hope recognises the need to offer particular support to those who are rendered vulnerable by familial instability.

School differences

The analyses regarding the influence of religiously affiliated schools reported in chapters nine, ten and eleven have demonstrated the following points. According to chapter nine, although young people attending *Anglican schools* share a number of indicators of spiritual health in common with young people in non-denominational schools, there are significant differences between the two groups in respect of all four of Fisher's domains of spiritual health. In comparison with young people in non-denominational schools, young people in Anglican schools record signs of lower spiritual health in the personal domain (less likely to find life really worth living) and in the communal domain (less confident in relationships with others), and signs of better spiritual health in the environmental domain (more concern about world poverty) and in the transcendental domain (more likely to believe in God, although they are also more likely to believe in fortune-tellers). The positive interpretation of these findings is that Anglican secondary schools may be working with less advantaged young people in the urban environment (as indicated by the lower spiritual health in the personal and communal domains) and nonetheless adding value to their spiritual health (as indicated by better spiritual health in the environmental and transcendental domains). According to this account Anglican schools add hope to the urban environment.

According to chapter ten, although young people attending *Catholic schools* share a number of indicators of spiritual health in common with young people in non-denominational schools, there are significant differences between the two groups in respect of all four of Fisher's domains of spiritual health. In the personal domain young people in Catholic schools show better spiritual health in terms of enjoying more sense of purpose in life. In the communal domain young people in Catholic schools show poorer spiritual health in terms of greater anxiety about relationships and bullying. In the environmental domain young people in Catholic schools show better spiritual health in terms of greater concern for world development. In the transcendental domain young people in Catholic schools show better spiritual health in terms of greater commitment to traditional religion, but poorer spiritual health in terms of commitment to non-traditional religious beliefs. The positive interpretation of these findings is that Catholic secondary schools bring to the urban environment communities in which belief in God is the norm. Pupils educated in this environment develop a greater sense of purpose in their own lives, hold a greater commitment to world development, and are as open in their attitudes to other groups as young people educated in non-denominational schools. According to this account Catholic schools contribute greatly to the common good and add hope to the urban environment.

According to chapter eleven, there are significant ways across all of Fisher's four domains in which young people attending *Christian schools* enjoy a higher level of spiritual health compared with young people in non-denominational schools. Within the personal domain young people in Christian schools benefit from a greater sense of purpose in life. Within the communal domain young people in Christian schools benefit from closer relationships with friends and from less fear of being bullied. Within the environmental domain young people in Christian schools are less racist in their attitudes and more concerned about world development issues. Within the transcendental domain young people in Christian schools are better rooted in traditional religious beliefs and less susceptible to non-traditional beliefs. The positive interpretation of these findings is that Christian schools bring to the urban environment communities committed to shaping purposive young lives capable of contributing to the common good on both local and global levels. Such communities are constructive rather than divisive of urban hope for the future.

The Christian theology of hope remains committed to the

physical health, psychological wellbeing and spiritual development of all God's people. Involvement in and through processes and systems of education have long reflected the Christian Church's commitment to this practical out-working of the theology of hope. There remain, however, strongly divided opinions within the Christian community regarding the best ways in which this commitment is expressed in practice. Some see the best reflection of the Christian theology of hope to be through radical commitment to the whole of the educational system. In this sense the Christian vocation to teach is expressed by Christians working in all schools. Others see the best reflection of the Christian theology of hope to be through the development and continuing maintenance of distinctive church-related schools. Chapters nine, ten and eleven have illustrated the three distinctive educational and theological perspectives of the Anglican Church, the Catholic Church and the independent Christian school movement. The data demonstrate that these differences in educational and theological perspectives are also reflected in differences in the levels of spiritual health reported by the pupils attending different forms of schools. Proper weight given to the methodology of contextual theology recognises that the Christian theology of hope needs to be sensitive to and responsive to the social context within which the Church is located. The theology of education provides an interesting test for this contextual perspective, since the theological arguments for and against church-related schools may carry very different weights in social contexts heavily influenced by the Christian tradition and in social contexts in which the Christian tradition is largely marginal.

Attitudinal differences

The analysis regarding social factors presented in chapter twelve has demonstrated that there is no clear-cut relationship between *social engagement* and spiritual health. Within the personal domain young people with high social engagement record better spiritual health, especially in terms of a greater sense of purpose in life and less susceptibility to feelings of depression. Within the communal domain young people with high social engagement enjoy better spiritual health on some indicators (less fear of being bullied) but poorer spiritual health on other indicators (less support from close friends). Within the environmental domain young people with high levels of social engagement record poorer spiritual health, especially in terms of holding more racist attitudes and in terms of feeling powerless in the face of the world's problems. Within the transcendental domain overall no clear pattern emerges between social engagement and spiritual health. The Christian theology of hope acknowledges that external resources and provisions are important for nurturing human growth and development both as individuals and as social beings. However, external factors are by themselves insufficient and inadequate to transform the human heart and to shape the human soul. External resources and provisions are ineffective without the internal will, commitment and understanding which can generate meaning, purpose, significance, self-fulfilment and service to others.

The analysis regarding personal factors presented in chapter thirteen has demonstrated that there is an overall clear relationship between *personal prayer* and spiritual health. Young people who pray have a clear profile of better spiritual health in the transcendental domain, but this strength is also reflected through the other three domains proposed by Fisher's model of spiritual health. Young people who pray enjoy better spiritual health in the personal domain (especially as reflected in a stronger sense of purpose in life), in the communal domain (especially as reflected in greater support from parents and close friends) and in the environmental domain (especially as reflected in more inclusive social attitudes and in greater concern for matters of global citizenship and sustainable development). There are, nevertheless, some important negative correlates of personal prayer. In the personal domain young people who pray are more likely to suffer from self-doubts. In the communal domain young people who pray are more likely to fall victim to bullying at school. The Christian theology of hope understands well the pivotal place of prayer in nurturing the Christian soul. Prayer is crucial in the human response to the two great commandments to love 'the Lord your God' and to love 'your neighbour as yourself'.

Religious affiliation

The analyses presented in chapters fourteen, fifteen, sixteen, seventeen and eighteen have examined in turn the contribution made by affiliation with five faith traditions clearly visible in contemporary society and culture: Christianity, Islam, Judaism, Hinduism and Sikhism. Chapter fourteen has demonstrated that there is an overall clear relationship between self-assigned affiliation with the *Christian tradition* in England and Wales and spiritual health. Young people who regard themselves as Christian affiliates demonstrate better levels of spiritual health across all four domains proposed by Fisher's model. In the personal domain young Christian affiliates display better spiritual health in terms of enjoying a greater sense of purpose in life. In the communal domain young Christian affiliates display better spiritual health in terms of having better relationships with parents and with close friends. In the environmental domain young Christian affiliates display better spiritual health in terms of holding less racist attitudes and in terms of being more positive about the contribution which they could make to the world's future. In the transcendental domain, young Christian affiliates display better spiritual health in terms of displaying a more positive and confident attitude toward traditional religious beliefs.

Chapter fifteen has demonstrated that there are significant ways in which young people affiliated with the *Islamic tradition* enjoy higher levels of spiritual health in comparison with young

people who belong to no religious tradition. This difference is reflected most strongly in the transcendental domain where young
Islamic affiliates demonstrate high commitment to traditional
religion and greater rejection of non-traditional religious beliefs.
In the environmental domain young Islamic affiliates display
greater concern for world development issues. In the communal
domain young Islamic affiliates experience greater support from
their mothers. In the personal domain young Islamic affiliates
express a greater sense of purpose in life. There are, however,
some significant warning signs in these data. In spite of enjoying
overall better spiritual health, young Islamic affiliates are as likely
as young non-affiliates to feel disempowered to influence world
events. They are more likely to experience low self-esteem and
much more likely to be worried about being bullied at school.

Chapter sixteen has demonstrated that there are significant
ways in which young people affiliated with the *Jewish tradition* enjoy higher levels of spiritual health in comparison with
young people who belong to no religious tradition. Moreover,
this finding holds true across all four domains of spiritual health
proposed by Fisher. In the personal domain young Jewish affiliates enjoy a significantly greater sense of purpose in life. In the
communal domain young Jewish affiliates enjoy better and closer
relationships with family and with friends, and especially with
their mother. In the environmental domain young Jewish affiliates display higher levels of concern for matters relevant to global
citizenship and sustainable development. In the transcendental
domain young Jewish affiliates display greater commitment to
belief in God and greater respect for religious traditions. The one
significant warning sign highlighted by these data concerns the
vulnerability of young Jewish affiliates to higher risks of bullying
at school.

Chapter seventeen has demonstrated that young people affiliated with the *Hindu tradition* enjoy higher levels of spiritual
health compared with young people who belong to no religious

tradition across three of the four domains defined by Fisher. In the personal domain young Hindu affiliates enjoy a significantly greater sense of purpose in life. In the environmental domain young Hindu affiliates demonstrate a more positive attitude to matters of global development and hold a more hopeful view of the contribution which they themselves can make to the world's future. In the transcendental domain young Hindu affiliates affirm belief in God and value the contribution of other religious traditions. It is in the communal domain, however, that this positive view of the spiritual health of young Hindu affiliates is questioned. Young Hindu affiliates are significantly more likely than young non-affiliates to live under the fear of being bullied at school, and they are more likely to be anxious about their relationships with other people.

Chapter eighteen has demonstrated that young people affiliated with the *Sikh tradition* follow a somewhat different profile of spiritual health from that followed by young people affiliated with the other religious traditions examined in the preceding chapters. A few key statistics draw attention to this difference in the personal domain and in the communal domain. Within the personal domain of spiritual health, there is a general tendency for religious affiliates to enjoy a greater sense of purpose in life. While 50% of the young non-affiliates felt their life has a sense of purpose, the proportions rose to 60% among the young Christian affiliates, to 66% among the young Islamic affiliates, to 67% among the young Jewish affiliates, and to 62% among the young Hindu affiliates. Among the young Sikh affiliates the proportion stood at 52%, very close to the non-affiliates. Within the communal domain of spiritual health, there is a general tendency for religious affiliates to enjoy a closer relationship with their parents. While 48% of the young non-affiliates found it helpful to talk about their problems with their mother, the proportions rose to 52% among the young Christian affiliates, to 52% among the young Islamic affiliates, and to 76% among the young Jewish affiliates. Among the young Hindu affiliates the proportion fell to 41% and among the young Sikh affiliates to 45%.

In the environmental domain and in the transcendental domain, however, young Sikh affiliates share more in common with the profile of spiritual health shaped by young people affiliated with the other religious traditions examined in the preceding chapters. A few key statistics draw attention to these similarities. Within the environmental domain of spiritual health, there is a general tendency for religious affiliates to show greater commitment to world development. While 52% of the young non-affiliates are concerned about the poverty of the third world, the proportions rose to 66% among the young Christian affiliates, to 62% among the young Islamic affiliates, to 66% among the young Jewish affiliates, to 74% among the young Hindu affiliates and to 63% among the young Sikh affiliates. Within the transcendental domain of spiritual health, young religious affiliates tend to have a worldview shaped by belief in life after death. While 38% of the young non-affiliates believed in life after death, the proportions rose to 50% among the young Christian affiliates, to 69% among the young Islamic affiliates, to 43% among the young Jewish affiliates, to 73% among the young Hindu affiliates, and to 58% among the young Sikh affiliates.

There remains one aspect of poor spiritual health which the young Sikh affiliates share in common with the young affiliates of other religious traditions, namely a higher level of anxiety regarding victimisation. While 25% of the young non-affiliates were worried about being bullied at school, the proportions rose to 30% among the young Christian affiliates, to 34% among the young Islamic affiliates, to 34% among the young Jewish affiliates, to 34% among the young Hindu affiliates, and to 36% among the young Sikh affiliates.

The Christian theology of hope rejoices alongside all those who, in their own ways, bring signs of hope to the urban environment. Working together men and women shaped by different faith traditions are able to raise the quality of life of urban dwellers and to raise aspirations above the mundane and above the material to recognise the claims of the transcendent upon human lives. Today the Christian theology of hope needs to embrace not only interdenominational collaboration but interfaith dialogue, in full recognition of the ways in which different faith traditions contribute to the spiritual health of their adherents.

Appendix

Statistical tables

3. Overall health check

3.1 Personal domain: overview

	yes %	? %	no %
I feel my life has a sense of purpose	56	35	10
I find life really worth living	70	21	9
I feel I am not worth much as a person	13	22	65
I often feel depressed	52	19	29
I have sometimes considered taking my own life	27	15	58
I often long for someone to turn to for advice	35	26	39
I am happy in my school	71	17	12

3.2 Communal domain: overview

	yes %	? %	no %
I am worried about my attractiveness to the opposite sex	34	23	43
I am worried about how I get on with other people	51	22	27
I find it helpful to talk about my problems with my mother	50	20	31
I find it helpful to talk about my problems with my father	32	23	45
I find it helpful to talk about my problems with close friends	64	19	18
I am worried about being bullied at school	28	22	51
I like the people I go to school with	90	7	3

	yes %	? %	no %
3.3 Environmental domain: overview			
There are too many black people living in this country	17	15	68
I think that immigration into Britain should be restricted	32	39	30
There is too much violence on television	20	22	58
I am concerned about the risk of pollution to the environment	64	26	11
I am concerned about the poverty of the third world	59	27	14
I am concerned about the risk of nuclear war	55	26	19
There is nothing I can do to help solve the world's problems	26	31	43
3.4 Transcendental domain: overview			
I believe in God	43	32	26
I believe in life after death	45	38	17
The Church seems irrelevant to life today	27	45	28
The Bible seems irrelevant to life today	30	41	29
I believe in my horoscope	35	29	36
I believe fortune-tellers can tell the future	20	30	50
I believe it is possible to contact the spirits of the dead	31	32	37

4. Male and female

4.1 Personal domain: male and female

	male %	female %	X²	P<
I feel my life has a sense of purpose	56	55	0.6	NS
I find life really worth living	74	65	193.8	.001
I feel I am not worth much as a person	12	15	34.7	.001
I often feel depressed	45	60	549.2	.001
I have sometimes considered taking my own life	24	31	125.7	.001
I often long for someone to turn to for advice	29	41	352.5	.001
I am happy in my school	70	72	10.9	.001

4.2 Communal domain: male and female

	male %	female %	X²	P<
I am worried about my attractiveness to the opposite sex	29	40	318.4	.001
I am worried about how I get on with other people	47	55	142.8	.001
I find it helpful to talk about my problems with my mother	43	57	460.8	.001
I find it helpful to talk about my problems with my father	39	25	530.3	.001
I find it helpful to talk about my problems with close friends	48	79	2328.7	.001
I am worried about being bullied at school	25	31	102.4	.001
I like the people I go to school with	88	91	53.1	.001

4.3 Environmental domain: male and female

	male %	female %	X^2	P<
There are too many black people living in this country	24	10	649.2	.001
I think that immigration into Britain should be restricted	41	22	946.7	.001
There is too much violence on television	16	24	268.0	.001
I am concerned about the risk of pollution to the environment	64	63	0.8	NS
I am concerned about the poverty of the third world	54	65	278.9	.001
I am concerned about the risk of nuclear war	54	56	10.6	.01
There is nothing I can do to help solve the world's problems	31	21	283.6	.001

4.4 Transcendental domain: male and female

	male %	female %	X^2	P<
I believe in God	40	46	91.2	.001
I believe in life after death	44	46	7.5	.01
The Church seems irrelevant to life today	33	22	349.6	.001
The Bible seems irrelevant to life today	35	25	284.0	.001
I believe in my horoscope	24	47	1324.3	.001
I believe fortune-tellers can tell the future	14	26	478.7	.001
I believe it is possible to contact the spirits of the dead	29	33	36.1	.001

223

5. Growing older

5.1 Personal domain: growing older

	year 9 %	year 10 %	X^2	P<
I feel my life has a sense of purpose	56	55	0.4	NS
I find life really worth living	69	70	1.5	NS
I feel I am not worth much as a person	14	13	5.6	.05
I often feel depressed	52	52	0.1	NS
I have sometimes considered taking my own life	27	27	0.4	NS
I often long for someone to turn to for advice	35	35	0.1	NS
I am happy in my school	72	70	11.0	.001

5.2 Communal domain: growing older

	year 9 %	year 10 %	X^2	P<
I am worried about my attractiveness to the opposite sex	34	34	0.4	NS
I am worried about how I get on with other people	51	51	0.8	NS
I find it helpful to talk about my problems with my mother	52	48	39.1	.001
I find it helpful to talk about my problems with my father	33	31	8.1	.01
I find it helpful to talk about my problems with close friends	62	65	25.3	.001
I am worried about being bullied at school	31	25	84.6	.001
I like the people I go to school with	90	90	0.1	NS

	year 9 %	year 10 %	X^2	P<
5.3 Environmental domain: growing older				
There are too many black people living in this country	16	19	21.5	.001
I think that immigration into Britain should be restricted	29	35	95.4	.001
There is too much violence on television	21	19	12.1	.001
I am concerned about the risk of pollution to the environment	64	64	0.2	NS
I am concerned about the poverty of the third world	59	60	6.7	.01
I am concerned about the risk of nuclear war	57	54	24.9	.001
There is nothing I can do to help solve the world's problems	27	25	10.4	.01
5.4 Transcendental domain: growing older				
I believe in God	44	41	12.1	.001
I believe in life after death	45	46	4.8	.05
The Church seems irrelevant to life today	26	29	21.4	.001
The Bible seems irrelevant to life today	29	32	25.8	.001
I believe in my horoscope	34	36	3.4	NS
I believe fortune-tellers can tell the future	20	20	0.1	NS
I believe it is possible to contact the spirits of the dead	30	32	3.8	.05

6. North and south

	north %	south %	X^2	P<
6.1 Personal domain: north and south				
I feel my life has a sense of purpose	55	55	0.9	NS
I find life really worth living	69	72	19.4	.001
I feel I am not worth much as a person	13	13	0.6	NS
I often feel depressed	52	53	0.2	NS
I have sometimes considered taking my own life	28	26	8.7	.01
I often long for someone to turn to for advice	35	36	0.7	NS
I am happy in my school	72	71	2.4	NS
6.2 Communal domain: north and south				
I am worried about my attractiveness to the opposite sex	36	33	10.4	.01
I am worried about how I get on with other people	51	49	6.1	.05
I find it helpful to talk about my problems with my mother	50	50	0.0	NS
I find it helpful to talk about my problems with my father	32	32	0.1	NS
I find it helpful to talk about my problems with close friends	63	64	2.2	NS
I am worried about being bullied at school	31	24	93.6	.001
I like the people I go to school with	90	89	4.4	.05

6.3 Environmental domain: north and south

	north %	south %	X^2	P<
There are too many black people living in this country	16	21	74.0	.001
I think that immigration into Britain should be restricted	31	36	39.3	.001
There is too much violence on television	20	19	5.5	.05
I am concerned about the risk of pollution to the environment	64	60	35.7	.001
I am concerned about the poverty of the third world	57	61	20.4	.001
I am concerned about the risk of nuclear war	51	60	145.1	.001
There is nothing I can do to help solve the world's problems	26	27	5.2	.05

6.4 Transcendental domain: north and south

	north %	south %	X^2	P<
I believe in God	43	41	5.9	.05
I believe in life after death	47	41	64.7	.001
The Church seems irrelevant to life today	26	27	3.3	NS
The Bible seems irrelevant to life today	28	31	16.8	.001
I believe in my horoscope	37	32	47.1	.001
I believe fortune-tellers can tell the future	22	15	134.1	.001
I believe it is possible to contact the spirits of the dead	31	29	9.9	.01

7. Employed fathers

	not %	employed %	X^2	P<
7.1 Personal domain: employed fathers				
I feel my life has a sense of purpose	51	57	40.2	.001
I find life really worth living	64	71	90.4	.001
I feel I am not worth much as a person	16	13	35.3	.001
I often feel depressed	57	51	37.4	.001
I have sometimes considered taking my own life	31	26	46.3	.001
I often long for someone to turn to for advice	37	35	11.6	.001
I am happy in my school	63	73	148.7	.001
7.2 Communal domain: employed fathers				
I am worried about my attractiveness to the opposite sex	33	34	2.1	NS
I am worried about how I get on with other people	50	51	0.4	NS
I find it helpful to talk about my problems with my mother	49	50	4.7	.05
I find it helpful to talk about my problems with my father	26	34	83.2	.001
I find it helpful to talk about my problems with close friends	61	64	11.4	.001
I am worried about being bullied at school	31	27	23.7	.001
I like the people I go to school with	87	90	26.8	.001

7.3 Environmental domain: employed fathers

	not %	employed %	X^2	P<
There are too many black people living in this country	18	17	0.7	NS
I think that immigration into Britain should be restricted	27	33	45.2	.001
There is too much violence on television	23	19	39.7	.001
I am concerned about the risk of pollution to the environment	60	64	30.3	.001
I am concerned about the poverty of the third world	53	61	92.0	.001
I am concerned about the risk of nuclear war	50	56	50.0	.001
There is nothing I can do to help solve the world's problems	29	25	29.1	.001

7.4 Transcendental domain: employed fathers

	not %	employed %	X^2	P<
I believe in God	44	43	2.4	NS
I believe in life after death	48	45	13.7	.001
The Church seems irrelevant to life today	25	28	15.0	.001
The Bible seems irrelevant to life today	28	31	15.7	.001
I believe in my horoscope	37	35	10.0	.01
I believe fortune-tellers can tell the future	25	19	74.3	.001
I believe it is possible to contact the spirits of the dead	33	31	12.1	.001

8. Broken homes

8.1 Personal domain: broken homes

	intact %	broken %	X^2	P<
I feel my life has a sense of purpose	57	52	39.5	.001
I find life really worth living	71	65	81.2	.001
I feel I am not worth much as a person	13	16	40.0	.001
I often feel depressed	51	58	91.3	.001
I have sometimes considered taking my own life	25	33	140.3	.001
I often long for someone to turn to for advice	34	39	4.4	.001
I am happy in my school	73	65	131.4	.001

8.2 Communal domain: broken homes

	intact %	broken %	X^2	P<
I am worried about my attractiveness to the opposite sex	34	35	1.9	NS
I am worried about how I get on with other people	50	52	3.3	NS
I find it helpful to talk about my problems with my mother	51	48	7.0	.01
I find it helpful to talk about my problems with my father	33	28	53.8	.001
I find it helpful to talk about my problems with close friends	63	66	12.0	.001
I am worried about being bullied at school	28	28	0.6	NS
I like the people I go to school with	90	89	3.9	.05

	intact %	broken %	X^2	P<
8.3 Environmental domain: broken homes				
There are too many black people living in this country	17	18	1.1	NS
I think that immigration into Britain should be restricted	32	31	2.3	NS
There is too much violence on television	20	19	3.1	NS
I am concerned about the risk of pollution to the environment	65	60	35.7	.001
I am concerned about the poverty of the third world	61	55	49.1	.001
I am concerned about the risk of nuclear war	56	53	13.2	.001
There is nothing I can do to help solve the world's problems	25	28	15.6	.001
8.4 Transcendental domain: broken homes				
I believe in God	44	37	103.1	.001
I believe in life after death	45	46	1.6	NS
The Church seems irrelevant to life today	27	29	7.6	.01
The Bible seems irrelevant to life today	30	32	6.1	.05
I believe in my horoscope	33	41	114.5	.001
I believe fortune-tellers can tell the future	18	25	128.8	.001
I believe it is possible to contact the spirits of the dead	29	37	127.9	.001

9. Anglican schools

9.1 Personal domain: Anglican schools

	non-denom %	Anglican %	X^2	P<
I feel my life has a sense of purpose	54	51	2.4	NS
I find life really worth living	69	64	10.0	.01
I feel I am not worth much as a person	14	17	8.7	.01
I often feel depressed	52	58	9.5	.01
I have sometimes considered taking my own life	28	30	1.3	NS
I often long for someone to turn to for advice	34	39	6.3	.05
I am happy in my school	70	69	0.6	NS

9.2 Communal domain: Anglican schools

	non-denom %	Anglican %	X^2	P<
I am worried about my attractiveness to the opposite sex	33	37	4.7	.05
I am worried about how I get on with other people	49	54	5.7	.05
I find it helpful to talk about my problems with my mother	50	52	1.6	NS
I find it helpful to talk about my problems with my father	31	31	0.0	NS
I find it helpful to talk about my problems with close friends	63	64	0.7	NS
I am worried about being bullied at school	28	34	14.1	.001
I like the people I go to school with	90	90	0.0	NS

9.3 Environmental domain: Anglican schools

	non-denom %	Anglican %	X^2	P<
There are too many black people living in this country	18	19	0.1	NS
I think that immigration into Britain should be restricted	31	32	0.1	NS
There is too much violence on television	20	26	20.9	.001
I am concerned about the risk of pollution to the environment	63	68	8.3	.01
I am concerned about the poverty of the third world	57	62	10.2	.01
I am concerned about the risk of nuclear war	55	56	0.1	NS
There is nothing I can do to help solve the world's problems	27	24	3.0	NS

9.4 Transcendental domain: Anglican schools

	non-denom %	Anglican %	X^2	P<
I believe in God	37	51	60.1	.001
I believe in life after death	43	54	39.8	.001
The Church seems irrelevant to life today	28	28	0.0	NS
The Bible seems irrelevant to life today	31	29	1.1	NS
I believe in my horoscope	36	36	0.0	NS
I believe fortune-tellers can tell the future	20	24	5.7	.05
I believe it is possible to contact the spirits of the dead	32	33	0.4	NS

10. Catholic schools

	non-denom %	Catholic %	X²	P<
10.1 Personal domain: Catholic schools				
I feel my life has a sense of purpose	54	64	83.4	.001
I find life really worth living	69	69	0.0	NS
I feel I am not worth much as a person	14	13	1.7	NS
I often feel depressed	52	52	0.1	NS
I have sometimes considered taking my own life	28	26	3.2	NS
I often long for someone to turn to for advice	34	37	7.3	.01
I am happy in my school	70	69	2.9	NS
10.2 Communal domain: Catholic schools				
I am worried about my attractiveness to the opposite sex	33	33	0.0	NS
I am worried about how I get on with other people	49	54	14.4	.001
I find it helpful to talk about my problems with my mother	50	49	0.1	NS
I find it helpful to talk about my problems with my father	31	33	2.2	NS
I find it helpful to talk about my problems with close friends	63	63	0.0	NS
I am worried about being bullied at school	28	31	10.5	.01
I like the people I go to school with	90	89	2.5	NS

10.3 Environmental domain: Catholic schools

	non-denom %	Catholic %	X^2	P<
There are too many black people living in this country	18	17	0.6	NS
I think that immigration into Britain should be restricted	31	33	1.7	NS
There is too much violence on television	20	20	0.5	NS
I am concerned about the risk of pollution to the environment	63	61	1.1	NS
I am concerned about the poverty of the third world	57	64	43.6	.001
I am concerned about the risk of nuclear war	55	51	14.6	.001
There is nothing I can do to help solve the world's problems	27	27	0.5	NS

10.4 Transcendental domain: Catholic schools

	non-denom %	Catholic %	X^2	P<
I believe in God	37	71	844.2	.001
I believe in life after death	43	56	123.0	.001
The Church seems irrelevant to life today	28	25	9.3	.01
The Bible seems irrelevant to life today	31	29	4.8	.05
I believe in my horoscope	36	39	6.8	.01
I believe fortune-tellers can tell the future	20	24	13.2	.001
I believe it is possible to contact the spirits of the dead	32	34	5.4	.05

11. Christian schools

	non-denom %	Christian %	X^2	P<
11.1 Personal domain: Christian schools				
I feel my life has a sense of purpose	54	75	39.9	.001
I find life really worth living	69	74	3.0	NS
I feel I am not worth much as a person	14	12	0.7	NS
I often feel depressed	52	38	16.7	.001
I have sometimes considered taking my own life	28	15	16.9	.001
I often long for someone to turn to for advice	34	33	0.2	NS
I am happy in my school	70	66	2.5	NS
11.2 Communal domain: Christian schools				
I am worried about my attractiveness to the opposite sex	33	38	2.6	NS
I am worried about how I get on with other people	49	58	6.5	.05
I find it helpful to talk about my problems with my mother	50	51	0.2	NS
I find it helpful to talk about my problems with my father	31	37	3.2	NS
I find it helpful to talk about my problems with close friends	63	75	14.7	.001
I am worried about being bullied at school	28	19	8.4	.01
I like the people I go to school with	90	84	8.8	.01

	non-denom %	Christian %	X^2	P<
11.3 Environmental domain: Christian schools				
There are too many black people living in this country	18	6	22.1	.001
I think that immigration into Britain should be restricted	31	29	0.8	NS
There is too much violence on television	20	35	34.9	.001
I am concerned about the risk of pollution to the environment	63	61	0.2	NS
I am concerned about the poverty of the third world	57	71	18.0	.001
I am concerned about the risk of nuclear war	55	32	47.0	.001
There is nothing I can do to help solve the world's problems	27	17	10.6	.01
11.4 Transcendental domain: Christian schools				
I believe in God	37	83	203.1	.001
I believe in life after death	43	74	90.9	.001
The Church seems irrelevant to life today	28	13	24.5	.001
The Bible seems irrelevant to life today	31	14	28.1	.001
I believe in my horoscope	36	8	75.4	.001
I believe fortune-tellers can tell the future	20	13	7.0	.01
I believe it is possible to contact the spirits of the dead	32	21	12.6	.001

12. Social engagement

12.1 Personal domain: social engagement

	low %	high %	X^2	P<
I feel my life has a sense of purpose	53	60	56.3	.001
I find life really worth living	63	72	86.7	.001
I feel I am not worth much as a person	15	13	9.4	.01
I often feel depressed	54	49	25.9	.001
I have sometimes considered taking my own life	27	28	2.0	NS
I often long for someone to turn to for advice	35	35	0.2	NS
I am happy in my school	68	71	11.2	.001

12.2 Communal domain: social engagement

	low %	high %	X^2	P<
I am worried about my attractiveness to the opposite sex	36	33	10.3	.01
I am worried about how I get on with other people	54	52	3.8	NS
I find it helpful to talk about my problems with my mother	51	50	1.9	NS
I find it helpful to talk about my problems with my father	27	38	132.4	.001
I find it helpful to talk about my problems with close friends	66	60	36.6	.001
I am worried about being bullied at school	32	27	21.1	.001
I like the people I go to school with	88	90	13.7	.001

12.3 Environmental domain: social engagement

	low %	high %	X^2	P<
There are too many black people living in this country	13	18	46.0	.001
I think that immigration into Britain should be restricted	27	33	46.4	.001
There is too much violence on television	21	19	7.2	.01
I am concerned about the risk of pollution to the environment	66	69	8.9	.01
I am concerned about the poverty of the third world	60	60	0.1	NS
I am concerned about the risk of nuclear war	54	58	14.1	.001
There is nothing I can do to help solve the world's problems	24	26	7.2	.01

12.4 Transcendental domain: social engagement

	low %	high %	X^2	P<
I believe in God	43	42	0.2	NS
I believe in life after death	45	48	6.7	.01
The Church seems irrelevant to life today	26	28	4.4	.05
The Bible seems irrelevant to life today	30	30	0.0	NS
I believe in my horoscope	37	34	9.9	.01
I believe fortune-tellers can tell the future	23	20	14.8	.001
I believe it is possible to contact the spirits of the dead	31	33	7.4	.01

13. Personal prayer

13.1 Personal domain: personal prayer

	never %	sometimes %	daily %	X^2	P<
I feel my life has a sense of purpose	48	60	73	702.8	.001
I find life really worth living	69	69	74	28.5	.001
I feel I am not worth much as a person	13	14	14	7.2	.05
I often feel depressed	49	56	51	100.0	.001
I have sometimes considered taking my own life	27	28	26	5.1	NS
I often long for someone to turn to for advice	30	40	39	265.4	.001
I am happy in my school	67	74	74	147.7	.001

13.2 Communal domain: personal prayer

	never %	sometimes %	daily %	X^2	P<
I am worried about my attractiveness to the opposite sex	29	39	40	251.2	.001
I am worried about how I get on with other people	45	57	57	338.4	.001
I find it helpful to talk about my problems with my mother	45	54	59	273.7	.001
I find it helpful to talk about my problems with my father	30	33	39	77.7	.001
I find it helpful to talk about my problems with close friends	58	69	70	290.0	.001
I am worried about being bullied at school	23	32	33	248.9	.001
I like the people I go to school with	90	90	87	17.3	.001

13.3 Environmental domain: personal prayer

	never %	sometimes %	daily %	X²	P<
There are too many black people living in this country	21	14	13	178.1	.001
I think that immigration into Britain should be restricted	34	30	27	62.4	.001
There is too much violence on television	15	22	34	537.3	.001
I am concerned about the risk of pollution to the environment	57	69	73	419.8	.001
I am concerned about the poverty of the third world	48	68	77	1156.2	.001
I am concerned about the risk of nuclear war	49	61	63	378.5	.001
There is nothing I can do to help solve the world's problems	32	22	18	357.4	.001

13.4 Transcendental domain: personal prayer

	never %	sometimes %	daily %	X²	P<
I believe in God	17	59	92	6786.7	.001
I believe in life after death	34	52	68	1305.1	.001
The Church seems irrelevant to life today	35	20	16	751.6	.001
The Bible seems irrelevant to life today	40	23	16	971.4	.001
I believe in my horoscope	33	39	29	116.5	.001
I believe fortune-tellers can tell the future	19	22	20	25.3	.001
I believe it is possible to contact the spirits of the dead	31	32	29	8.7	.05

14. Christians

14.1 Personal domain: Christians

	none %	Christians %	X^2	P<
I feel my life has a sense of purpose	50	60	195.4	.001
I find life really worth living	68	71	26.5	.001
I feel I am not worth much as a person	14	13	4.0	.05
I often feel depressed	51	54	10.8	.01
I have sometimes considered taking my own life	28	26	14.7	.001
I often long for someone to turn to for advice	33	37	46.8	.001
I am happy in my school	67	74	151.7	.001

14.2 Communal domain: Christians

	none %	Christians %	X^2	P<
I am worried about my attractiveness to the opposite sex	31	37	75.9	.001
I am worried about how I get on with other people	48	54	77.9	.001
I find it helpful to talk about my problems with my mother	48	52	50.0	.001
I find it helpful to talk about my problems with my father	31	33	13.3	.001
I find it helpful to talk about my problems with close friends	61	66	76.5	.001
I am worried about being bullied at school	25	30	55.3	.001
I like the people I go to school with	90	90	0.1	NS

14.3 Environmental domain: Christians

	none %	Christians %	X^2	P<
There are too many black people living in this country	19	16	43.8	.001
I think that immigration into Britain should be restricted	32	33	3.5	NS
There is too much violence on television	17	21	78.5	.001
I am concerned about the risk of pollution to the environment	60	67	93.0	.001
I am concerned about the poverty of the third world	52	66	390.3	.001
I am concerned about the risk of nuclear war	53	58	73.5	.001
There is nothing I can do to help solve the world's problems	29	23	89.5	.001

14.4 Transcendental domain: Christians

	none %	Christians %	X^2	P<
I believe in God	24	56	2187.2	.001
I believe in life after death	38	50	297.2	.001
The Church seems irrelevant to life today	33	22	310.4	.001
The Bible seems irrelevant to life today	36	25	320.8	.001
I believe in my horoscope	35	35	0.0	NS
I believe fortune-tellers can tell the future	20	20	2.4	NS
I believe it is possible to contact the spirits of the dead	33	31	10.0	.01

15. Muslims

15.1 Personal domain: Muslims

	none %	Muslims %	X^2	P<
I feel my life has a sense of purpose	50	66	49.7	.001
I find life really worth living	68	69	0.4	NS
I feel I am not worth much as a person	14	17	5.1	.05
I often feel depressed	51	48	1.9	NS
I have sometimes considered taking my own life	28	30	0.8	NS
I often long for someone to turn to for advice	33	39	8.2	.01
I am happy in my school	67	77	25.3	.001

15.2 Communal domain: Muslims

	none %	Muslims %	X^2	P<
I am worried about my attractiveness to the opposite sex	31	28	2.2	NS
I am worried about how I get on with other people	48	45	1.9	NS
I find it helpful to talk about my problems with my mother	48	52	4.3	.05
I find it helpful to talk about my problems with my father	31	31	0.0	NS
I find it helpful to talk about my problems with close friends	61	62	0.6	NS
I am worried about being bullied at school	25	34	17.7	.001
I like the people I go to school with	90	88	2.3	NS

15.3 Environmental domain: Muslims

	none %	Muslims %	X^2	P<
There are too many black people living in this country	19	14	2.7	NS
I think that immigration into Britain should be restricted	32	18	42.6	.001
There is too much violence on television	17	38	151.6	.001
I am concerned about the risk of pollution to the environment	60	62	0.5	NS
I am concerned about the poverty of the third world	52	62	17.5	.001
I am concerned about the risk of nuclear war	53	50	1.2	NS
There is nothing I can do to help solve the world's problems	29	29	0.0	NS

15.4 Transcendental domain: Muslims

	none %	Muslims %	X^2	P<
I believe in God	24	91	1091.2	.001
I believe in life after death	38	69	193.5	.001
The Church seems irrelevant to life today	33	23	20.0	.001
The Bible seems irrelevant to life today	36	24	32.0	.001
I believe in my horoscope	35	23	30.0	.001
I believe fortune-tellers can tell the future	20	17	3.3	NS
I believe it is possible to contact the spirits of the dead	33	16	57.9	.001

16. Jews

16.1 Personal domain: Jews

	none %	Jews %	X^2	P<
I feel my life has a sense of purpose	50	67	5.9	.05
I find life really worth living	68	87	8.7	.05
I feel I am not worth much as a person	14	11	0.3	NS
I often feel depressed	51	43	1.3	NS
I have sometimes considered taking my own life	28	19	2.1	NS
I often long for someone to turn to for advice	33	39	1.0	NS
I am happy in my school	67	83	6.3	.05

16.2 Communal domain: Jews

	none %	Jews %	X^2	P<
I am worried about my attractiveness to the opposite sex	31	37	0.7	NS
I am worried about how I get on with other people	48	55	1.0	NS
I find it helpful to talk about my problems with my mother	48	76	17.4	.001
I find it helpful to talk about my problems with my father	31	41	2.4	NS
I find it helpful to talk about my problems with close friends	61	68	1.2	NS
I am worried about being bullied at school	25	34	2.1	NS
I like the people I go to school with	90	89	0.1	NS

16.3 Environmental domain: Jews

	none %	Jews %	X^2	$P<$
There are too many black people living in this country	19	17	0.1	NS
I think that immigration into Britain should be restricted	32	40	1.6	NS
There is too much violence on television	17	20	0.5	NS
I am concerned about the risk of pollution to the environment	60	76	5.5	.05
I am concerned about the poverty of the third world	52	66	4.0	.05
I am concerned about the risk of nuclear war	53	57	0.4	NS
There is nothing I can do to help solve the world's problems	29	26	0.2	NS

16.4 Transcendental domain: Jews

	none %	Jews %	X^2	$P<$
I believe in God	24	64	45.0	.001
I believe in life after death	38	43	0.4	NS
The Church seems irrelevant to life today	33	27	0.9	NS
The Bible seems irrelevant to life today	36	23	4.3	.05
I believe in my horoscope	35	35	0.0	NS
I believe fortune-tellers can tell the future	20	17	0.4	NS
I believe it is possible to contact the spirits of the dead	33	31	0.0	NS

17. Hindus

	none %	Hindus %	X^2	P<
17.1 Personal domain: Hindus				
I feel my life has a sense of purpose	50	62	8.2	.01
I find life really worth living	68	64	0.9	NS
I feel I am not worth much as a person	14	10	2.0	NS
I often feel depressed	51	49	0.2	NS
I have sometimes considered taking my own life	28	27	0.1	NS
I often long for someone to turn to for advice	33	44	8.9	.01
I am happy in my school	67	80	11.6	.001
17.2 Communal domain: Hindus				
I am worried about my attractiveness to the opposite sex	31	40	5.4	.05
I am worried about how I get on with other people	48	60	8.3	.01
I find it helpful to talk about my problems with my mother	48	41	2.9	NS
I find it helpful to talk about my problems with my father	31	28	0.5	NS
I find it helpful to talk about my problems with close friends	61	68	3.8	NS
I am worried about being bullied at school	25	34	6.3	.05
I like the people I go to school with	90	93	1.6	NS

248

17.3 Environmental domain: Hindus

	none %	Hindus %	X^2	P<
There are too many black people living in this country	19	9	4.1	.05
I think that immigration into Britain should be restricted	32	14	22.7	.001
There is too much violence on television	17	23	4.1	.05
I am concerned about the risk of pollution to the environment	60	67	2.9	NS
I am concerned about the poverty of the third world	52	74	28.2	.001
I am concerned about the risk of nuclear war	53	45	3.6	NS
There is nothing I can do to help solve the world's problems	29	20	5.4	.05

17.4 Transcendental domain: Hindus

	none %	Hindus %	X^2	P<
I believe in God	24	80	248.0	.001
I believe in life after death	38	73	79.3	.001
The Church seems irrelevant to life today	33	19	12.8	.001
The Bible seems irrelevant to life today	36	23	12.0	.001
I believe in my horoscope	35	40	1.4	NS
I believe fortune-tellers can tell the future	20	21	0.0	NS
I believe it is possible to contact the spirits of the dead	33	21	8.8	.01

18. Sikhs

18.1 Personal domain: Sikhs

	none %	Sikhs %	X^2	P<
I feel my life has a sense of purpose	50	52	0.3	NS
I find life really worth living	68	65	1.0	NS
I feel I am not worth much as a person	14	16	1.3	NS
I often feel depressed	51	56	2.1	NS
I have sometimes considered taking my own life	28	29	0.1	NS
I often long for someone to turn to for advice	33	40	5.6	.05
I am happy in my school	67	71	2.2	NS

18.2 Communal domain: Sikhs

	none %	Sikhs %	X^2	P<
I am worried about my attractiveness to the opposite sex	31	34	0.6	NS
I am worried about how I get on with other people	48	51	1.1	NS
I find it helpful to talk about my problems with my mother	48	45	0.4	NS
I find it helpful to talk about my problems with my father	31	27	1.5	NS
I find it helpful to talk about my problems with close friends	61	63	0.3	NS
I am worried about being bullied at school	25	36	14.8	.001
I like the people I go to school with	90	87	2.1	NS

18.3 Environmental domain: Sikhs

	none %	Sikhs %	X^2	P<
There are too many black people living in this country	19	7	4.2	.05
I think that immigration into Britain should be restricted	32	16	27.0	.001
There is too much violence on television	17	20	2.1	NS
I am concerned about the risk of pollution to the environment	60	62	0.3	NS
I am concerned about the poverty of the third world	52	63	11.9	.001
I am concerned about the risk of nuclear war	53	52	0.0	NS
There is nothing I can do to help solve the world's problems	29	25	1.5	NS

18.4 Transcendental domain: Sikhs

	none %	Sikhs %	X^2	P<
I believe in God	24	75	336.5	.001
I believe in life after death	38	58	40.0	.001
The Church seems irrelevant to life today	33	22	11.9	.001
The Bible seems irrelevant to life today	36	20	27.5	.001
I believe in my horoscope	35	42	5.1	.05
I believe fortune-tellers can tell the future	20	32	18.6	.001
I believe it is possible to contact the spirits of the dead	33	23	10.9	.001

References

Abbas, T. (2003), The impact of religio-cultural norms and values on the education of young South Asian women, *British Journal of Sociology of Education*, 24, 411–28.

Amato, P.R. and Cheadle, J. (2005), The long reach of divorce: divorce and child well-being across three generations, *Journal of Marriage and Family*, 67, 191–206.

Ambert, A.M. and Saucier, J.F. (1986), Adolescents' overt religiosity and parents' marital status, *International Journal of Comparative Sociology*, 27, 87–95.

Anwar, M. (1994), *Young Muslims in Britain: attitudes, educational needs and policy implications*, Leicester, The Islamic Foundation.

Anyadike-Danes, M. (2004), The real north–south divide? Regional gradients in UK male non-employment, *Regional Studies*, 38, 85–95.

Archbishop of Canterbury's Commission On Urban Priority Areas (1985), *Faith in the City*, London, Church House Publishing.

Archer, L. (2001), 'Muslim brothers, black lads, traditional Asians': British Muslim young men's constructions of race, religion and masculinity, *Feminism and Psychology*, 11, 79–105.

Argyle, M. and Beit-Hallahmi, B. (1975), *The Social Psychology of Religion*, London, Routledge and Kegan Paul.

Aseltine, R.H. (1996), Pathways linking parental divorce with adolescent depression, *Journal of Health and Social Behaviour*, 37, 133–48.

Austin, A. (1977), *Four Critical Years*, San Francisco, Jossey-Bass.

Bailey, R. (1999), Play, health and physical development, in T. David (ed.), *Young Children Learning*, pp 46–66, London, Paul Chapman Publishers.

Bailey, R. (2005), Evaluating the relationship between physical education, sport and social inclusion, *Educational Review,* 57, 71–90.

Balding, J. (1993), *Young People in 1992,* Exeter, Schools Health Education Unit, University of Exeter.

Balding, J. (1997), *Young People in 1996,* Exeter, Schools Health Education Unit, University of Exeter.

Balding, J. (1998), *Young People in 1997,* Exeter, Schools Health Education Unit, University of Exeter.

Balding, J. (1999), *Young People in 1998,* Exeter, Schools Health Education Unit, University of Exeter.

Baron, S., Field, J. and Schuller, T. (eds) (2001), *Social Capital: critical perspective,* Oxford, Oxford University Press.

Barrett, A.E. and Turner, R.J. (2005), Family structure and mental health: the mediating effects of socioeconomic status, family process and social stress, *Journal of Health and Social Behaviour,* 46, 156–69.

Barry, M. (2001), *Challenging Transitions: young people's views and experiences of growing up,* London, Save the Children.

Basit, N.T. (1997), *Eastern Values, Western Milieu: identities and aspirations of adolescent British Muslim girls,* Aldershot, Ashgate.

Batson, C.D., Schoenrade, P. and Ventis, W.L. (1993), *Religion and the Individual: a social-psychological perspective,* Oxford, Oxford University Press.

Beinart, S., Anderson, B., Lee, S. and Utting, D. (2002), *Youth at Risk? a national survey,* London, Communities that Care.

Berger, P. (1967), *The Sacred Canopy: elements of a sociology of religion,* New York, Doubleday.

Berger, P. (1969), *A Rumour of Angels: modern society and the rediscovery of the supernatural,* New York, Doubleday.

Berntsson, L.J., Kohler, L. and Gustafsson, J.E. (2001), Psychosomatic complaints in school children: a Nordic comparison, *Scandinavian Journal of Public Health,* 29, 44–54.

Bhanot, S. and Santosh, R. (2003), *The Hindu Youth Research Project 2001,* Oxford, Oxford Centre for Hindu Studies.

Bibby, R.W. (1985), Religious encasement in Canada: an argument for Protestant and Catholic entrenchment, *Social Compass,* 16, 287–303.

Bibby, R.W. (1987), *Fragmented Gods: the poverty and potential of religion in Canada*, Toronto, Irwin Publishing.

Borkhuis, G.W. and Patalano, F. (1997), MMPI personality differences between adolescents from divorced and non-divorced families, *Psychology*, 34, 37–41.

Bouma, G.D. (1992), *Religion: meaning, transcendence and community in Australia*, Melbourne, Longman Cheshire.

Bourdieu, P. (1997), The forms of capital, in A.H. Halsey, H. Lauder, P. Brown and A. Stuart (eds), *Education: culture, economy, society*, Oxford, Oxford University Press.

Boyle, J.J. and Francis, L.J. (1986), The influence of differing church aided school systems on pupil attitude towards religion, *Research in Education*, 35, 7–12.

Bradburn, N.M. (1969), *The Structure of Psychological Well-being*, Chicago, Illinois, Aldine.

Braddock, J.H. (1981), Race, athletics, and educational attainment, *Youth and Society*, 12, 335–50.

Brothers, J. (1964), *Church and School: a study of the impact of education on religion*, Liverpool, University of Liverpool Press.

Brown, A.S. and Lankshear, D.W. (2000), *The National Society's Handbook for Inspection under Section 23* (third edition), London, National Society and Church House.

Brown, C.G. (2001), *The Death of Christian Britain*, London, Routledge.

Brown, L.B. (1994), *The Human Side of Prayer: the psychology of praying*, Birmingham, Alabama, Religious Education Press.

Bruce, S. (2002), *God is Dead: secularisation in the west*, Oxford, Blackwell.

Bufford, R.K., Paloutzian, R.F. and Ellison, C. (1991), Norms for the Spiritual Well-Being Scale, *Journal of Psychology and Theology*, 19, 56–70.

Burke, B. (1993), Wellness in the healing ministry, *Health Progress*, 74 (7), 34–7.

Byrd, R.C. (1988), Positive therapeutic effects of intercessory prayer in a coronary care unit population, *Southern Medical Journal*, 81, 826–9.

Carr, D. (1995), Towards a distinctive conception of spiritual education, *Oxford Review of Education*, 21, 83–98.

Chadwick, P. (1997), *Shifting Alliances: church and state in English education*, London, Cassell.

Chadwick, P. (2001), The Anglican perspective on church schools, *Oxford Review of Education*, 27, 475–87.

Choquet, M. (1995), Illicit drug consumption among adolescents: results of an epidemiologic survey of 12,391 adolescents aged 11 to 19 (1993), *Bulletin De L'Academie Nationale de Medecine*, 179, 249–64.

Clark, J. and Barber, B.L. (1994), Adolescents in post divorce and always-married families: self-esteem and perceptions of fathers' interest, *Journal of Marriage and the Family*, 56, 608–14.

Coe, G.A. (1916), *The Psychology of Religion*, Chicago, University of Chicago Press.

Coleman, J. (1988), Social capital in the creation of human capital, *American Journal of Sociology*, 94, 95–120.

Coward, D.D. and Reed, P.G. (1996), Self-transcendence: a reason for healing at the end of life, *Issues in Mental Health Nursing*, 17, 275–88.

Crossman, S.M., Shea, J.A. and Adams, G.R. (1980), Effects of parental divorce during early childhood on ego development and identity formation of college students, *Journal of Divorce*, 3, 263–72.

Cruickshank, M. (1963), *Church and State in English Education*, London, Macmillan.

Curran, M. and Francis, L.J. (1996), Measuring 'Catholic identity' among pupils in Catholic secondary schools, in L.J. Francis, W.K. Kay and W.S. Campbell (eds), *Research in Religious Education*, pp 383–91, Leominster, Gracewing.

Curtice, J. (1988), One nation? in R. Jowell, S. Witherspoon and L. Brook (eds), *British Social Attitudes: the fifth report*, pp 127–45, Aldershot, Gower.

Curtice, J. (1992), The north–south divide, in R. Jowell, L. Brook, G. Prior and B. Taylor (eds), *British Social Attitudes: the ninth report*, pp 71–87, Aldershot, Dartmouth.

Curtice J. (1996), One nation again? in R. Jowell, J. Curtice, A. Park,

L. Brook and K. Thompson (eds), *British Social Attitudes: the thirteenth report*, pp 1–14, Aldershot, Dartmouth.

Curtice, J. and Stead, M. (1986), Proportionality and exaggeration in the British electoral system, *Electoral Studies*, 5, 209–28.

Curtice, J. and Stead, M. (1988), Analysis, in D. Butler and D. Kavanagh (eds), *The British General Election of 1987*, pp 316–62, London, Macmillan.

Cuttance, P. (1989), The effectiveness of Scottish schooling, in D. Reynolds, B.P.M. Creemers and T. Peters (eds), *School Effectiveness and Improvement*, pp 153–68, Cardiff, School of Education, University of Wales.

Davie, G. (1994), *Religion in Britain since 1945: believing without belonging*, Oxford, Blackwell.

de Goede, M., Spruijt, E., Maas, C. and Duindam, V. (2000), Family problems and youth unemployment, *Adolescence*, 35, 587–601.

Deakin, R. (1989), *The New Christian Schools*, Bristol, Regius Press.

Dearing Report (2001), *The Way Ahead: Church of England schools in the new millennium*, London, Church House Publishing.

Delaney, W. and Lee, C. (1995), Self-esteem and sex-roles among male and female high-school-students: their relationship to physical activity, *Australian Psychologist*, 30 (2), 84–7.

Department of Education and Science (1983), *Young People in the 80s: a survey*, London, Her Majesty's Stationery Office.

Department of Education and Science (1989), *The Education Reform Act 1988: religious education and collective worship*, London, DES, circular 3/89.

Doran, T., Drever, F. and Whitehead, M. (2004), Is there a north–south divide in social class inequalities in health in Great Britain? cross sectional study using data from the 2001 census, *British Medical Journal*, 328, 1043–5.

Douglas, J.W.B. (1970), Broken families and child behaviour, *Journal of the Royal College of Physicians*, 4, 203–10.

Dowling, E.M. and Scarlett, W.G. (eds) (2006), *Encyclopaedia of Religious and Spiritual Development*, Thousand Oaks, California, Sage.

Drury, B. (1991), Sikh girls and the maintenance of an ethnic culture, *New Community*, 17, 387–400.

Egan, J. (1985), An evaluation of the implementation of the principles of Catholic education in the Catholic comprehensive schools in Wales, Unpublished Ph.D. dissertation, University of Wales (Cardiff).

Egan, J. (1988), *Opting Out: Catholic schools today*, Leominster, Fowler Wright.

Egan, J. and Francis, L.J. (1986), School ethos in Wales: the impact of non-practising Catholic and non-Catholic pupils on Catholic secondary schools, *Lumen Vitae*, 41, 159–73.

Elliott, B.J. and Richards, M.P.M. (1991), Children and divorce: educational performance and behaviour before and after parental separation, *International Journal of Law and the Family*, 5, 258–76.

Ellison, C. (1983), Spiritual well-being: conceptualization and measurement, *Journal of Psychology and Theology*, 11, 330–40.

Ely, M., Richards, M.P.M., Wadsworth, M.E.J. and Elliott, B.J. (1999), Secular changes in the association of parental divorce and children's educational attainment: evidence from three British birth cohorts, *Journal of Social Policy*, 28, 437–55.

Fane, R.S. (1999), Is self-assigned religious affiliation socially significant?, in L.J. Francis (ed.), *Sociology, Theology and the Curriculum*, pp 113–24, London, Cassell.

Fehring, R., Miller, J. and Shaw, C. (1997), Spiritual well-being, religiosity, hope, depression, and other mood states in elderly people coping with cancer, *Oncology Nursing Forum*, 24, 663–71.

Ferri, E. (1976), *Growing Up in a One-Parent Family*, Slough, National Foundation for Educational Research.

Finney, J.R. and Malony, H.N. (1985), Contemplative prayer and its use in psychotherapy: a theoretical model, *Journal of Psychology and Theology*, 13, 172–81.

Fisher, J.W. (1998), Spiritual health: its nature, and place in the school curriculum. Unpublished PhD dissertation, The University of Melbourne.

Fisher, J.W. (2000), Being human, becoming whole: understanding spiritual health and well-being, *Journal of Christian Education*, 43, 37–52.

Fisher, J.W. (2001), Comparing levels of spiritual well-being in State,

Catholic and Independent schools in Victoria, Australia, *Journal of Beliefs and Values*, 22, 99–105.

Fisher, J.W. (2004), Feeling good, living life: a spiritual health measure for young children, *Journal of Beliefs and Values*, 25, 307–15.

Fisher, J.W., Francis, L.J. and Johnson, P. (2000), Assessing spiritual health via four domains of spiritual wellbeing: the SH4DI, *Pastoral Psychology*, 49, 133–45.

Fisher, J.W., Francis, L.J. and Johnson, P. (2002), The personal and social correlates of spiritual well-being among primary school teachers, *Pastoral Psychology*, 51, 3–11.

Fisher, S. and Holder, S. (1981), *Too Much Too Young: today's generation speaks out on being young in the eighties*, London, Pan.

Francis, L.J. (1979), School influence and pupil attitude towards religion, *British Journal of Educational Psychology*, 49, 107–23.

Francis, L.J. (1982a), *Youth in Transit: a profile of 16–25 year olds*, Aldershot, Gower.

Francis, L.J. (1982b), *Experience of Adulthood: a profile of 26–39 year olds*, Aldershot, Gower.

Francis, L.J. (1984a), *Young and Unemployed*, Tunbridge Wells, Costello.

Francis, L.J. (1984b), *Teenagers and the Church: a profile of church-going youth in the 1980s*, London, Collins Liturgical Publications.

Francis, L.J. (1986a), Denominational schools and pupil attitude towards Christianity, *British Educational Research Journal*, 12, 145–52.

Francis, L.J. (1986b), Roman Catholic secondary schools: falling rolls and pupil attitudes, *Educational Studies*, 12, 119–27.

Francis, L.J. (1987), *Religion in the Primary School: partnership between church and state?* London, Collins Liturgical Publications.

Francis, L.J. (1992), The influence of religion, gender and social class on attitudes toward school among eleven year olds in England, *Journal of Experimental Education*, 60, 339–48.

Francis, L.J. (1997), The psychology of gender differences in religion: a review of empirical research, *Religion*, 27, 81–96.

Francis, L.J. (2001a), *The Values Debate: a voice from the pupils*, London, Woburn Press.

Francis, L.J. (2001b), Religion and values: a quantitative perspective, in L.J. Francis, J. Astley and M. Robbins (eds), *The Fourth R for the Third Millennium: education in religion and values for the global future*, pp 47–78, Dublin, Lindisfarne Books.

Francis, L.J. (2002), Catholic schools and Catholic values: a study of moral and religious values among 13–15 year old pupils attending non-denominational and Catholic schools in England and Wales, *International Journal of Education and Religion*, 3, 69–84.

Francis, L.J. (2003), Religion and social capital: the flaw in the 2001 census in England and Wales, in P. Avis (ed.), *Public Faith: the state of religious belief and practice in Britain*, pp 45–64, London, SPCK.

Francis, L.J. (2005a), Prayer, personality and purpose in life among churchgoing and non-churchgoing adolescents, in L.J. Francis, M. Robbins and J. Astley (eds), *Religion, Education and Adolescence: international empirical perspectives*, pp 15–38, Cardiff, University of Wales Press.

Francis, L.J. (2005b), Gender role orientation and attitude toward Christianity: a study among older men and women in the United Kingdom, *Journal of Psychology and Theology* (in press).

Francis, L.J. (2005c), *Faith and Psychology: personality, religion and the individual*, London, Darton, Longman and Todd.

Francis, L.J. (2005d), Independent Christian schools and pupil values: an empirical investigation among 13–15-year-old boys, *British Journal of Religious Education*, 27, 2, 127–41.

Francis, L.J. and Astley, J. (eds) (2001), *Psychological Perspectives on Prayer: a reader*, Leominster, Gracewing.

Francis, L.J. and Burton, L. (1994), The influence of personal prayer on purpose in life among Catholic adolescents, *Journal of Beliefs and Values*, 15, 2, 6–9.

Francis, L.J. and Carter, M. (1980), Church aided secondary schools, religious education as an examination subject and pupil attitudes towards religion, *British Journal of Educational Psychology*, 50, 297–300.

Francis, L.J. and Evans, T.E. (1996), The relationship between personal prayer and purpose in life among churchgoing and non-churchgoing 12–15 year olds in the UK, *Religious Education*, 91, 9–21.

Francis, L.J. and Jewell, A. (1992), Shaping adolescent attitude towards the church: comparison between Church of England and county secondary schools, *Evaluation and Research in Education*, 6, 13–21.

Francis, L.J. and Kay, W.K. (1995), *Teenage Religion and Values*, Leominster, Gracewing.

Francis, L.J. and Martineau, J. (2001), *Rural Youth*, Stoneleigh Park, Acora Publishing.

Francis, L.J., Robbins, M. and Astley, J. (eds) (2005), *Religion, Education and Adolescence: international, empirical perspectives*, Cardiff, University of Wales Press.

Francis, L.J. and Wilcox, C. (1996), Religion and gender orientation, *Personality and Individual Differences,* 20, 119–21.

Francis, L.J. and Wilcox, C. (1998), Religiosity and femininity: do women really hold a more positive attitude toward Christianity? *Journal for the Scientific Study of Religion,* 37, 462–9.

Frankl, V.E. (1978), *The Unheard Cry for Meaning: psychotherapy and humanism*, New York, Simon and Schuster.

Freedman, D.S., Khan, L.K., Dietz, W.H., Srinivasan, S.R. and Berenson, G.S. (2001), Relationship of childhood obesity to coronary heart disease risk factors in adulthood: the Bogalusa Heart Study, *Pediatrics*, 108, 712–18.

Furnham, A. and Gunter, B. (1989), *The Anatomy of Adolescence: young people's social attitudes in Britain*, London, Routledge.

Furnham, A. and Stacey, B. (1991), *Young People's Understanding of Society*, London, Routledge.

Gabardi, L. and Rosén, L.A. (1991), Differences between college students from divorced and intact families, *Journal of Divorce and Remarriage*, 15, 3/4, 175–91.

Gahler, M. (1998), Self-reported psychological well-being among adult children of divorce in Sweden, *Acta Sociologica*, 41, 209–25.

Garber, R.J. (1991), Long-term effects of divorce on the self-esteem of young adults, *Journal of Divorce and Remarriage*, 17, 1/2, 131–7.

Gilbert, A.D. (1980), *The Making of Post-Christian Britain*, London, Longman.

Gill, R. (1999), *Churchgoing and Christian Ethics*, Cambridge, Cambridge University Press.

Giuliani, C., Iafrate, R. and Rosnati, R. (1998), Peer-group and romantic relationships in adolescents from intact and separated families, *Contemporary Family Therapy*, 20, 95–105.

Glock, C.Y., Wuthnow, R., Piliavin, J.A. and Spencer, M. (1975), *Adolescent Prejudice*, New York, Harper and Row.

Goldman, R.J. (1964), *Religious Thinking from Childhood to Adolescence*, London, Routledge and Kegan Paul.

Gomez, R. and Fisher, J.W. (2003), Domains of spiritual well-being and development and validation of the Spiritual Well-Being Questionnaire, *Personality and Individual Differences*, 35, 1975–91.

Gomez, R. and Fisher, J.W. (2005), Item response theory analysis of the spiritual well-being questionnaire, *Personality and Individual Differences*, 38, 1107–21.

Goodloe, R. and Arreola, P. (1992), Spiritual health: out of the closet, *Health Education*, 23, 221–6.

Gordon, J. and Grant, G. (eds) (1997), *How We Feel: an insight into the emotional world of teenagers*, London, Jessica Kingsley Publishers.

Grace, G. (2001), The state and Catholic schooling in England and Wales: politics, ideology and mission integrity, *Oxford Review of Education*, 27, 489–500.

Greenberg, E. and Nay, W. (1982), The intergenerational transmission of marital instability reconsidered, *Journal of Marriage and the Family*, 44, 335–47.

Guijarro, S., Naranjo, J., Padilla, M., Gutierez, R., Lammers, C. and Blum, R.W. (1999), Family risk factors associated with adolescent pregnancy: study of a group of adolescent girls and their families in Ecuador, *Journal of Adolescent Health*, 25, 166–72.

Gunther, N., Slavenburg, B., Feron, F. and van Os, J. (2003), Childhood social and early development factors associated with mental health service use, *Social Psychiatry and Psychiatric Epidemiology*, 38, 101–8.

Hammond, C. (ed.) (1991), *Creation Spirituality and the Dreamtime*, Newtown, New South Wales, Millennium.

Hanks, M.P. and Eckland, B.K. (1976), Athletics and social participation in the educational attainment process, *Sociology and Education*, 49, 271–94.

Harris, W.S., Gowda, M., Kolb, J.W., Strychacz, C.P., Vacek, J.L., Jones, P.G., Forker, A., O'Keefe, J.H. and McCallister, B.D. (1999), A randomised, controlled trial of the effects of remote, intercessory prayer on outcomes in patients admitted to the coronary care unit, *Archives of Internal Medicine,* 159, 2273–8.

Hateley, B.J. (1983), *Spiritual Well-Being Through Life Histories,* Annual Scientific Meeting of the Gerontological Society, San Francisco. Nov. 1983. (ED 241 877).

Hendry, L.B., Shucksmith, J., Love, J.G. and Glendinning, A. (1993), *Young People's Leisure and Lifestyle,* London, Routledge.

Heyer, D.L. and Nelson, E.S. (1993), The relationship between parental marital status and the development of identity and emotional autonomy in college students, *Journal of College Student Development,* 34, 432–6.

Hills, A.P. (1998), Scholastic and intellectual development and sport, in K.-M. Chan and L.J. Mitchell (eds), *Sports and Children,* pp 76–88, Champaign, Illinois, Human Kinetics.

Hodge, A. (1931), *Prayer and its Psychology,* London, SPCK.

Hood, R.W., Morris, R.J. and Watson, P.J. (1987), Religious orientation and prayer experience, *Psychological Reports,* 60, 1201–02.

Hood, R.W., Morris, R.J. and Watson, P.J. (1989), Prayer experience and religious orientation, *Review of Religious Research,* 31, 39–45.

Hood-Morris, L.E. (1996), A spiritual well-being model: use with older women who experience depression, *Issues in Mental Health Nursing,* 17, 439–55.

Hornsby-Smith, M.P. (1978), *Catholic Education: the unobtrusive partner,* London, Sheed and Ward.

Hughes, M. and Lloyd, E. (1996), Young people: stake holders in the educational system, in H. Roberts and D. Sachdev (eds), *Young People's Social Attitudes: the views of 12–19 year olds,* pp 99–117, Barkingside, Barnardos.

Jackson, R. (1989), Hinduism: from ethnographic research to curriculum development in religious education, *Panorama,* 1(2), 59–77.

Jackson, R. (1996), The construction of 'Hinduism' and its impact on religious education in England and Wales, *Panorama,* 8(2), 86–104.

Jackson, R. and Nesbitt, E.M. (1993), *Hindu Children in Britain*, Stoke on Trent, Trentham.

James, W. (1902), *The Varieties of Religious Experience*, New York, Longmans Green.

Janssen, J., de Hart, J. and den Draak, C. (1989), Praying practices, *Journal of Empirical Theology*, 2(2), 28–39.

Jenkins, J.E. and Zunguze, S.T. (1998), The relationship of family structure to adolescent drug use, peer affiliation, and perception of peer acceptance of drug use, *Adolescence*, 33, 811–22.

Jennings, A.M., Salts, C.J. and Smith, T.A. Jr (1991), Attitudes toward marriage: effects of parental conflict, family structure, and gender, *Journal of Divorce and Remarriage*, 17, 1/2, 67–79.

Kay, W.K. and Francis, L.J. (1996), *Drift from the Churches: attitude toward Christianity during childhood and adolescence*, Cardiff, University of Wales Press.

Kay, W.K., Francis, L.J. and Gibson, H.M. (1996), Attitude toward Christianity and the transition to formal operational thinking, *British Journal of Religious Education*, 19, 45–55.

Kierkus, C.A. and Baer, D. (2002), A social control explanation of the relationship between family structure and delinquent behaviour, *Canadian Journal of Criminology Review*, 44, 425–58.

Kiernan, K.E. and Cherlin, A.J. (1999), Parental divorce and partnership dissolution in adulthood: evidence from a British cohort study, *Population Studies: a journal of demography*, 53, 39–48.

Kitwood, T. (1980), *Disclosures to a Stranger*, London, Routledge and Kegan Paul.

Kremer, J., Trew, K. and Ogle, S. (eds) (1997), *Young People's Involvement in Sport*, London, Routledge.

Kuhlthau, K.A. and Perrin, J.M. (2001), Child health status and parental employment, *Archives of Pediatrics and Adolescent Medicine*, 155, 1346–50.

Lankshear, D.W. (2005), The influence of Anglican secondary schools on personal, moral and religious values, in L.J. Francis, M. Robbins and J. Astley (eds), *Religion, Education and Adolescence: international empirical perspectives*, pp 55–69, Cardiff, University of Wales Press.

Lawlor, M. (1965), *Out of this World: a study of Catholic values*, London, Sheed and Ward.

Likert, R. (1932), A technique for the measurement of attitudes, *Archivesof Psychology*, 140, 1–55.

Livingston, R.B. and Kordinak, S.T. (1990), The long term effect of parental divorce: marital role expectations, *Journal of Divorce and Remarriage*, 14, 2, 91–105.

Lopez, F.G., Campbell, V.L. and Watkins, C.E. Jr (1988), The relation of parental divorce to college student development, *Journal of Divorce*, 12, 1, 83–98.

Lundborg, P. (2002), Young people and alcohol: an econometric analysis, *Addiction*, 97, 1573–82.

McCann-Erickson Advertising Agency (1977), *You Don't Know Me: a survey of youth in Britain*, London, McCann-Erickson Advertising Agency.

McCullough, M.E. (1995), Prayer and health: conceptual issues, research review, and research agenda, *Journal of Psychology and Theology*, 23, 15–29.

McLeish, J. (1970), *Student Attitudes and College Environments*, Cambridge, Institute of Education.

McNeish, D. (1996), Young people, crime, justice and punishment, in H. Roberts and D. Sachdev (eds), *Young People's Social Attitudes: the views of 12–19 year olds*, pp 71–98, Barkingside, Barnardos.

Market and Opinion Research International (1979), *Youth in Britain: attitudes and life style*, London, MORI.

Marfleet, A. (1992), Whose spirituality? *Spectrum*, 24 (1), 21–7.

Marsh, H.W. (1993), The effects of participation in sport during the last two years of high school, *Sociology of Sport Journal*, 10, 18–43.

Martin-Lebrun, E., Poussin, G., Barumandzadeh, T. and Bost, M. (1997), Psychological consequences of parental separation on children, *Archives de Pediatrie*, 4, 886–92.

Matthews, S.W. (1982), Rethinking sociology through a feminist perspective, *American Sociologist*, 17, 29–35.

Martin, D.A. (1967), *A Sociology of English Religion*, London, SCM.

Max, D.A., Brokaw, B.F. and McQueen, N.M. (1997), The effects of marital disruption on the intergenerational transmission of religious values, *Journal of Psychology and Theology*, 25, 199–207.

Modestin, J., Furrer, R. and Malti, T. (2005), Different traumatic experiences are associated with different pathologies, *Psychiatric Quarterly*, 76, 19–32.

Monck, E., Graham, P., Richman, N. and Dobbs, R. (1994), Adolescent girls: self-reported mood disturbance in a community population, *British Journal of Psychiatry*, 165, 760–9.

Montgomery, A. and Francis, L.J. (1996), Relationship between personal prayer and school-related attitudes among 11–16 year old girls, *Psychological Reports*, 78, 787–93.

Morgan, D.H.J. (1986), Gender, in R.G. Burgess (ed.), *Key Variables in Social Investigation*, pp 31–53, London, Routledge and Kegan Paul.

Morris, A.B. (1994), The academic performance of Catholic schools, *School Organisation*, 14, 81–9.

Morris, A.B. (1995), The Catholic school ethos: its effect on post-16 student academic achievement, *Educational Studies*, 21, 67–83.

Morris, A.B. (1997), Same mission, same methods, same results? Academic and religious outcomes from different methods of Catholic schooling, *British Journal of Educational Studies*, 45, 378–91.

Morris, A.B. (1998a), So far, so good: levels of academic achievement in Catholic schools, *Educational Studies*, 24, 83–94.

Morris, A.B. (1998b), By their fruits you will know them: distinctive features of Catholic education, *Research Papers in Education*, 13, 87–112.

Morris, A.B. (2001), Patterns of performance of Catholic schools in England, *Networking*, 3(1), 17–21.

Morris, A.B. (2005), Diversity, deprivation and the common good: pupil attainment in Catholic schools in England, *Oxford Review of Education*, 31, 311–30.

Muldoon, M. and King, N. (1995), Spirituality, health care, and bioethics, *Journal of Religion and Health*, 34, 329–49.

Murphy, J. (1971), *Church, State and Schools in Britain 1800–1970*, London, Routledge and Kegan Paul.

Mutrie, W. and Parfitt, G. (1998), Physical activity and its link with mental, social and moral health in young people, in S. Biddle, J. Sallis and N. Cavill (eds), *Young and Active? young people and health enhancing physical activity, evidence and implications,* pp 49–68, London, HEA.

National Curriculum Council (1993), *Spiritual and Moral Development,* London, National Curriculum Council.

National Interfaith Coalition on Aging (1975), *Spiritual Wellbeing: a definition,* Athens, Georgia, NICA.

Neher, L.S. and Short, J.L. (1998), Risk and protective factors for children's substance use and antisocial behaviour following parental divorce, *American Journal of Orthopsychiatry,* 68, 154–61.

Nesbitt, E.M. (1995), *The Religious Lives of Sikh Children in Coventry,* Unpublished PhD dissertation, University of Warwick.

Nesbitt, E.M. (1997a), Splashed with goodness: the many meanings of *Amrit* for young British Sikhs, *Journal of Contemporary Religion,* 12, 17–33.

Nesbitt, E.M. (1997b), Sikhs and proper Sikhs: young British Sikhs' perceptions of their identity, in P. Singh and N.G. Barrier (eds), *Sikh Identity: continuity and change,* pp 315–34, Delhi, Manohar.

Nesbitt, E.M. (1998), British, Asian and Hindu: identity, self-narration and the ethnographic interview, *Journal of Beliefs and Values,* 19, 189–200.

Nesbitt, E.M. (1999), Being religious shows in your food: young British Hindus and vegetarianism, in T.S. Rukmani (ed.), *Hindu Diaspora: global perspectives,* pp 397–425, Montreal, Quebec, Concordia University.

Nesbitt, E.M. (2001), What young British Hindus believe: some issues for the researcher and the RE teacher, in H.-G. Heimbrock, C. Scheilke and P. Schreiner (eds), *Towards Religious Competence: diversity as a challenge for education in Europe,* pp 150–62, Münster, Lit-Verlag.

Nesbitt, E.M. (2005), Young British Sikhs and religious devotion: issues arising from ethnographic research, in A. King and J. Brockington (eds), *The Intimate Other: love divine in Indic religions,* pp 310–16, New Delhi, Orient Longman.

Nesbitt, E.M. and Jackson, R. (1992), Christian and Hindu children:

their perceptions of each other's religious traditions, *Journal of Empirical Theology*, 5(2), 39–62.

Nesbitt, E.M. and Jackson, R. (1993), Aspects of cultural transmission in a Diaspora Sikh Community, *Journal of Sikh Studies*, 18, 52–66.

Nesbitt, E.M. and Jackson, R. (1995), Sikh children's use of 'God': ethnographic fieldwork and religious education, *British Journal of Religious Education*, 17, 108–20.

Newman, T. (1996), Rights, rites and responsibilities: the age of transition to the adult world, in H. Roberts and D. Sachdev (eds), *Young People's Social Attitudes: the views of 12–19 year olds,* pp 6–22, Barkingside, Barnardos.

Nurco, D.N., Kinlock, T.W., O'Grady, K.E. and Hanlon, T.E. (1998), Differential contributions of family and peer factors to the etiology of narcotic addiction, *Drug and Alcohol Dependence*, 51, 229–37.

O'Connor, T.E., Thorpe, K., Dunn, J. and Golding, J. (1999), Parental divorce and adjustment in adulthood, findings from a community sample, *Journal of Child Psychology and Psychiatry and Allied Disciplines*, 40, 777–89.

O'Keeffe, B. (1992), A look at the Christian schools movement, in B. Watson (ed.), *Priorities in Religious Education*, pp 92–112, London, Falmer Press.

O'Neill, D. and Sweetman, O. (1998), Intergenerational mobility in Britain: evidence from unemployment problems, *Oxford Bulletin of Economics and Statistics*, 60, 431–47.

Oakley, A. (1981), *Subject Women*, Oxford, Martin Robertson.

Oakley, A. (1996), Gender matters: man the hunter, in H. Roberts and D. Sachdev (eds), *Young People's Social Attitudes: the views of 12–19 year olds,* pp 23–43, Barkingside, Barnardos.

Office for National Statistics (2001), *Social Capital: a review of the literature*, London, Office for National Statistics.

Otto, L.B. (1982), Extracurricular activities, in H.J. Walberg (ed.), *Improving Educational Standards and Productivity,* pp 217–33, Berkeley, California, McCuthan.

Otto, L.B. and Alwin, D.F. (1977), Athletics, aspirations, and attainments, *Sociology of Education*, 42, 102–13.

Papaioannou, A., Karastogiannidou, C. and Theodorakis, Y. (2004),

Sport involvement, sport violence and health behaviours of Greek adolescents, *European Journal of Public Health*, 14, 168–72.

Parish, T.S. (1981), The impact of divorce on the family, *Adolescence*, 16, 577–80.

Park, A., Phillips, M. and Johnson, M. (2004), *Young People in Britain: the attitudes and experiences of 12 to 19 year olds*, London, Department for Education and Skills.

Pedersen, W. (2001), Adolescent victims of violence in a welfare state, *British Journal of Criminology*, 41, 1–21.

Pedersen, W., Mastekaasa, A. and Wichstrøm, L. (2001), Conduct problems and early cannabis indication: a longitudinal study of gender differences, *Addiction*, 96, 415–31.

Phillips, C.P. and Asbury, C.A. (1990), Relationship of parental marital dissolution and sex to selected mental health and self concept indicators in a sample of black university freshmen, *Journal of Divorce*, 13, 3, 79–91.

Poloma, M.M. and Pendleton, B.F. (1989), Exploring types of prayer and quality of life: a research note, *Review of Religious Research*, 31, 46–53.

Poyntz, C. and Walford, G. (1994), The new Christian schools: a survey, *Educational Studies*, 20, 127–43.

Putnam, R.D. (2000), *Bowling Alone: the collapse and revival of American community*, New York, Touchstone.

Quensel, S., McArdle, P., Brinkley, A., Wiegersma, A., Blom, M., Fitzgerald, M., Johnson, R., Kolte, B., Michels, I., Pierolini, A., Pos, R. and Stoekel, I. (2002), Broken homes or drug using peers: 'significant relations'? *Journal of Drug Issues*, 32, 467–89.

Quesnell, M.D. (2000), An analysis of selected beliefs and values among Czech fourteen and fifteen year old public school students, unpublished PhD dissertation, University of Wales, Trinity College, Carmarthen.

Quesnell, M.D. (2002), *Co Si Myslime, Čemu Věřime a Kdo Jsme*, Praha, Vydala Academia.

Ramsey, I. (1970), *The Fourth R*, London, National Society and SPCK.

Rebellon, C.J. (2002), Reconsidering the broken homes/delinquency relationship and exploring its mediating mechanism(s), *Criminology*, 40, 103–35.

Reed, R.H. (1950), *Eighty Thousand Adolescents*, London, George Allen and Unwin.

Rees, G., Francis, L.J. and Robbins, M. (2005), *Spiritual Health and the Well-Being of Urban Young People*, London, The Children's Society.

Regnier, R. (1994), The sacred circle: a process pedagogy of healing, *Interchange*, 25, 129–44.

Roberts, H. (1996), It wasn't like that in our day: young people, religion and right and wrong, in H. Roberts and D. Sachdev (eds), *Young People's Social Attitudes: the views of 12–19 year olds*, pp 128–40, Barkingside, Barnardos.

Roberts, H. and Sachdev, D. (eds) (1996), *Young People's Social Attitudes: the views of 12–19 year olds*, Barkingside, Barnardos.

Robinson, A. (1994), Spirituality and risk: toward an understanding, *Holistic Nursing Practice*, 8(2), 1–7.

Roehlkepartain, E.C., King, P.E., Wagener, L. and Benson, P.L. (eds) (2005), *The Handbook of Spiritual Development in Childhood and Adolesence*, Thousand Oaks, California, Sage.

Rona, R.J. and Chinn, S. (1991), Fathers unemployment and height of primary-school children in Britain, *Annals of Human Biology*, 18, 441–8.

Rubenstein, J.L., Halton, A., Kasten, A., Rubin, C. and Stechler, G. (1998), Suicidal behaviour in adolescents: stress and protection in different family contexts, *American Journal of Orthopsychiatry*, 68, 274–84.

Sahin, A. (2002), Critical/dialogic Islamic education: attitudes towards Islam and modes of religious subjectivity among British Muslim youth, Unpublished PhD dissertation, University of Birmingham.

Sahin, A. and Francis, L.J. (2002), Assessing attitude toward Islam among Muslim adolescents: the psychometric properties of the Sahin Francis scale, *Muslim Educational Quarterly*, 19(4), 35–47.

Sanders, C.E., Field, T.M., Diego, M. and Kaplan, M. (2000), Moderate involvement in sports is related to lower depression levels among adolescents, *Adolescence*, 35, 793–7.

Scholefield, L. (2001), The spiritual, moral, social and cultural values of students in a Jewish and a Catholic secondary school, *International Journal of Children's Spirituality*, 6, 41–53.

Segrin, C., Taylor, M.E. and Altman, J. (2005), Social cognitive mediators and relational outcomes associated with parental divorce, *Journal of Social and Personal Relationships*, 22, 361–77.

Shephard, R.J. (1997), Curricular physical activity and academic performance, *Pediatric Exercise Science*, 9, 113–26.

Shucksmith, J. and Hendry, L.B. (1998), *Health Issues and Adolescence: growing up, speaking out*, London, Routledge.

Simmons, C. and Wade, W. (1984), *I Like to say What I Think: a study of the attitudes, values and beliefs of young people today*, London, Kogan Page.

Smith, A.G.C. (2002), *The Nature and Significance of Religion among Adolescents in the Metropolitan Borough of Walsall*, Unpublished PhD dissertation, University of Wales, Bangor.

Smith, A.G.C. (2006), *Growing up in Multifaith Britain: explorations in youth, ethnicity and religion*, Cardiff, University of Wales Press.

Smith, D. (1989), *North and South: Britain's economic, social and political divide*, Harmondsworth, Penguin.

Snyder, E.E. and Spreitzer, E. (1990), High school athletic participation as related to college attendance among Black, Hispanic and White males: a research note, *Youth and Society*, 21, 390–8.

Spencer, A.E.C.W. (1968), An evaluation of Roman Catholic educational policy in England and Wales 1900–1960, in P. Jeff (ed.), *Religious Education: drift or decision?* pp 165–221, London, Darton, Longman and Todd.

Spencer, P., Beange, R. and Curtice, J. (1992), *The 1992 Election and the North–South Divide*, London, Lehman Bros.

Spruijt, E. and de Goede, M. (1997), Transitions in family structure and adolescent well-being, *Adolescence*, 32, 897–911.

Steptoe, A. and Butler, N. (1996), Sports participation and emotional wellbeing in adolescents, *The Lancet*, 347, 1789–92.

Suh, T., Schutz, C.G. and Johanson, C.E. (1996), Family structure and initiating non-medical drug use among adolescents, *Journal of Child and Adolescent Substance Abuse*, 5(3), 21–36.

Sund, A.M., Larsson, B. and Wichstrøm, L. (2003), Psychosocial correlates of depressive symptoms among 12–14 year old Norwegian adolescents, *Journal of Child Psychology and Psychiatry and Allied Disciplines*, 44, 588–97.

Taylor, D.L. (1995), A comparison of college athletic participants and non-participants and self-esteem, *Journal of College Student Development*, 36, 444–51.

Thatcher, A. (1996), 'Policing the sublime': a wholly (holy?) ironic approach to the spiritual development of children, in J. Astley and L.J. Francis (eds), *Christian Theology and Religious Education: connections and contradictions*, pp 117–39, London, SPCK.

Thompson, E.H. (1991), Beneath the status characteristics: gender variations in religiousness, *Journal for the Scientific Study of Religion*, 30, 381–94.

Tillich, P. (1952), *The Courage to Be*, New Haven, Connecticut, Yale University Press.

Tritter, J. (1992), An educated change in moral values: some effects of religious and state schools on their students, *Oxford Review of Education*, 18, 29–43.

Vance, J.E., Bowen, N.K., Fernandez, G. and Thompson, S. (2002), Risk and protective factors as predictors of outcome in adolescents with psychiatric disorder and aggression, *Child and Adolescent Psychiatry*, 41, 36–43.

van Driel, L. and Kole, I.A. (1987), *Bij-tijds Leren Geloven: verkenning van het educatief klimaat in een drietal kerkelijke gemeenten*, Kampen, J.H. Kok.

Vess, J.D., Schwebel, A.I. and Moreland, J. (1983), The effects of early parental divorce on the sex role development of college students, *Journal of Divorce*, 7, 1, 83–95.

Waddington, R. (1984), No apology for theology, chapter 4 in *A Future in Partnership*, London, National Society.

Walford, G. (1994), Weak choice, strong choice and the new Christian schools, in J.M. Halstead (ed.), *Parental Choice and Education: principles, policies and practice*, pp 139–50, London, Kogan Page.

Walford, G. (1995a), *Educational Politics: pressure groups and faith-based schools*, Aldershot, Avebury.

Walford, G. (1995b), The Christian schools campaign: a successful educational pressure group? *British Educational Research Journal*, 21, 451–64.

Walford, G. (1995c), Faith-based grant-maintained schools: selective international policy borrowing from the Netherlands, *Journal of Educational Policy*, 10, 245–57.

Walford, G. (2000), *Policy and Politics in Education: sponsored grant-maintained schools and religious diversity*, Aldershot, Ashgate.

Walford, G. (2001a), Evangelical Christian schools in England and the Netherlands, *Oxford Review of Education*, 27, 529–41.

Walford, G. (2001b), The fate of the new Christian schools: from growth to decline? *Educational Studies*, 27, 465–77.

Walford, G. (2001c), Building identity through communities of practice: evangelical Christian schools in the Netherlands, *International Journal of Education and Religion*, 2, 126–43.

Walford, G. (2001d), Funding for religious schools in England and the Netherlands: can the piper call the tune? *Research Papers in Education*, 16, 359–80.

Walford, G. (2002), Classification and framing of the curriculum in evangelical Christian and Muslim schools in England and the Netherlands, *Educational Studies*, 28, 403–19.

Walford, G. (2003), Separate schools for religious minorities in England and the Netherlands: using a framework for the comparison and evaluation of policy, *Research Papers in Education*, 18, 281–99.

Walker, D. (1996), Young people, politics and the media, in H. Roberts and D. Sachdev (eds), *Young People's Social Attitudes: the views of 12–19 year olds*, pp 44–70, Barkingside, Barnardos.

Wallerstein, J.S. and Lewis, J.M. (2004), The unexpected legacy of divorce: report of a 25-year study, *Psychoanalytic Psychology*, 21, 353–70.

Wallis, R. and Bruce, S. (1992), Secularization: the orthodox model, in S. Bruce (ed.), *Religion and Modernization: sociologists and historians debate the secularization thesis*, pp 8–30, Oxford, Clarendon Press.

Watson, K. and MacKenzie, P. (1996), The new Christian schools in England and Wales: an analysis of current issues and controversies, *Journal of Research on Christian Education*, 5, 179–208.

Wilson, B. (1966), *Religion in Secular Society*, London, Watts.

Wolfinger, N.H. (1998), The effects of parental divorce on adult tobacco and alcohol consumption, *Journal of Health and Social Behaviour*, 39, 254–69.

Woodroffe, C., Glickman, M., Barker, M. and Power, C. (1993), *Children, Teenagers and Health: the key data*, Buckingham, Open University Press.

Yankelovich, D. (1974), *The New Morality: a profile of American youth in the 1970s*, New York, McGraw-Hill.

Yeung, R.R. and Hemsley, D.R. (1997), Personality, exercise and psychological well-being: static relationships in the community, *Personality and Individual Differences*, 22, 47–53.

Young, E. (1984), Spiritual health: an essential element in optimum health, *Journal of American College Health*, 32, 273–6.

Zaharopoulos, E. and Hodge, K.P. (1991), Self-concept and sport participation, *New Zealand Journal of Psychology*, 20, 12–16.

Zavalloni, M. (1975), Social identity and the recording of reality: its relevance for cross-cultural psychology, *International Journal of Psychology*, 10, 197–217.

Name Index

Subject Index

277